Intolerant Britain?

Intolerant Britain?

Hate, citizenship and difference

Derek McGhee

Open University Press

Open University Press
McGraw-Hill Education
McGraw-Hill House
Shoppenhangers Road
Maidenhead
Berkshire
England
SL6 2QL

email: enquiries@openup.co.uk
world wide web: www.openup.co.uk

and Two Penn Plaza, New York, NY 10121-2289, USA

First published 2005

A catalogue record of this book is available from the British Library

ISBN-13 978 0335 21674 1 (pb)   978 0335 21675 8 (hb)
ISBN-10 0 335 21674 9 (pb)   0 335 21675 7 (hb)

Library of Congress Cataloging-in-Publication Data
CIP data applied for

Typeset by RefineCatch Limited, Bungay, Suffolk
Printed in the UK by Bell & Bain Ltd, Glasgow

Contents

Acknowledgements   ix

Introduction   1
**1 Over-policed and under-protected: race and policing from
    Scarman to Lawrence**   15
2 Trouble up north: building community cohesion in Bradford   41
3 Asylum hysteria: insecure borders, anxious havens   65
4 Faith-hate in post-9/11 UK   92
5 Building trust – policing homophobia   118
**6 Beyond toleration: privacy, citizenship and sexual minorities
    in England and Wales**   141
7 Cosmopolitan citizenship: New Labour, 'new Britain'   163

Notes   186
Bibliography   206
Index   227

In memory of Stephen Lawrence, Firsat Dag and David Morley

Acknowledgements

The seeds of the ideas for the chapters contained in this book came to me in the summer of 2001. At this time I had begun to collect documents and reports, mostly examples of what I call here institutional reflexivity, in relation to minority communities. I started with various reports produced by local government, local authority, police, and lesbian and gay organizations in relation to taking homophobic hate crime seriously in Southampton (see Chapter 5). An early version of this research was eventually published in 2003 as 'Joined-up government, "community safety" and lesbian, gay, bisexual and transgender active citizens' in *Critical Social Policy*, Vol. 23, pp. 345–75. At the same time, I increasingly found my attention being drawn away from 'lesbian and gay issues' towards issues and communities remote from my 'specialist' area, for example the Pakistan–Muslim community in Bradford, Oldham and Burnley (see Chapter 2). I published an earlier version of this research on community cohesion in Bradford in 2003 as 'Moving to "our" common ground – a critical examination of community cohesion discourse in twenty-first century Britain' in *Sociological Review*, Vol. 51, pp. 376–404. What interested me about these two areas of research was that much of the terminology I had encountered in the documents referring to the lesbian and gay community in Southampton were also appearing in the archive of documents and reports that emerged in relation to the 2001 disturbances in Bradford, Oldham and Burnley. I found these similarities intriguing, especially in the diagnosis of the 'problem' and also the suggested 'solutions' in these very different archives of official documents.

It was from these observations, and talking about these issues with friends and colleagues, who also read early drafts of chapters and made suggestions during presentations (especially Dr Wendy Bottero, Dr Caroline Knowles, Dr Graham Crow, Prof. Les Moran, Dr Paul Bridgen, Prof. Rosemary Pringle), that I began to realize that if I strayed even further from lesbian and gay studies into, for example, race and policing, asylum and immigration, Islamophobia in the post-9/11 context, etc., that it would be possible to make further connections between seemingly disparate issues, and understand even more about the wider context of the problematization of prejudice, intolerance and hatred in contemporary British society through an exploration of how racism, virulent asylophobia, rampant Islamophobia, as well as homophobia (and the institutionalized varieties of these prejudices) were being constructed by government, police, pressure groups and other organizations as social problems.

This multi-focused analysis of the construction and suggested solutions to these often very different social problems has led me to consider wider questions in relation to tolerance, intolerance, British national identity, British citizenship, and ultimately of difference in contemporary British society. These are intriguing developments in a particular moment in British history; this book attempts to plot these developments and see the connections between their diverse elements. There is much to celebrate in this wider ethos of 'protective inclusionism', however, in each chapter I also offer critical insights in relation to some of the inconsistencies, limitations, contradictions and ambivalences that lie behind many of the discourses, policies, legislation and initiatives examined here.

There are a number of people I would like to thank in relation to the various processes that came together during the writing of this book. First, to all my colleagues in the Sociology and Social Policy Division in the University of Southampton, thanks for the support, encouragement and lunch time banter. I also had specific support from various groups of people outside of the University of Southampton. First, at Open University Press and McGraw-Hill Education, especially my commissioning editor Mark Barratt for his encouragement and support for the project. Second, the three book proposal referees selected by Mark: Dr Claire Alexander, Prof. John Solomos and Prof. Les Moran, who all in very different ways helped to shape my ideas and sharpen my focus, and through their comments encouraged me to write a better book. Third, I would like to thank the three colleagues in the division who read my first complete draft of the book during the Easter break in 2004, Dr Caroline Knowles, Dr Graham Crow and Dr Wendy Bottero; their comments and suggestions were invaluable to the final completion of the project. And many thanks to Dr Claire Alexander for her useful and challenging comments on the manuscript. Special thanks must go to my patron and eulogist Dame Caress Camellia for her unstinting commitment and support despite her advancing years. I would also like to thank various family members including my parents John and Jeannette; the Cullis family (especially Robert, Gwenneth and Les); as well as friends Lee Price, Caroline Jones, Traute Meyer and Sue Heath, for all of their support during the writing of the book.

Finally, I would like to thank Andrew and Jem Cullis for all their love and support.

Introduction

The social problem of hate

In the early twenty-first century, hatred, prejudice, intolerance and antagonism between groups are commonplace in the UK, just as they are throughout the world. In most cases, hatred embodies a set of fears about difference; it often forms around the unknown rather than the known in relation to racial, religious, cultural, sexual and gendered 'others' (Eisenstein 1996). Hatreds, like prejudices, are complex and multiple phenomena. Some prejudices (e.g. anti-fascist) are considered good, some (e.g. preference for tall people over short people) relatively innocuous, but other prejudices increasingly provoke strong social and political censure (Jacobs and Potter 1998). Some of these so-called 'bad prejudices' are examined in this book, in particular racism, Islamophobia, homophobia and asylophobia (the fear and hatred of asylum seekers).

To understand the nature of hating and the formation of prejudices, attempts have been made to classify the different varieties of prejudices and hatreds. For example, Allport (1954), in his book *The Nature of Prejudice*, distinguished between 'hate-prejudice' and 'love-prejudice'. Love-prejudices occur when the very act of affirming a group's or individual's way of life is associated with a perceived outside threat to their privileged position in society. This form of prejudice has many associations with the preservationist motivations of Far Right and fundamentalist groups, who attempt to mobilize hatred as a defence against a myriad number of others. On the other hand, hate-prejudices are driven by the desire to eradicate the object of hate. This hatred is extropunitive, which means that the hater is sure that the fault lies in the object of hate and thus the hatred is justified and sustained through the continuing existence of the other.

Like Allport, Young-Breuhl (1996) also attempts to make sense of the different types of prejudices and hatreds in her book *The Anatomy of Prejudice*. She distinguishes between primary ('bad') prejudices, such as sexism, racism, anti-Semitism and homophobia, and secondary, relatively harmless prejudices, for example not liking certain foods. For Young-Breuhl, the primary prejudices can be further categorized as 'obsessional prejudice', 'hysterical prejudice' and 'narcissistic prejudice' (p. 137). People holding obsessional prejudices, by her definition, see their hate-objects as omnipresent conspirators, or enemies set on one's destruction, who therefore must be eliminated. Hysterical prejudice, on the other hand, interprets the 'hated' individual as 'other', as inferior and often sexually threatening. And individuals with narcissistic prejudices 'cannot tolerate the idea that other people who are not like them exist' (Young-Breuhl 1996: 33–5).

Elements of these classifications of prejudice-hatreds will be explored in the chapters that follow in relation to: racism (Chapter 1); institutionalized prejudices, for example institutional racism (Chapter 1) and institutional homophobia (Chapter 5); inter-community violence and segregation (Chapter 2); the growing fear and hatred of asylum seekers and Muslims alike (Chapters 3 and 4); and the combination of all three of Young-Breuhl's prejudices in the form of homophobia[1] (Chapters 5 and 6).

Hatred is often associated, as Allport and Young-Breuhl's classifications demonstrate, with the processes of defensive (and often futile) border maintenance and the fear of the other, which are both in turn closely associated with psychoanalytic theory. According to Zizek, psychoanalysis can help to unravel a group's, community's or nation's fantasies and investments in the other, for example:

> This relationship towards a Thing, structured by means of fantasies, is what is at stake when we speak of the menace to our 'way of life' presented by the other; it is what is threatening when, for example, a white Englishman is panicked because of the growing presence of 'aliens'.
>
> (Zizek 1990: 51–2)

The collective investment in the other is rarely satiated by violence. The power of the other, according to Zizek (1994), is paradoxical. He cites the example of the Jews in Nazi Germany: 'the more they were ruthlessly exterminated, the more horrifying were the dimensions acquired by those who remained' (p. 78). A similar over-investment in the other occurred apropos the Serbian hatred of Muslims in Bosnia: 'the more they slaughtered and starved out, the more powerful was the danger of "Muslim fundamentalism" in Serbian eyes' (p. 78).

Thus, hatred can be strongly associated with love – of country, of self, of community and of sexual desire, especially when sexual desire is repressed. Hatred can also be associated with defensiveness – of one's way of life, of one's perceived privilege, purity and superiority. And hatred, as will be demonstrated in this book, is often associated with the unbearable intimacy (or proximity) of a psychically invested other who is the object of an individual's or group's 'psychic fixation' (Yanay 2002). This type of theorizing concerning the projection onto, and the power of, the other is crucial for understanding the social relations of hating. However, this type of theorizing[2] can be limited, just as the theories of 'prejudice' and 'hate' (for example, Allport and Young-Breuhl above) are also somewhat limited as they tend to essentialize and pathologize 'prejudice' through employing stereotypes that depict 'prejudiced individuals' (Rattansi 1992: 25) who consistently display a, b or c type prejudices. According to Jock Young, the problem with these types of theories is they:

> tend to depict such othering or demonization as a cultural universal, a product of the ever-present problems of human psychology or group formation. Instead we need to locate such processes in time and social context, we need to specify who is more likely to demonize, to explain the context of the labels applied to outsiders, to understand the mechanisms of exclusion and describe the likely outcome of such othering. In short we need to know the when, why, who, what, how and whether of demonization.
>
> (Young 2003: 256)

In many ways, this book takes up Young's challenge for a sociology of othering, as it is a sustained and multi-focused analysis of racism, asylophobia, Islamophobia and homophobia in the UK, in relation to specific locations (e.g. Brixton in London, Bradford, Oldham and Burnley, Sighthill in Glasgow, Caia Park in Wrexham, North Wales and Southampton on the south coast) and the particular problems experienced there. However, I also explore the institutionalized varieties of racism, asylophobia, Islamophobia and homophobia, as well as the institutional response to accusations of institutionalized prejudice in contemporary Britain. Therefore, rather than just focusing on why people hate, and the contexts and motivations of prejudice, each chapter also includes a critical examination of official anti-hate discourses, policies, initiatives and legislation, as well as the processes through which organizations are attempting to deal with institutionalized prejudices.

This element of the book is an attempt to explore some of the ambivalent aspects of this ethos of 'protective inclusionism', in relation to some of the limitations, inconsistencies and contradictions within these developments. When viewed collectively, these developments in relation to anti-racism, anti-Islamophobia, anti-extremism and anti-homophobia are tantamount to the othering of 'bad' prejudices. Even though many of us welcome these developments (and could perhaps benefit from them), this does not mean that sociologists should be any less vigilant or critical in their scrutiny of them. We must be attentive to how 'prejudice', 'hatred' and 'intolerance' as social problems are being constructed and are currently being used in specific ways by various organizations and institutions within government and the criminal justice system, especially when these are reduced to 'cultural' and 'individual' problems that divert attention away from the often wider socio-economic structural contexts of their emergence.

Hate and institutional reflexivity

In many ways, the emergence of hate, intolerance and prejudice as social problems in advanced western societies is associated with the uneasy co-existence of what Beck, Giddens and Lash refer to as reflexive modernization and counter-modernization. According to Lash (1999), there are two aspects of reflexive modernization in the work of Beck and Giddens. The first is associated with the contingency, risk and ambivalence that is forced upon us with the relative decline of institutions in an age of reflective judgement; the second is associated with our attempt to create order for ourselves and others through reflection on these social processes. However, Beck (1997) suggests that this ordering process can become 'counter-modern' in orientation, in that it can become too rigid, defensive and past-oriented. Beck suggests that defensive intra-group hatred, prejudice and intolerance are associated with the process of counter-modernization that inscribes, promises and elaborates new and old rigidities in the face of our powerlessness in the simultaneous processes of reflexive modernization, wherein our securities and certainties are continually being eroded and our insecurities broadened. Thus, whereas reflexive modernization describes the process in 'practically all fields of social activity' of the gradual or eruptive collapse of previously applicable basic certainties, counter-modernization is viewed as an unfortunate side-effect (in the form of a social 'bad') that has emerged as an antidote to reflexive modernization (Beck 1997: 11).

Lash (1994a: 116) suggests that in Beck and Giddens, reflexivity 'aims to achieve the minimization of insecurity' in relation to social order [Giddens] and social change [Beck]. For Beck and Giddens, reflexive modernization is primarily concerned with institutions and 'institutional reflexivity' in relation to the side-effects, the dangers or the 'bads' that stem from the modern production of goods (Lash 1994b). In this book, the focus is less on the institutional response to the bio-hazards of risk society[3] or the 'emergent institutions' arising in response to the disruption of gender, love and familial relationships in the context of modernization (as in Beck and Giddens), and more on the institutional response to risk, uncertainty and ambivalence in the form of social bads and social problems (including counter-modern phenomena) associated with late modern cultural diversity in multi-ethnic, multicultural, multi-faith Britain.

Beck (1997) lists nationalism, ethnocentrism, xenophobia and violence as counter-modern social responses to reflexive modernization. Giddens adds the rise of fundamentalism to Beck's list of counter-modern responses. Giddens (1994a) suggests (as does Beck) that there is nothing mysterious about the rise of such social phenomena in the late modern world; for example, 'fundamentalism' assumes the sense it does only against a background of the prevalence of radical doubt associated with the erosion of boundaries of classes, business sectors, nations, continents, families, gender roles and so on. Counter-modernization, in response to the latter, asserts, draws, creates and attempts to solidify boundaries again (Beck 1997) through attempting to resurrect the pillars of 'communal security' (Hier 2003). The emotions associated with the processes of attempting to construct and maintain firm boundaries in an age of fluid and porous boundaries is seen by Beck as negative, other-focused acts of social defence. The problem with this type of emoting is that it is too strong and often results in antagonizing the communities and social groups that are its objects.

According to Furedi (2004), contemporary culture does not simply applaud emotions (for example, getting in touch with our feelings, men in particular becoming more emotionally literate), as not all emotions are appropriate. Contemporary culture also demands that feelings and emotions that are too strong should be curbed and moderated. Just as varieties of prejudice are distinguished by desirability and undesirability, emotions are similarly categorized as positive and negative phenomena. Furedi points out that there is evidence of a process of 'cultural cooling' in contemporary cultures, in that the members of society are being obliged to curb and moderate strong feelings. This cultural cooling of especially strong, 'inappropriate' or 'bad' emotions and prejudices associated with other-directed hatred, prejudice, intolerance, as well as the impulses of segregation, is directly related to Beck's depiction of counter-modern, emotionally charged, constructed certitude. According to Beck (1997: 65), 'counter-modern constructions are founded in emotions (compulsions to act or, more exactly, to defend oneself). This is the source of their (convincing) force and power. Emotion and active assertion are their main ingredient'.

Richard Sennett offers a similar description of the link between intolerance and the defensive maintenance of identity and community through the hyping of emotion (Sennett 1974: 309). Hatred, prejudice, intolerance and inter-group antagonism are not therefore the eruption of atavistic primordial hatreds associated with insufficiently civilized and socialized individuals and groups. According to Beck, these phenomena are the emotional response to de-traditionalization, geographical and social mobility, and unprecedented diversity, and are often associated with social groups who feel that they have been abandoned or left behind in a fast-paced and ever-changing world where community, culture, tradition and identity provide certainty, and become something to defend and fight for.

In many ways, this book is an examination of how counter-modern 'hot' emotions such as the incitement and violent expression of hatred and group antagonisms are being interpreted by 'reflexive institutions' and other organizations as particular social problems. At the same time, this problematization of the social bads of antagonism, prejudice and hatred is part of a wider project associated with the re-imagination of British national identity under the New Labour government. The strength of this book is that it combines diverse and often separate areas of research (racism, Islamophobia, homophobia and asylophobia) in an attempt to provide a wider analysis of institutional reflexivity in the form of discourses, policies, programmes and legislation that have been, are planned or are being rolled-out to deal with these diverse social problems and what they are associated with – that is, the crisis in British citizenship. One of the most striking findings in relation to this multi-focused analysis of these social problems is the similarities between them in terms of how they are conceptualized and especially how they are to be ameliorated. For example:

(1) All of these phenomena have, in recent years, been subject to institutional reflection. In many cases, this institutional reflexivity involves these institutions and organizations reflecting on the part they have played in perpetuating these social problems. The police in particular have been in a process of reviewing and acknowledging their role in perpetuating and sustaining counter-modern 'social bads' through the institutionalization of prejudice (see Chapters 1, 4, 5 and 6). At the same time, the police are, through the process of review, also attempting to become increasingly 'opened-up' to critique and contestation (Lash 1994b) through the expansion of consultative mechanisms with the communities they serve (see Chapters 1, 5 and 6). Thus, institutional reflexivity, especially in relation to policing, is a central theme running throughout the book, in which new institutional reflexivity and collaborative methods of enquiry are being encouraged (Misztal 1996) to better serve previously oppressed social groups in society, especially ethnic and sexual minority groups.

(2) At the same time, the counter-modern tendencies of social groups who attempt to construct strong boundaries against and encroaching other – for example, in the form of 'poor' white communities feeling under threat from non-white neighbouring communities (see Chapter 2 in relation to Bradford, Oldham and Burnley), or in the widespread fear and loathing (referred to here as asylophobia) targeted at asylum seekers (see Chapter 3) are seen as a serious problem of community cohesion directly related to the failure of multicultural integration strategies.[4] What will be observed in various places throughout this book (especially in Chapters 2 and 7) is an attempt to erode these defensive boundaries in the form of excessive loyalty and commitment to a community's cultural traditions and identity to promote less exclusive and thus less 'separatist-prone' forms of belonging. At the heart of this process is the attempt to re-imagine a variety of British citizenship suitable for

the twenty-first century. In Chapter 7, it is suggested that this process can be described as a social strategy beyond the multicultural respect of culture, tradition and identity in which citizenship is being redefined through processes of cosmopolitanization, which on the surface appears progressive yet in practice could prove to have a darker underbelly of social engineering.

(3) In relation to (1) and (2), the social problems associated with hatred, intolerance, institutional prejudice and group antagonisms that are explored in this book are also being subjected to similar risk or 'insecurity-minimizing' strategies in the form of policy solutions, all of which are associated with promoting active forms of citizenship. The policy goal in all of these initiatives is to increase trust and confidence in marginalized or antagonized communities through promoting participation and dialogue between communities or between communities and key organizations (e.g. the police). This is a common feature of the pursuit of community cohesion in Bradford, Oldham and Burnley (see Chapter 2), as well as the attempt to transform the lesbian, gay, bisexual and transgender (lgbt) communities in Southampton from hidden communities (and hidden targets of hate crime) into active citizens – that is, active in the protection of their communities through mechanisms of participatory policing (see Chapters 5 and 6). In both these cases, these strategies are dedicated to breaking down barriers between communities and often between minority communities and organizations. 'Trust building' here is associated with what Giddens (1994b: 187) refers to as the promotion of 'active trust', which is trust that is won, achieved and actively sustained through an 'opening out to the other'. Like the emergence of a cosmopolitanized British citizenship, this variety of active, participatory and dialogic citizenship, although 'progressive' on the surface in its inclusivity of minority groups previously excluded, could be conceived as a governmental strategy associated with the shift from 'private' and 'insular' to more public spheres of control.

(4) Related to (3) is the attempt to legislate against the violent and damaging extremes of hatred, especially when the expression of this hatred is an 'officially designated prejudice' (Jacobs and Potter 1998) that is targeted at identified vulnerable minority communities. In this book, these designated communities are: ethnic minority communities, religious minority communities and some sexual minority communities (that is, lgbt communities rather than other sexual minority communities such as paedophiles). So-called 'hate crimes' achieved common currency in the United Kingdom only in the aftermath of the 1999 Stephen Lawrence Inquiry Report (see Chapter 1) and after the high-profile neo-Nazi nail-bombing campaign that targeted symbolic locations – Brixton (the Black community), Brick Lane (the Asian community) and Soho (the gay community) – across London in April 1999 (McLaughlin 2002). This new batch of legislation, in particular the sentence enhancement provisions for racially aggravated

offences in section 28 of the Crime and Disorder Act (see Chapter 1) and incitement to racial and religious hatred legislation (see Chapter 4), has been described as declaratory legislation, which performs two major functions: (1) they are intended to send a message to wider society that hate crime will not be tolerated, and (2) it sends a message to the groups targeted by hatred that their rights, interests and needs as victims of hate crime will be taken seriously by the criminal justice system. Thus, in many ways, hate crime legislation can be described as the deployment of a 'good' violence (that is, legal institutional violence encoded through the power to punish offenders) to counter 'bad' forms of violence fuelled by prejudice and hatred (Moran and Skeggs 2004). Or, in other words, 'hate crime' legislation can be described as a decivilizing mechanism designed to promote increased civility (Van Krieken 1999) – that is, to demonstrate how much 'we' in advanced western societies hate those who hate. In various chapters (especially 1, 4, 6 and 7), it is suggested that these developments are indicative of a redrawing of boundaries in contemporary British society in relation to inclusion, toleration and citizenship through an observable and wide-ranging commitment to the protection of 'vulnerable' social groups from hatred, which is, in turn, related to a wider project associated with the cosmopolitanization of British citizenship. However progressive this sounds, there are problems with this interpretation in practice. It will be demonstrated in Chapters 1 and 4 in particular that hate crime laws are being put to very limited use in England and Wales. The function of hate crime laws, as explicitly stated by representatives of the Home Office (see Chapter 4), seems to be more declaratory than punitive in orientation.

The intolerance of intolerance

In many ways this book, as its title suggests, is an examination of the shifting boundaries of tolerance and intolerance in contemporary British society in response to the construction of hatred and other counter-modern characteristics as social problems. According to Ingrid Creppell:

> The current interest in toleration comes from negative reasons more than positive ones: rampant genocide in the twentieth century; religious fundamentalism around the world; continued Israeli–Palestinian, Catholic–Protestant, and Muslim–Hindu conflict; ethnic and religious wars in Eastern Europe; outbreaks of mass killing in Africa and other regions. In everyday life in developed countries racism and intolerance of gays, Jews and Muslims continue to be major issues.
>
> (Creppell 2003: 1)

However, despite this renewed interest in tolerance in the face of these and other social problems, tolerance itself has in recent years also become the object of much institutional (academic) reflexivity and redefinition. For example, I suggest that in the institutional reflexivity currently unfolding in late modern multi-ethnic, multi-faith and multicultural advanced Western societies (such as contemporary Britain), the emphasis of tolerance is less on the tolerance of the 'other' (e.g. minority ethnic communities, minority religious communities and minority sexual communities) than on the intolerance of the intolerance that is often targeted at these minority communities.

To understand this shift in the relations of tolerance, it is important first to consider how tolerance is defined in social and political science. In these literatures, tolerance and acts of toleration are defined as two interdependent activities: disapproval and restraint. That is, to be tolerant of a person or group, one must first disapprove of a person or social group, or find aspects of a person's or group's practices or beliefs disagreeable. However, despite their well founded objections, the tolerators restrain themselves from imposing their disapproval (Creppell 2003). According to Raz:

> Toleration, then, is the curbing of an activity likely to be unwelcome to its recipient or of an inclination so to act which is in itself morally valuable and which is based on a dislike or an antagonism towards that person or a feature of his life, reflecting a judgment that these represent limitations or deficiencies in him, in order to let that person have his way or in order for him to gain or keep some advantage.
>
> (Raz 1986: 402)

Thus, toleration is the act of not interfering with or coercing another (person or group) despite one's (or one's group's) morally justifiable negative response to them. Intolerance is the opposite – it is the act of interfering with or coercing another (person or group) motivated by one's (or one's group's) negative response to them (Creppell 2003). According to Creppell, both tolerance and intolerance so defined can be described as 'negative' responses towards another or another's group. That is, intolerance suggests an unconstrained (and possibly violent) reaction to, or action taken against, the other.

However, tolerance or an act of toleration, although merciful, is also a negative action as it involves condescension (Creppell 2003). At the same time, both tolerance and intolerance so defined share another negative characteristic – both do not lead to progressive social relationships with the other, as both tolerance and intolerance are associated with the construction of protective or defensive boundaries between groups. Misztal (1996) concurs with this assessment when she suggests that tolerance is a short-term remedy rooted in indifference. Thus, both acts of intolerance and acts of tolerance pose a particular problem for ensuing social relationships between groups. Misztal suggests that the indifference to the other associated with the act of toleration is no longer an adequate answer to many of our modern dilemmas, which are forcing us to ask if it is enough to 'live and let live', or does toleration require a positive welcoming of difference. At the same time, the literatures on toleration are often unhelpful for examining the context of tolerance or intolerance in relation to many contemporary inter-group conflicts and prejudices, as they are too focused on the morality or immorality of the original disapproval or disagreement in the first part of the act. Thus, the major source of concern in these literatures is whether the act of restraint is based on a moral (acceptable) or immoral (unacceptable) disapproval or disagreement, in the form of a 'good' or justifiable prejudice or a 'bad' or unjustifiable prejudice. For example, Heyd (1996) is adamant that any mode of restraint by a German skinhead to a Turk living in Germany could not be described as tolerance because the original disapproval or disagreement was patently immoral; neither can the homophobe's restraint towards homosexual behaviour be defined as a case of toleration because 'there are no good reasons to object to the behaviour in the first place' (pp. 3–5). According to Creppell, this distinction between morally justifiable and morally unjustifiable disapproval, disagreement or objection to another person or group makes the discussion of toleration irrelevant to most social and political conflicts today and therefore it 'must be rejected'. What Creppell (2003) suggests instead is that the basic two-step unilateral model of toleration should: (1) be less concerned with the morality or immorality of the act of toleration, and (2) should be modified by adding a third component to the definition: 'that one may disapprove and then restrain oneself but, crucially, one stays in a relationship with the person or group with whom one is in conflict' (p. 4). Thus, the indifference to the other at the heart of an act of toleration is replaced with an attempt to understand and communicate with them (Misztal 1996). Creppell suggests that:

> the restraint associated with an act of toleration is only meaningful because the parties remain in the presence of one another in a non-trivial way. Toleration essentially implies a continued relationship of some significant level of accommodation.
>
> (Creppell 2003: 4)

Creppell's modified model of toleration, based on the accommodation of differences (including disapproval and disagreement) and active processes of engagement between groups, is directly related to many of the discourses, policies and programmes included in the chapters in this book in relation to the promotion of active citizenship, the building of trust and the attempt to increase confidence in ethnic, religious, migrant and sexual minority groups. What this modified model of toleration through active engagement or dialogue between groups suggests is that intolerance in the form of unrestrained disapproval of another person or group poses a particular social danger in society (as did the former model of toleration), in that it is associated with the creation of distance, indifference and overt antagonisms between social groups that are antithetical to communication, dialogue and finding common ground between such groups.

Emergent British citizenship

In the chapters that follow, I demonstrate how these revitalized and renewed models of 'toleration in dialogue with the other' are becoming increasingly evident in the discourses, policies and initiatives deployed in the context of Third Way politics. I also suggest that the social and political significance of the promotion of this variety of toleration should not be underestimated as merely political 'lip-service'. Rather, this model of tolerance (and intolerance) should be viewed as having wide-ranging implications (progressive and draconian) for the associated processes whereby 'Britishness' and British citizenship are being themselves re-imagined. In this emergent culture of tolerance where hot emotions and excessive (counter-modern) attachments and loyalties are being systematically cooled to foster understanding and communication between different social groups; intolerance is becoming increasingly intolerable. Even liberal definitions and models of tolerance are becoming increasingly intolerable in this climate in that the White, male, Christian and heterosexual power to tolerate non-White, female, non-Christian and non-heterosexual others is now also being viewed as problematic. Intolerance in the form of unrestrained hatred and antagonism targeted at groups and individuals is presented by various official organizations (e.g. the Home Office, the police) as a particular injury in which 'society' is the ultimate victim (see Chapters 1, 5 and 6). At the same time as suggesting the wider social injury associated with hatred, these official discourses can also be described as providing the justification for learning the lessons of the past, abandoning strategies that have failed to deliver a British society at ease with its own diversity (e.g. multiculturalism; see Chapter 7) and devising new strategies to replace them.

Much of the developments, policy innovations, strategies and the evolution of 'social problems' in British society associated with hatred, prejudice and intolerance depicted here can be described as an exploration of reflexive modernization within the context of the British Third Way socio-political context. According to Giddens (2000), the Third Way, above all else, is an endeavour to respond to change built around the cornerstones of progressive equal opportunities, personal responsibility and the mobilization of citizens and communities. In many ways, this book suggests that reflexive modernization within Third Way politics might be more than 'the great moving nowhere show', as it was famously described by Stuart Hall (1998a) in his comparison with radical and transformative political ideologies, for example Thatcherism. I suggest that Third Way politics in the end does not, as Hall perhaps too hastily suggests, just accept the world as it is rather than truly seeking to transform it (Giddens 2000). In this book I show that the Third Way ideals of increased equal opportunities and personal responsibilities through the facilitation of active citizens in active communities are implicated in wider strategies of attempting to achieve commonality, of moving to and finding 'common ground' in relation to the shared values and standards of an emergent citizenship for a multi-ethnic, multi-lingual and multi-faith Britain. However, this is not to say that the journey, the movement to this common ground, will be a smooth ride. As stated above, there is much to celebrate in this emergent culture of intolerance of intolerance; yet, at the same time, there are emerging sources of concern.

Chapter summaries

Chapter 1 focuses on the relationship between the police and the African-Caribbean community in London through the analysis of two significant inquiries: the Scarman Inquiry (report published in 1981) and the Stephen Lawrence Inquiry (report published in 1999). The emphasis in this chapter is on the shift in policing discourses from 'black' being a social problem to be managed to racism in the form of racist incidents, and institutional racism being constructed as a major social problem in society. Chapter 1 also provides the context for the emergence of hate crime legislation in the UK and the community safety ethos introduced in the provisions of the Crime and Disorder Act 1998, which is explored in subsequent chapters.

Chapter 2 examines the emergence of concerns in relation to 'community cohesion' in a number of official responses to the disturbances and 'riots' that occurred in Oldham, Burnley and Bradford in the summer of 2001. Some of the themes introduced above – for example, the problems associated with the recourse to counter-modern identifications as defences against a spatially proximate 'enemy-other' – will be explored here through an examination of the polarization and antagonism between the segregated White and Pakistani communities in these areas. It is in this chapter that the germ of the theme of active citizens in active communities will be introduced as the antidote to excessive loyalty and commitment to both White and Asian identities, cultures and traditions. This chapter takes particular issue with the limitations of 'cultural'-centric programmes and harsh criminal justice measures in these post-'riot' contexts, which systematically de-emphasize (1) the extent of material deprivation and (2) the role 'self-' or 'community defence' (from oppressive policing and Far Right insurgences) played in these 'disturbances'.

Chapter 3. This chapter explores the symbiosis of state-generated and popular 'tabloid' racism in relation to asylum seekers in Britain. The emphasis is on the management of the 'asylum problem' in relation to the integration (through citizenship initiatives) of migrant communities and through the government strategy of getting tough on asylum to calm the counter-modern mobilization of 'Middle England' against the perceived 'threat' of asylum seekers. This chapter contains case studies (in Scotland and North Wales) dedicated to examining the asylophobic reaction to the government's asylum dispersal policy in recent years.

Chapter 4 focuses on the progress of, and problems with, attempting to pass legislation in the House of Commons and Lords dedicated to the incitement of religious hatred. The chapter also describes the emergence of Islamophobia as an officially designated category of hatred, which has increased in Britain since the 9/11 attacks in the USA in 2001. Contradictory concerns in relation to protection will be examined here with reference to Britain's Muslim community as potential 'inner enemies', and as a community in need of protection from Far Right organized hate campaigns. The chapter concludes with the suggestion that perhaps incitement legislation should be expanded to protect other groups in society, for example the lesbian and gay community.

Chapters 5 and 6 change the emphasis of the book somewhat in that attention shifts from race relations and religious intolerance to the intolerance of sexual minority communities (especially lgbt communities), usually expressed in the form of homophobia. In this chapter, many of the developments outlined in Chapter 1 in relation to the policing of racist incidents, institutionalized prejudice in police forces and the police–community 'consultation' requirements included in the provisions of the Crime and Disorder Act of 1998, will be re-examined in relation to the process whereby the problems associated with institutional homophobia and homophobic incidents are also being taken seriously alongside institutional racism and racist incidents by police. Chapter 6 includes an examination of what these developments in the policing of lgbt communities, and of the reforms of certain sexual offences legislation, mean for minority sexual citizenship in the twenty-first century.

Chapter 7 is dedicated to exploring many of the common themes and problems that emerge in the preceding chapters and to contextualize them in wider developments associated with the Labour government's attempts to imagine a new Britain. Many of the themes introduced above will be more fully explored in this concluding chapter, in particular institutional reflexivity, counter-modernization, the failure of multiculturalism and the re-coding of British citizenship through what Beck refers to as the processes of re-traditionalization and cosmopolitanization.

1 Over-policed and under-protected: race and policing from Scarman to Lawrence

Introduction

In this chapter, I examine Lord Scarman's Inquiry into the Brixton disturbances of 1981 alongside the MacPherson Inquiry into the death of Stephen Lawrence in 1993 to map the trajectory of the initial denial, and eventual acknowledgement, of institutional racism in the Metropolitan Police Service. In many ways, this chapter contextualizes the official (police and government) responses and policy developments in relation to the recognition of institutional prejudice directed at minority groups in British society that will be examined in subsequent chapters in the form of institutional asylophobia, Islamophobia and homophobia. In addition to the central theme of this chapter – that is, the process whereby organizations (such as the police) reflect (or are being forced to reflect) on their institutional racism – other themes that recur throughout the book, such as trust, consultation, citizenship (including the right to fair and equitable policing) and the necessity of protecting minority groups from hate crime, will also be examined. The Stephen Lawrence Inquiry, as will be demonstrated below, is a crucial event in the history of race relations in the UK. The hate crime that resulted in the murder of Stephen Lawrence, and the inquiry into the murder and police investigation of it, has resulted in the beginnings of a re-coding of race and a redrawing of the boundaries of toleration in British society, in which racism and racists rather than ethnic minority groups are increasingly being presented as social problems (or diseases) to be removed from society.

In the first section of the chapter, I examine the significance of Stephen Lawrence's murder, the Lawrence family's campaign and the eventual inquiry chaired by Sir William MacPherson. This is followed by a section that examines the failure of the Metropolitan Police Service to serve the Black (African-Caribbean) community in London fairly and equally in the light of both the Scarman and Stephen Lawrence inquiries. Two sections are then dedicated to exploring the denial of institutional racism (in the Scarman Inquiry) through to the acknowledgement (and definitions) of the various forms that racism can take in public institutions (in the Stephen Lawrence Inquiry). The construction of the social problem of race in the Scarman Report is contrasted with its seeming reversal in the Stephen Lawrence Inquiry, in which racism, and not race, is seen as the social problem to be addressed in contemporary British society. As well as acknowledging the significance of the definitions of the various forms of racism that can be found in the Stephen Lawrence Inquiry, I suggest that these definitions and the recommendations made by the Stephen Lawrence Inquiry might not have gone far enough.

The remainder of the chapter addresses: (1) the recommendations from Scarman to the Stephen Lawrence Inquiry and beyond into the Crime and Disorder Act 1998 with regard to the development of mechanisms of consultation between the police and ethnic minority communities to improve the relationship between them; and (2) the recommendations from Scarman to the Stephen Lawrence Inquiry in relation to stop and search policies, which have been and always will be a major source of resentment because of the disproportionate stopping and searching of the members of the African-Caribbean community, especially young men. Finally, the following question is addressed: Can the police ever police with the consent of the ethnic minority communities if their stop and search policy remains unregulated by race relations legislation? The continual use of stop and search is presented as one of the major inhibitors of the development of 'active trust' between the Metropolitan Police Service and London's ethnic minority communities.

The significance of Stephen Lawrence

Stephen Lawrence was murdered on 22 April 1993. On that evening Stephen and his friend Duwayne Brooks were on their way home, waiting for a bus in Eltham, south-east London. As they waited, a group of five or six White youths crossed the road towards them shouting racist abuse, such as referring to Lawrence and Brooks as 'niggers'. During this confrontation, Stephen Lawrence was stabbed twice, in the chest and in the arm. Both of these stab wounds severed arteries and Stephen was dead by the time the ambulance arrived at the scene. This incident, according to the inquiry, probably lasted no more than 15–20 seconds (MacPherson 1999: 1.1). The results of the inquiry into the murder were published almost 6 years later on 24 February 1999 and were greeted with a great deal of national (and even international) media attention.[1] On the publication of the inquiry report, the murder of Stephen Lawrence dominated terrestrial and satellite television, radio and the print media[2] for several days in Britain (Bowling 1999: xi). But why did this particular murder and this inquiry receive such attention?

According to McLaughlin and Murji (1999), the Stephen Lawrence Inquiry was more than just a high-profile inquiry into the murder of an African-Caribbean teenager and the failure to convict his killers. This inquiry had been transformed into a matter of urgent public importance in which: (1) the Metropolitan Police were subjected to unprecedented public scrutiny; (2) the construction of young African-Caribbean men as street criminals and drug dealers by the police was challenged; and (3) previous campaigns for justice were remembered and reconnected to public debate. Bowling (1999) describes the Stephen Lawrence Inquiry and the report of it as being a lightning rod which has drawn down and focused energies from diffuse, private grievances and frustrations, transforming them into highly charged issues of public policy. Variously described as a 'landmark' and a 'watershed' by journalists and social scientists alike, the inquiry facilitated a period of unprecedented introspection, examination, reflection and catharsis regarding race relations in Britain.

The wide appeal of the inquiry can be explained through the breadth of recommendations that emanated from it in relation to general policies on race relations, racism, education and social policy, as well as a wide range of related issues (Solomos 1999). As a result, the inquiry has been described as initiating 'a flurry of activity on tackling racism', mostly in the form of conferences, internal reviews and 'race and diversity training' in many public institutions and voluntary sector organizations throughout the country (Sivanandan 2000: 6). However, without the Lawrence family's campaign, this inquiry would have never taken place in the manner that it eventually did (Bowling 1999; McLaughlin and Murji 1999; Sivanandan 2000). The Lawrence family, especially Stephen's parents Doreen and Neville Lawrence, were described as being relentless in their campaign in the face of official indifference and denial (Bowling 1999; Sivanandan 2000). The members of the Lawrence family can also be described as being at the centre of a re-coding of race in Britain through the drawing in the tabloid press, especially in the *Daily Mail*, of a boundary between 'ordinary, decent Britons – white and black – and the racist "savages" from South London who killed Stephen Lawrence' (McLaughlin and Murji 1999: 377).

At the same time, the impact of this murder and the inquiry can be described as the aperture through which so-called 'hate crimes', and the inadequate policing of them, came to public attention as social problems simultaneously. According to Jenness and Broad (1997), social problems such as hate crime and the discriminatory practices of public institutions in relation to minority groups targeted by hate crime are rarely fully constituted until its victims are made apparent. The Stephen Lawrence murder fits with Jenness and Broad's description of the emergence of a symbolic victim associated with a social problem – that is, an injured person who is harmed by forces outside of his or her control – who is essentially innocent and thus worthy of others' concern. Stephen Lawrence and his family's 'victim status' is undeniable in terms of his death through a racially motivated murder and the family's, and other witnesses' unsatisfactory treatment by the Metropolitan Police Service, both factors Stephen and his family had little control over. At the same time, Stephen was an 'attractive victim', a young man with a future, from a middle-class, church-going Christian family, whose innocence in his attack was easily dramatized, thus rendering him worthy of others' concern through what Jenness and Broad (1997) describe as 'the projections of collective sentiments' (p. 6).

The Lawrence family campaign and the Stephen Lawrence Inquiry itself are significant components in the process of memorialization, whereby symbolic victims and especially the surviving relatives (mostly parents) of high-profile violent incidents usually involving young people and children become powerful agents of legislative change or legislative review (Valier and Lippens 2004).

Race and policing

In this section of the chapter, I examine the similarities and differences between the two most significant reviews of race relations in the UK (albeit in the context of policing in London): the Scarman Inquiry into the Brixton disturbances of 1981 and the Stephen Lawrence Inquiry. The events that triggered these inquiries are rather different. Although the Stephen Lawrence Inquiry had an extremely wide remit, it was inspired by the murder of one young man, and the inquiry into the murder took place 6 years later. The Scarman Inquiry, on the other hand, was ordered by the then Home Secretary, William Whitelaw, two days after some of the most serious disturbances to take place on mainland Britain in the twentieth century (Bowling 1999). The disturbances in Brixton between 10 and 12 April 1981 were not isolated events. Between 1980 and 1981, Toxteth in Liverpool, Moss Side in Manchester, the St. Paul's district in Bristol and the Handsworth area in Birmingham experienced similar disturbances, all involving young African-Caribbean (and sometimes Asian) men in confrontations with police. These events, including the Brixton disturbances, unleashed a wave of anxious insecurity in the country, which was evident in the official commentary at that time. For example, commenting on the Brixton disturbances, Lord Scarman himself stated that:

> the rioters . . . found a ferocious delight in arson, criminal damage to property, and in violent attacks upon police, the fire brigade, and the ambulance service. Their ferocity, which made no distinction

between the police and the members of the rescue services is, perhaps, the most frightening aspect of this terrifying weekend.

(Scarman 1981: 3.109)

Lord Scarman and others depicted these events in particularly racialized terms, as an indication of 'something new and sinister in our long national history' (Sir John Stokes, MP for Halesowen and Stourbridge, cited in Benyon 1984a: 4).

Despite the differences in the events that inspired the Scarman and Stephen Lawrence inquiries, they both share a central concern related to the failure of the Metropolitan Police Service to police ethnic minority groups in London fairly. In relation to the Brixton disorders, the Metropolitan Police Service was accused of oppressive styles of policing in general but especially in the run up to the weekend of 10 April, in particular the police operation known by its now famous codename, Swamp '81. Operation Swamp as it has come to be known was singled out by the Scarman Inquiry as a particularly 'flawed' and 'inflexible' policing method, characterized by 'hard-policing' and an unwillingness to solicit or consult local opinion on such methods (Scarman 1981: 4.70, 4.71). Operation Swamp, which was directed primarily against street crime, employed three policing methods: the use of special patrol groups, the use of the 'sus' law (to deal with suspected persons loitering with intent to commit an arrestable offence) and the exercise of the statutory power to stop and search (Scarman 1981: 4.2).

The decision to go ahead with this operation was described by the Scarman Inquiry as being 'unwise' (Scarman 1981: 3.27), in that tensions in the area were already high due to an attempt by the police to come to the aid of a young African-Caribbean male stab-wound victim on the previous day. During this incident on 9 April, a crowd of African-Caribbean residents from the area attempted to seize the stab-wound victim from the police, even though the police, according to the inquiry, were attempting in this instance to help the injured man (Scarman 1981: 3.23). This confrontation ended with a 'sinister twist', in that after the crowd seized the stab-wound victim, the police radioed for assistance, which came in the form of a sub-stantial number of officers, resulting in the further escalation of tensions (Scarman 1981: 3.25). The wise course, according to the inquiry, would have been not to go ahead with Operation Swamp in the light of the tensions in the area the day before (Scarman 1981: 3.27). The Swamp '81 operation, however, did go ahead and on 10 April 112 officers were deployed with the intention of making extensive use of the stop and search power provided by Section 66 of the Metropolitan Police Act 1839 (Benyon 1984b).[3] According to Benyon, 943 'stops' were made during this operation; just over half of those stopped were African-Caribbean and over two-thirds were under 21. The Scarman Inquiry lists the number of arrests at 118 (75 charges resulted), but these included only one for robbery, one for attempted burglary and 20 charges of theft or attempted theft (Scarman 1981: 4.37–4.40). As Benyon (1984b) points out, and this criticism will be further developed below, judged by its own aims (to arrest burglars and robbers) the operation was not very successful and resulted in over 850 'innocent' people being inconvenienced and irritated. There was a complete lack of consultation on this operation within the Metropolitan Police Service. Even the beat officers involved in the day-to-day policing of the area, and who had been involved in tensions just the day before, were not consulted; nor were local community leaders. The Scarman Inquiry described this as 'a serious mistake' (Scarman 1981: 4.75–4.80). Operation Swamp, in a context of raised police–community tension in an area characterized by police–community antagonism, became 'the accelerator event' (Taylor 1984: 28) that triggered the weekend of disturbances in Brixton on 10–12 April.

The problems identified by the Stephen Lawrence Inquiry were of a different order, yet still related to the Metropolitan Police Service's incompetence in dealing with members of ethnic minority communities. For example, the principal witness to the murder, Duwayne Brooks, was mistakenly considered by the Metropolitan Police Service to be a perpetrator initially and was marginalized as a witness in their subsequent investigations. Mrs Lawrence was patronized by the members of the Metropolitan Police Service throughout the investigation, and the Lawrence family's solicitor, Imran Khan, was subjected to a campaign by the Metropolitan Police designed to discredit him. Above all, the main mistake by the Metropolitan Police Service in relation to this murder was their failure to acknowledge how race and racism impacted upon the circumstances of the murder and all aspects of the routine police work associated with the investigation (McLaughlin and Murji 1999). The terms of reference of the inquiry were announced in Parliament by the then Home Secretary Jack Straw as the following: 'To inquire into the matters arising from the death of Stephen Lawrence on the 22nd April 1993 to date, in order to particularly identify the lessons to be learned from the investigation and prosecution of racially motivated crimes' (cited in MacPherson 1999: 6).

The lessons to be learned by the Scarman and Stephen Lawrence inquiries into the policing of ethnic minority groups by the Metropolitan Police Service can be described as being structured around (a) the denial of institutional racism (in the Scarman Inquiry) and (b) the acknowledgement of institutional racism (in the Stephen Lawrence Inquiry). These are explored in turn below.

'Bad apples' and weak families

In his report of the inquiry into the Brixton disturbances of 1981, Lord Scarman introduced what has been described since as the 'bad apple thesis' (Bowling 1999; Bowling and Phillips 2002) to explain the existence of racism in the Metropolitan Police Service. According to Scarman:

> the direction and policies of the Metropolitan Police are not racist. I totally and unequivocally reject the attack made on the integrity and impartiality of the senior direction of the force. The criticism lies elsewhere – in errors of judgement, in a lack of imagination and flexibility, but not in deliberate bias or prejudice.
>
> (Scarman 1981: 4.62)

For Scarman:

> Racial prejudice does manifest itself occasionally in the behaviour of a few officers on the streets. It may be only too easy for some officers, faced with what they must see as the inexorably rising tide of street crime, to lapse into an unthinking assumption that all young black people are potential criminals. I am satisfied however, that such a bias is not to be found amongst senior police officers.
>
> (Scarman 1981: 4.62)

Part of the problem, according to Lord Scarman, was not racist policing, but rather the belief among ethnic minority communities that the police are racist, a belief which is reinforced by the 'power of gossip and rumour':

> I have little doubt that behind some of the criticisms lies the power of gossip and rumour. There must be the temptation in every young criminal – black or white – stopped in the street or arrested in Brixton to allege misconduct by a police officer . . . Whether justified or not, many in Brixton believe that the police routinely abuse their powers and mistreat alleged offenders. The belief here is as important as the fact. One of the most serious developments in recent years has been the way in which the older generation of black people in Brixton has come to share the belief of the younger generation that the police routinely harass and ill-treat black youngsters.
>
> (Scarman 1981: 4.66–4.67)

Scarman's assertions can be described as a political diversion strategy, in which he reduced objective, institutional racism (in the form of a conscious matter of policy originating from senior ranks) to a matter of a small, but regrettable, number of low-ranking prejudiced officers. And the perception of the local community in Brixton that the police were racist was equally dismissed as the gossip and rumour mongering of 'criminals'. By not dealing with racism head on, Lord Scarman has gone down in history as the person responsible for shifting the object of anti-racist struggle from public institutions to the individual, from an emphasis on changing society to focusing on the problems of the African-Caribbean community in Brixton (Bourne 2001). Thus, for Scarman, institutional racism, as he understood it, did not exist in Britain (Scarman 1981: 2.22); however, what did exist in Brixton (although exacerbated by flawed and unimaginative policing practices) and elsewhere in the country were African-Caribbean communities blighted by 'racial disadvantage' (Bourne 2001: 11). Thus, Scarman managed to turn the inquiry away from the legal and political questions of institutional racism and discrimination by the police against the African-Caribbean community, to a focus on the social problems associated with racial disadvantage, as being at the root of the problems in Brixton.

Gilroy (1992) describes Lord Scarman's Report as a crucial document in the history of 'black' criminality. For Gilroy, the Scarman Report provided the official seal to the definition of the origins and extent of African-Caribbean crime through tying these to distinct patterns of protest and family life that were presented as being characteristic of African-Caribbean culture. This shift in emphasis in the Scarman Report, as depicted by Gilroy, was evident in the media reporting of police and Conservative politicians' statements in the summer of 1981, which focused on violent street rioting and the alleged weakness of the family unit in West Indian communities (Solomos and Rackett 1991), which was viewed as being incapable of disciplining young people. The Prime Minister at the time, Margaret Thatcher, was quick to place the responsibility for the riots with the families of the 'rioters'. She was reported in *The Times* on 10 July 1981 as saying that if the parents concerned could not control the actions of their children, what could the government do to stop them (cited in Solomos and Rackett 1991: 55). Scarman himself also attributed the drift of African-Caribbean youngsters into crime and violence to weak family units, weakened by the 'change in circumstances' through migration in which West Indian traditional family structures, especially the roles of the West Indian mothers at the centre of those families, were being undermined by new demands, such as female paid work (Scarman 1981: 2.17). With West-Indian mothers away from the family home as wage earners, and West Indian fathers at worst absent and therefore of little or no significance and at best a distant and supportive (but seldom dominant) figure, Scarman attempted to define the problem in Brixton as one associated with cycles of racial disadvantage. Like the American African-Caribbean, inner-city underclass theory of Charles Murray (Murray 1990; Herrnstein and Murray 1994) and others that would achieve social and political prominence in the 1980s and into the 1990s, the instability of the 'matriarchal' West Indian family identified by Scarman was predictive of a whole host of social problems, including high rates of 'illegitimacy', children in care, low educational achievement, exclusion from job markets and, eventually, crime (Scarman 1981: 2.17). Scarman thus diverted attention away from the social problems associated with the institutional racism of public institutions such as the police to focus instead on the social problems associated with West Indian families. This is part of a wider history of the political response to African-Caribbean immigration, which is deeply infused with the common sense notion that 'black' is intrinsically a social problem (Solomos and Rackett 1991). The circularity of the argument is evident in the following, which although sympathetic to the plight of inner-city African-Caribbean youth, manages to further distance the consideration of institutional racism from public debate through focusing instead upon the compound social problems resulting from racial disadvantage which explain African-Caribbean hostility to the police:

> would it be correct to conclude that young black people are wholly alienated from British society as a result of the deprivations they suffer? But it would be surprising if they did not feel a sense of frustration and deprivation. And living much of their lives on the streets, they are brought into contact with the police who appear to them as the visible symbols of the authority of a society which has failed to bring them its benefits or do them justice.
>
> (Scarman 1981: 2.23)

When we fast-forward to the Stephen Lawrence Inquiry, we see that Lord Scarman's quasi-sociological theory of the social problem of African-Caribbean 'culture' (as associated with social disadvantage and hostility against the police and as the cause of social disadvantage and hostility against police) was challenged. For example, the Institute of Race Relations, in their submission to part two of the Stephen Lawrence Inquiry, sets the scene for the reversal in the conceptualization of *the* social problem of race with regard to the policing of the African-Caribbean community, to focus instead on the social problems associated with racism through suggesting that policy be redirected in two major ways. First, policy should no longer focus on African-Caribbean people as a source of social problems, but instead should focus on the need for all institutions in this society, not least the police, to respect civil rights and afford ethnic minority groups the proper protection against racial harassment and attacks. Second, it is racism, not ethnic minority groups, that needs to be targeted for remedial action, not just in policing but across a wide range of social, educational and legal policies (Institute of Race Relations 1999).

The acknowledgment of institutional racism

Jenny Bourne (2001) captures the reversal in terms of conceptualizing the social problem associated with the policing of the African-Caribbean community from Scarman to Lawrence when she suggests that the emphasis of the Scarman Inquiry Report had been about managing 'them', the problem; what the Macpherson-led inquiry emphasized in contrast was that racism in Britain was *the* problem and this was shaming for the nation through bringing home to Britain the extent of racist violence and the way miscarriages of justice could take place through incompetent and racist policing. In contrast to Lord Scarman's rejection of the accusation that Britain was an institutionally racist country (Scarman 1981: 2.22), MacPherson acknowledged the existence of racism in a wide range of institutions. The result was that Scarman's bad apple thesis was replaced in the Stephen Lawrence Inquiry by a thesis that implied that the apple tree, if not the whole orchard, was infected with the disease of institutional racism:

> racism, institutional or otherwise, is not the prerogative of the Police Service. It is clear that other agencies including, for example, those dealing with housing and education also suffer from the disease. If racism is to be eradicated there must be specific and co-ordinated action both within the agencies themselves and by society at large, particularly through the education system, from primary school upwards and onwards.
>
> (MacPherson 1999: 6.54)

In the view of the MacPherson-led inquiry, institutional racism in the Metropolitan Police Service was apparent in relation to what they had seen and heard throughout the process of their enquiries in relation to the following: (a) the police investigation (and treatment of witnesses) in relation to the murder of Stephen Lawrence; (b) a general concern relating to the policing of the African-Caribbean community in Britain in relation to, for example, disproportionate application of police stop and search powers; (c) concerns related to the under-reporting of racist incidents due to a lack of trust in police by many members of the African-Caribbean community; and (d) concerns about the evident lack of police training in racism awareness that emerged in relation to the specific inquiry into the murder and in the inquiry's hearings around the country which were recorded in part 2 of the report[4] (MacPherson 1999: 6.45). Thus rather than being an intermittent problem (with a few bad apples), the Stephen Lawrence Inquiry diagnosed a systematic, institutional-ized problem that required root and branch reform (Bowling and Phillips 2002). Institutional racism was defined thus in the report in relation to the concerns listed above:

> The collective failure of an organization to provide an appropriate and professional service to people because of their colour, culture, or ethnic origin. It can be seen or detected in processes, attitudes and behaviour which amount to discrimination through unwitting prejudice,[5] ignorance, thoughtlessness and racist stereotyping which disadvantage minority ethnic people.
>
> (MacPherson 1999: 6.34)

Even though this definition was welcomed as going some way to re-focusing the problem at the heart of the policing of the African-Caribbean community, this definition is inadequate. For example, Solomos (1999) describes the definition as not being rigorous enough. In fact, Solomos suggests that the Stephen Lawrence Inquiry offers a 'rather limited, and in places contradictory, discussion of racism' (p. 2). Solomos's main problems with regard to the inquiry were that: (1) it did not come up with a satisfactory definition of what it means by institutional racism in relation to the police; and (2) it did not provide us with a framework of what kind of policy and political initiatives are necessary to tackle racism in institutions or in society. Solomos suggests that rather than focusing on the meaning of institutional racism and examining the mechanisms that would help us to understand the historical processes and the contemporary realities that shape relations between the police and ethnic minority communities, the inquiry emphasized instead 'discrimination through unwitting prejudice, ignorance, thoughtlessness and racist stereotyping which disadvantage minority ethnic people'.

Alongside the criticism that the inquiry did not go far enough (which will be expanded on below in relation to the definition of racist incidents), the other main criticism levelled at the inquiry was that its limited engagement with institutional racism has in turn resulted, in recent years, in similarly limited anti-racist reviews and agendas being perpetuated throughout the country in a wide range of organizations. There is a sense in the social science commentary on the inquiry of a missed opportunity simultaneous with the pronouncements of the inquiry's 'landmark' status. For Sivanandan (2000), the inquiry's recommendations have resulted in the development and pre-occupation with formulaic anti-racist procedures, which he describes as 'off-the-peg' blueprints for institutional reviews for 'every problem and every occasion' (p. 5). The result is that 'anti-racism itself has become institutional-ised' (Bourne 2001: 16) in the post-Stephen Lawrence Inquiry period mostly in the guise of the 'development' of 'staff competences'. The inquiry, according to Sivanandan (2000), did enough to put institutional racism on the map and to draw attention to its prevalence in society in general. The point, however, is not to look to this particular inquiry for a solution to racism in non-police organizations. Rather, these organizations should examine their particular roles, the context in which they work and the way in which racism has developed in their fields, not just to accept definitions derived from the Stephen Lawrence Inquiry, which might not be appropriate in every organizational context.

Another effect of the inquiry and the 6-year build-up to it was the re-coding of race in and through Stephen Lawrence and his parents, in which, according to McLaughlin and Murji (1999), 'inclusive gestures' from the print media, especially the *Daily Mail* and the *Daily Telegraph*, can be described as a significant development in which those tabloids that speak for 'Middle England' initiated a discourse that 'blackness' and Britishness are not mutually exclusive, through the process of readers sharing in the grief and anger of the Lawrence family. This seemingly positive development, however, has had unintended consequences, which in turn have also limited British society's thorough engagement with racism. According to McLaughlin and Murji (1999), this has occurred through the tabloids' demonization and pathologization of the five suspects[6] referred to 'as the racist "savages" from South London who killed Stephen Lawrence' (p. 377). The key achievement of this demonization of the five suspects was that racism is distanced from mainstream society. Racism was thus depicted as the overt and violent practices of a few dangerous people and not a social problem or a disease, to use an analogy employed by MacPherson, endemic in mainstream society. This re-coding of racism also resulted in the more right-wing tabloids' support of the Stephen Lawrence Inquiry and the Lawrence family's campaign as focusing exclusively on the need to bring the suspects to justice (thus punishing the explicitly racist 'few'), while at the same time arguing that the legacy of the inquiry should not be a 'general "witch hunt" against racism' (McLaughlin and Murji 1999: 377). Thus, for the tabloids, the mainstream or popular racism of society in general was not the problem, nor even in the end the Metropolitan Police Service's institutional racism; the problem became the overt racist violence synonymous with a small group of abnormal, excessively racist individuals. Despite this significant, yet ultimately limited re-coding of British identity against extreme racism in the tabloid media's response, recommendations made in the inquiry about the recording of racist incidents and for the criminalization of racist incidents would formalize this re-coding process in law.

Taking racist hate crime seriously

As well as the acknowledgement of institutional racism, the Stephen Lawrence Inquiry has also been lauded for its recommendations in relation to the policing of racist incidents. These recommendations emerge from the inquiry's recognition that there were inadequate measures in the criminal law for the protection of ethnic minority communities from the range of behaviours motivated by racist prejudice.[7] The recommendations for criminal legislation that would protect ethnic minority communities from racist incidents were in part related to the recognition in the Stephen Lawrence Inquiry that African-Caribbean people (and their families), even when they were the victims of a serious crime, were rarely seen as victims of crime. Thus, the recommendation in the inquiry that legislation covering racist incidents should be introduced was to ensure that crimes and incidents motivated by racism and perpetrated against the members of the African-Caribbean community and other minority racial groups[8] should not be subjected to a similar degree of ignorance and indifference that the Lawrence family, Duwayne Brooks and the family's solicitor experienced. Stephen Lawrence's father, Neville Lawrence, stated during the inquiry that 'it is clear to me that the police come in with the idea that the family of African-Caribbean victims are violent criminals who are not to be trusted' (MacPherson 1999: 4.4). In response to these and myriad other statements from the members of the African-Caribbean community and representatives of organizations, the recommendations of the inquiry for the introduction of legislative measures for dealing with racist incidents can be described as an attempt to re-classify African-Caribbean people in the procedures of the agencies of criminal justice as victims of crimes rather than criminals. This can be described as an attempt to disrupt the stereotyping and criminalization of all members of the African-Caribbean community, but especially young men, which has characterized the relationship between the police and the African-Caribbean community since the 1950s.

According to the Association of Chief Police Officers' (ACPO) *Guide to Identifying and Combating Hate Crime*, hate crime 'is a crime where the perpetrator's prejudice against any identifiable group of people is a factor in determining *who* is victimised' (ACPO 2000: 13). The ACPO's former definition of a 'racial' incident is similarly worded:

> A racial incident is any incident in which it appears to the reporting or investigating officer that the complaint involves an element of racial motivation, or any incident which includes an allegation of racial motivation made by any person.
>
> (cited in MacPherson 1999: 45.16)

According to the MacPherson-led inquiry, this widely used definition was problematic because: (a) it over-emphasized the perpetrator's motivation; (b) the definition was not victim-oriented enough; and (c) the words 'racial' and 'racially motivated' were deemed by the inquiry to be inaccurate and confusing and should be replaced with the adjective 'racist' (MacPherson 1999: 45.16–45.17). As a result of these problems, the definition of a racist incident (recommendation 12 of the inquiry), which has also been subsequently adopted by the ACPO,[9] is: 'a racist incident is any incident which is perceived to be racist by the victim or any other person' (MacPherson 1999: 45.17). In this definition, the victim of and witnesses to a racist incident are clearly given preference, in an attempt to ensure that they will be recognized by the agents and agencies of criminal justice and that their complaint will be taken seriously by them. This should lead to the protection of ethnic minority groups rather than the habitual stereotyping of whole sections of the African-Caribbean community, especially young men, as hostile 'anti-police' criminals, which has consistently de-emphasized the position of African-Caribbean people as victims.

A few months before the publication of the inquiry's report, on 30 September 1998, the Crime and Disorder Act came into force (after receiving Royal Assent on 31 July 1998). This legislation included new offences under Sections 28–32 which deal with the crimes of racist violence and harassment, in the form of 'racially aggravated offences'. In their guidance on these new offences, the government stated the purpose behind them:

> The Government introduced these new offences in order to deal with the problem of racist violence and harassment. The government recognises that racist crime does not simply injure the victim or their property, it affects the whole family and it erodes the standards of decency of the wider community. Trust and understanding built up over many years can be eroded by the climate of fear and anxiety which can surround a racist incident.
>
> (Home Office 1998a: 1.1)

Paul Iganski's (1999b) work on racially aggravated 'hate crime' legislation isolates the three main objectives for including racially aggravated crime legislation in the Crime and Disorder Act 1998. These are the 'deterrent-effect' or function of the legislation, the promotion of social cohesion and the impetus for a more effective response to incidents by the criminal justice system. In terms of the promotion of social cohesion, the symbolic force of this legislation was supposed to operate in two main ways. First, through the expression of collective social opprobrium against perpetrators and the acts they commit. The legislation was also expected to contribute to social cohesion by countering 'the marginalization experienced by communities targeted by attacks'

(Iganski 1999b: 389). Thus, in many ways this legislation offers those targeted by hate some protection from it. This legislation also performs a symbolic role in attempting to modify or correct undesirable behaviour in society not only in the name of greater protection for certain groups who are 'injured' by hate, but also in the name of protecting wider society from the negative impacts of a hate incident in the form of institutional mistrust, and the potential polarization between social groups. The legislation also emphasizes the destructive and often marginalizing impact of hate crimes such as racist incidents on the victim, family, neighbourhood, community and ultimately the nation.

The developments so far in relation to both racist incidents and racially aggravated offences can thus be described as mechanisms that attempt to overcome inequity in criminal justice service provision to ethnic minority groups, especially the members of the African-Caribbean community. However, they are also about winning the trust of the members of the African-Caribbean community and other ethnic minority groups through ensuring that the hate crimes and incidents they experience will be taken seriously by the police and other agencies. Thus, a victim-oriented definition of 'racist incidents' was introduced for the purposes of victim and witness reporting processes (as well as for the recording of them in local police and national criminal statistics). In contrast, racially aggravated offences were introduced for the purpose of punishing the racist 'aggravating factor' motivating or accompanying 'ordinary' offences such as assaults, criminal damage, public order offences and harassment. Racially motivated offences differ from these 'ordinary' offences in that stiffer sentences are available for people convicted of the new offences. Thus, hatred, prejudice or intolerance are not being punished here as separate offences; this is sentence enhancement legislation that increases punishment for conduct that was already a crime (Jacobs and Potter 1998) when racist bias or motivation can be proved as being a motivating factor during the commissioning of these offences.[10]

The creation of these types of offences and associated sentence enhancement is not without problems. The provision of sentence enhancement for hate crimes, including racially aggravated offences, has been both welcomed and the subject of concern in social science. According to Jacobs and Potter (1998), in talking about hate crime provisions in the USA, one of the problems associated with legislation such as this is that it could be targeted at the wrong type of offenders because the definition of racist aggravation is often too wide. The result is that many minor incidents, including the use of racist language during an altercation or assault, are being caught by the legislation. The use of racist language in these instances, according to Jacobs and Potter, is low-intensity prejudice, aberrant, *ad-hoc* or 'heat of the moment' behaviour that does not indicate the deep prejudice of, for example, a member of a Far Right organization. Jacobs and Potter note that there are many different forms of prejudice (as observed in the Introduction of this book), and that enhanced sentencing provisions for hate crimes can be interpreted too literally without distinguishing deeply held prejudices from, for example, a racist epithet spoken during a heated encounter. The fear is that low-level, surface racist incidents will be caught by this legislation, when its 'real' target should be deep-seated, ideological hatred.

In the UK, a number of commentators (Bourne 2002) and social scientists (Burney 2002; Ray and Smith 2002) have voiced similar concerns regarding Section 28 of the Crime and Disorder Act. Bourne (2002) suggests two main problems with the provisions. The first echoes Jacobs and Potter above, in that the literal interpretation of the presence of racist language during the commissioning of a crime has resulted in prosecuting authorities criminalizing the wrong people and in fact trivializing the issue of racial crime. I would disagree with this concern and with the distinction between the typology of hate criminals. This distinction is offender-centric, as it focuses on the motivation of the hater and thus ignores the victim-centred definitions of a racist incident in the Stephen Lawrence Inquiry. I do have more sympathy for Bourne's second major criticism associated with evidence in relation to the Crime and Disorder Act hate crime provisions. According to Bourne, whereas an assault on someone is objective and measurable, the motive for an assault is subjective and difficult to prove. Because of this, the Crown Prosecution Service brings only one in four racially aggravated crimes to court. This is an unsatisfactory outcome, as 'having a law on racial motivation which is available, but impossible of proof, has effectively put back the struggle to get the racial context of a crime treated as material evidence in trials' (Bourne 2002: 83).

'Hate crime laws' have been described by North American scholars as the 'next generation' of criminal laws which have been enacted to condemn traditionally and officially designated prejudices, such as racial, religious and gender prejudices, that are held, expressed and acted upon by individuals (Jacobs and Potter 1998). These types of criminal laws, according to Jacobs and Potter, are a product of increased race, gender and sexual orientation consciousness in contemporary Western societies. Hate crime categories are, as Jacobs and Potter suggest, a new component in the criminal law lexicon and to our way of thinking about 'the' crime problem. However, and despite the problems explored above, I would suggest that hate crime legislation, proposed legislation and the declaratory statements supporting hate crime initiatives (see also Chapters 4 and 5) also offer a new component in our way of thinking about 'social problems' in general. Hatred that is incited, expressed or acted out has been conceptualized as having an undesirable impact beyond the individual victim, his or her community, neighbourhood and town, culminating ultimately in injury to wider society. Thus, by taking hate crime seriously, the discourses, practices and legislation associated with it can be described as connecting with the government's wider concerns and objectives in that: (1) hate crime is presented as a particular social problem that has a negative impact well beyond the individual victim(s); (2) which is in turn connected to the failures of public institutions (e.g. institutional racism and institutional homophobia in the police) to deal with the victims and perpetrators of hate crime; (3) which is in turn connected to inclusive strategies dedicated to ameliorating the social detachment and marginalization of minority communities targeted by hate from the social mainstream. Thus, by taking the social problem of hate crime seriously, the wider strategy of increasing trust in public institutions and thus also attempting to increase political and civic participation (i.e. attempting to activate or re-activate the 'citizenship practices' of British ethnic minority groups) is exposed for our scrutiny.

However, North American writers (especially Jacobs and Potter) have suggested two significant problems with this potential political strategy in relation to hate crime legislation. First, hate crime legislation in the USA is a rather blunt weapon in the fight against bigotry in that it does not differentiate sufficiently between 'low-level' and 'high-level' episodes of prejudice (as mentioned above). However, Jacobs and Potter's second concern in relation to hate crime legislation is that it could prove to be the source of social division rather than social cohesion in society. That is, with the introduction of hate crime laws, social relations between groups could become increasingly 'balkanized' through the fragmentation of the criminal law into various offender/victim configurations, such as race, gender, religion and sexual orientation, and that this will inevitably heighten tensions and reinforce prejudices and mutual suspicions between groups. Thus, Jacobs and Potter fear that in the process whereby minority groups will be encouraged to lobby for recognition as victims of hate crime (already evident in the UK in relation to protecting many more target groups from the incitement of hatred, including Muslims; see Chapter 4), a central function of the criminal law as a vehicle for enhancing social solidarity, recognized by Durkheim, will be put in jeopardy.[11]

In relation to the first concern, the problem in the UK identified by Bourne (2002) is that too few, not too many, hate crime incidents (e.g. racist incidents), are finding their way into hate crime statistics due to the under-reporting of racist incidents by victims and witnesses and the under-recording of incidents as racist by police and other agencies.[12] And the UK hate crime legislation (including the incitement of racial hatred) is seen as declaratory legislation, which establishes boundaries and plugs legal loopholes, but is rarely used as a specific mechanism in law for punishing 'hate criminals' (this will be explored in greater detail in Chapter 4). In relation to Jacobs and Potter's (1998) apocalyptic perspective on hate crime provisions turning an advanced Western society such as the USA (or for that matter the UK) into 'the nightmare in the former Yugoslavia' (p. 132), this concern appears somewhat exaggerated, especially their suggestion that the violent fragmentation and balkanization of these societies is an inevitable result of the over-zealous introduction of hate crime provisions. In the UK, hate crime legislation is

being introduced as a means of making society more cohesive, more democratic and fairer through extending protection and participation to the social
groups injured and detached (from mainstream society and civic participation) by hate (a theme explored in Chapters 4–6 in particular). This is evident
in the following statement from the Association of Chief Police Officers:

> Social tolerance towards hate crime needs to drop to zero. Such
> behaviour must be regarded as totally unacceptable. It must be mar-
> ginalized and isolated from the mainstream. Hatred must be met by a
> hostile environment. Corresponding efforts must be made to draw
> isolated victims and victim groups into mainstream society by fair
> treatment, dialogue, respect and the inspiration of trust.
>
> (ACPO 2000: 51)

This is one of many similar statements from police and government
organizations that will feature in this book with regard to the 'war on hate
crime' in the wider context of the intolerance of intolerance. However, it is
important to note that the offer of increased protection from the harm of hate
for the communities targeted by it is part of a wider Third Way strategy in
which the right to these protections is offered in a social contract that expects
the groups that will benefit from this protection to become less insular, less
defensive and take up the obligations and responsibilities associated with the
wider political community. In the UK, therefore, hate crime provisions and the
taking of hate crimes seriously are ultimately matters of citizenship understood as rights with responsibilities – the right to be protected from harm in
the provisions of the criminal law with the understanding that this right is
accompanied by a re-orientation of commitments, loyalties and responsibilities to the wider political community. Instead of heating-up tensions and
competition between groups, as in Jacobs and Potter's (1998) 'balkanization
theory', hate crime provisions in the UK are part of the wider strategy
(explored in greater detail in Chapter 7) of cooling-down group tensions and
loyalties so that 'we' can all move to the common ground of shared values
through toleration forged in the presence of, and in active dialogue with,
others (Creppell 2003).

The politics of consultation

> Whatever was done 'after Scarman', it became clear during the
> Lawrence Inquiry that the loss of 'confidence and trust' among ethnic
> minority communities had, if anything, worsened in the intervening
> 18 years.
>
> (Bowling and Phillips 2002: 17)

In addition to the recommendations associated with 'racially aggravated' provisions, and the suggestions regarding the reporting and recording of racist incidents, a third component of the Stephen Lawrence Inquiry's recommendations was devoted to overcoming the antagonism and mistrust between minority groups and the police through mechanisms that would ensure greater police–community consultation. These recommendations were made in an attempt to overcome one of the most obvious indicators that ethnic minority groups did not trust police – that is, the under-reporting of racist incidents. To encourage the reporting of racist incidents, the Stephen Lawrence Inquiry recommended 'that all possible steps should be taken by police services at local level in consultation with local government and other agencies and local communities to encourage the reporting of racist incidents and crimes' (MacPherson 1999: recommendation 16). In the Crime and Disorder Act 1998, this recommendation became law through the statutory consultation requirement involving police services, local authorities, local agencies and communities in the form of crime prevention initiatives and 'crime reduction partnerships'. This legislative requirement placed a duty on the police as an organization to 'open-out' to the other (in this case, ethnic minority communities) to develop stable ties with them (Giddens 1994b). As already suggested in the Introduction to this book, this is an attempt to win, achieve and actively sustain trust. In relation to racist incidents and ethnic minority communities such as the African-Caribbean community, and as will be demonstrated in Chapter 5 in relation to sexual minority communities, the Stephen Lawrence Inquiry and the Crime and Disorder Act 'consultation' recommendations and requirements are part of a bridge-building strategy between the police and other agencies (in a multi-agency complex), as well as between police, local authorities and local communities with special reference to 'hard to reach groups', so designated through their enduring lack of trust in the police (this will be explored in greater detail in Chapters 5 and 6).

Police and minority community consultation is not a recent policy recommendation in that consultation was proposed but rarely (and problematically) implemented on the ground as a result of recommendations made by the Scarman Inquiry. The Scarman Inquiry suggested that a statutory framework should be developed to require local consultation between the Metropolitan Police Service and the African-Caribbean community at borough or police district level (Scarman 1981: 5.69). Keith (1993) describes the latter as a crucial development that placed consultation on the political agenda in a context which explicitly linked consultation to the prevention of public disorder and the resolution of the clashes between the police and African-Caribbean people in London. According to Holdaway (1996), Lord Scarman's ambition was to have police–community liaison or consultative committees established as a statutory duty on the Metropolitan Police Service to bring 'representative' public opinion to bear on local police policy to improve police race relations, especially through the presence of minority ethnic representation on the committees. Section 106 of the Police and Criminal Evidence Act 1984 made statutory requirements in London for all police constabularies to establish such consultation committees. However, Holdaway (1996) describes research conducted at the time (by Rod Morgan) as indicating that there was evidence of widespread confusion regarding non-London police forces that thought they were required to create such committees and those police forces that instituted them reported varying, yet limited success. Consultation between the police and ethnic minority groups was to be raised again as a mechanism for bridging the gap between the police and African-Caribbean communities during the Stephen Lawrence Inquiry and in the year in which the Crime and Disorder Act was implemented. For example, Her Majesty's Inspectorate of Constabularies (HMIC), in the Thematic Inspection Report on Police Community and Race Relations, noted there was a growing awareness that:

> the police cannot win the battle against crime without the support of the communities they serve. As communities become more plural, gaining their trust[13] will require both improvements in the quality of service they receive and the adoption – as a core element of all policing activity – of a community focused strategy which recognises diversity . . . In effect this means that all the various components . . . of the police organisation should reflect a community and race relations element in their individual plans and strategies.
>
> (HMIC 1997: 4)

The Stephen Lawrence Inquiry also recommended that the Metropolitan Police Service should include targets for the recruitment, progression and retention of 'minority ethnic staff', which was to be monitored by HMIC (MacPherson 1999: recommendations 64–66) to ensure that the Metropolitan Police Service is more representative of ethnic diversity in London, thus further attempting to 'change' the racist culture of the organization from the inside-out. On the whole, this legislation and these recommendations can be described as progressive attempts at developing a police force that polices with the consent of many more communities than those represented by White Middle England. It should also be noted that the aim of these consultation mechanisms (and increased recruitment and retention of ethnic minority police officers[14]) is not just to facilitate passive trust, but instead are attempts to promote 'active trust' through dialogue with the other in a wider process of institutional reflexivity (Lash 1994b).

In the Metropolitan Police Service, one of the most significant developments in relation to anti-hate crime initiatives has been the formation of the high-profile Diversity Unit (Stanko 2001), which has the remit of (i) monitoring incidents of hate crime across London and (ii) formulating strategic policy and promoting good practice for the investigation of such crimes. At the same time, special community safety units[15] were established in each of the Metropolitan Police Service's 32 boroughs. These units deal with racist and homophobic hate crime but mostly, according to Stanko (2001), with domestic violence, which accounts for four out of five community safety unit referrals.[16] The combination of these developments amounts to a commitment on the part of the Metropolitan Police Service, and increasingly police forces throughout Britain, to take racist (and other) hate crimes seriously and of attempting, through mechanisms of consultation, to promote dialogue between the police, other agencies and diverse community groups. However, despite all of these progressive developments, there remains at least one major problem regarding the policing of ethnic minority communities. All of these developments sit uncomfortably with one of the most persistent and virulent policies that impacts on the relationship between the police and many minority groups and 'subcultural' groups, in particular young people, and especially young African-Caribbean men – that is, police stop and search.

Over-policed still? Stop and search

> The cultural link between crime – the original cause of police interest in the Brixton area – and politics is not the only connection between them. Their common context – 'the street' – defines them both and reveals their essential similarity. Scarman's report indexes the gradual replacement of 'mugging' as the central sign for black criminality. The concept has been replaced in more recent pronouncements by police and politicians by the term 'street crime'.
>
> (Gilroy 1992: 106)

According to the Stephen Lawrence Inquiry, 'if there was one area of complaint which was universal it was the issue of stop and search. Nobody in ethnic minority communities believes that the complex arguments which are sometimes used to explain figures of stop and search are valid'. However, the inquiry noted that on the issue of stop and search:

> it is not within our terms of reference to resolve the whole complex argument on this topic. Whilst there are other factors at play we are clear that the perception and experience of minority communities that discrimination is a major element in the stop and search problem is correct.
>
> (MacPherson 1999: 45.8)

Despite the acknowledgement of the discriminatory effects of stop and search in the inquiry report as being the most historically enduring factor in the problematic relationship between the police and minority ethnic communities, this policing method was excluded from the recommendation 'that the full force of the Race Relations legislation[17] should apply to all police officers, and that Chief Officers of Police should be made vicariously liable for the acts and omissions of their officers relevant to this legislation' (MacPherson 1999: recommendation 11). The inquiry's recommendations with regard to stop and search were that the powers of the police under current legislation should remain unchanged. This decision was justified by the inquiry on the basis that this policing method was required 'for the prevention and detection of crime' (MacPherson 1999: recommendation 60). Several commentators (Anthias 1999; McLaughlin and Murji 1999; Lea 2000; Mooney and Young 2000), in particular Bridges (1999), have noted the inquiry's 'contradictory approach' when it comes to stop and search, in that they clearly acknowledge the problem and offer a hard-hitting rejection of police rationalizations for the vastly disproportionate use of stop and search against the Black community (Bridges 1999; MacPherson 1999: 6.45(b)). But crucially, despite this the inquiry did not recommend that stop and search procedures should be subjected to the full weight of law (in the Race Relations Amendment Act 2000). The inquiry instead suggested an administrative tightening of the procedures (Lea 2000) in the form of regulations found in recommendations 61–63 of the inquiry, which suggest that: records be kept by police officers of all stop and searches made under any legislative provision;[18] these records should be monitored, analysed, presented for HMIC review and the results of the latter should be published; and, finally, publicity campaigns should be introduced to promote the public's awareness of stop and search provisions (including their right to a receipt in all circumstances) (MacPherson 1999: recommendations 61–63). But is regulation, analysis and monitoring of these practices enough? And is stop and search really an efficient crime prevention and crime detection method?

In the rest of this section, the precarious balancing act between the Metropolitan Police's insistence that stop and search is an effective policing tool for fighting 'street crime' and the negative impact which this policing method has on minority ethnic communities will be examined through exploring the questions above. The concern expressed by many social science commentators regarding attempts to tighten stop and search procedures is that reasonable suspicion will remain a process very difficult to 'purify' of discriminatory factors such as ageism, racism and cultural differences while policing Britain's streets. The grounds of reasonable suspicion will, regardless of informing those stopped of their rights and each encounter being recorded and eventually monitored and reviewed,[19] still impact disproportionately on those members of society who are young, Black and male (the considerable increase in the stopping and searching of young Asian men since 9/11 2001 is seen as evidence of institutionalized Islamophobia; see Chapter 4). The problem is one of police discretion: the decision to stop and search will not be determined by law or policy, but by situationally justified reasons (Waddington 1999), which although subject to tighter regulation and monitoring, the type of behaviour that will arouse suspicion in a police officer will remain anomalous – that is, behaviour that is judged as being suspicious in terms of a general background understanding of what is 'normal'. It seems that the grounds of anomalous suspicion are strongly related to a suspect being young, African-Caribbean and male when the figures for police stop and search are reviewed. There is consistent evidence that the ratio of young African Caribbean men to young White men of the same age stopped and searched varies, yet is always disproportionately focused on African-Caribbean people, for example 5:1 (Home Office, in Waddington 1999: 6), 7.5:1 (Statewatch, in Kushnick 1999: 3–5) and 8:1 (Bowling,[20] in Dodd 2003: 1). These figures therefore support Gilroy's (1992) proposition that 'street crime', which encompasses the offences stop and search is designed to 'police', has a 'black' face and is indexical of the problem of 'black' criminality. One could be convinced that even though stop and search is one of the major stumbling blocks in the police winning the trust and confidence of ethnic minority communities in England and Wales, it must be an incredibly important tool in crime prevention and crime detection for the Stephen Lawrence Inquiry to have left it untouched by one of its major recommendations that all police operations should be brought within the terms of the Race Relations Act 2000. However, this too is subject to debate. For example, research has shown that stop and search is not an efficient policing method (see also conclusions drawn from the results of Operation Swamp above). For example, Wilkins and Addicott show that between 1986 and 1996 stop and search (under PACE regulations) rose over nine times in England and Wales as a whole; however, the proportion of such stops which led to an arrest fell over the same period from 17 to 10 per cent (Kushnick 1999: 230). According to Kushnick, such figures suggest that stop and search is anything but a useful method of apprehending criminal offenders. At the same time, Bridges (2001) noted that the Home Office's post-Stephen Lawrence research on stop and search (Miller *et al.* 2000) also disproved the basic premise that stop and search is required for the prevention and detection of crime when it was suggested that police forces with similar characteristics and crime rates (to the Metropolitan Police Service) make widely differing use of stop and search tactics. The conclusions of Home Office researchers Miller, Bland and Quinton on stop and search were that it has:

> a minor role in detecting offenders from the range of all crimes that they address, and the relatively small role in detecting offenders for such crime that come to the attention of the police ... searches

appear to have only a limited direct disruptive effect on crime by intercepting those going out to commit offences . . . it is not clear to what extent searches undermine criminal activity through the arrest and conviction of prolific offenders.

(Miller *et al.* 2000: v–vi)

For all its attempts to define institutional racism, unwitting racism and its acknowledgment of the specific policing methods and procedures that bear down more heavily on ethnic minorities, the Stephen Lawrence Inquiry has taken many steps forward since the Scarman Inquiry, yet one crucial step back. By suggesting that stop and search not be subjected to the full weight of race relations legislation and instead be more tightly regulated by police services and reviewed by HMIC, the inquiry has missed the opportunity to eradicate a significant source of police–ethnic minority community tension. Stop and search is one of the main procedures through which police services acquire their reputation for racism, at the same time as being the main police procedure through which ethnic minority community members' perceptions of police racism are reinforced. By excluding stop and search from the rigours of race relations legislation, the inquiry tipped the balance of their recommendations in favour of supporting existing policing practices over improving wider race relations. The assumption the inquiry made about stop and search was that policy or procedure could be uncoupled from outcome through tightening regulations. That a young African-Caribbean person is subjected to a more carefully monitored stop and search procedure will do little to restore his or her confidence in the police, if being repeatedly and disproportionately stopped and searched by police is part of their everyday experience. The central problem, according to Anthias (1999), was that the Stephen Lawrence Inquiry failed to distinguish between police mechanisms that unwittingly exclude and disadvantage groups through criteria that are not ethnically specific, and mechanisms that specifically and 'wittingly' are applied differently to different groups on the basis of ethnic membership or its perception, including the disproportionate stopping and searching of more African-Caribbean than White people. Thus in relation to stop and search, the inquiry needed, yet failed, to disassociate the unintentional effects of procedures from procedures that relate to the exercise of judgements and agency (Anthias 1999).

According to Lea (2000), the inquiry's recommendation that all stops be recorded with the aim of filtering out those stops not justified by reasonable suspicion is easily got round by police officers. For Lea, stop and search policy should be subjected to a more radical approach that would change the role of stop and search itself, from a largely ineffective mechanism for gathering information to one which takes place only on the basis of information gathered. Thus, the primacy of 'reasonable suspicion', so central to the accusation of institutional racism and to the universal complaint emanating from ethnic minority communities found in the inquiry, could be replaced by suspicion based on 'concrete evidence' (Mooney and Young 2000). Mooney and Young suggest that stop and search procedures in their current form, regardless of proposed improvements in recording and monitoring, have counterproductive effects, and on the whole have inconclusive crime prevention functions. As a result, Mooney and Young (2000) suggest that stop and search should be replaced with procedures that are 'a smaller, precision instrument, intelligence led and sharply focused' (p. 85). At the same time, rather than attempting to apprehend criminals and prevent crimes through stop and search mechanisms that are counterproductive to police–community trust and confidence building, an intelligence-led policy for stopping and searching suspects might also be fed by intelligence and information offered to police from the members of ethnic minority communities. Stop and search will always be a sign that police services do not trust communities to be the eyes and the ears of the police. By building trust in communities, by encouraging communities to have confidence in a fair and equitable police force, rather than antagonizing communities through policing methods (with uncertain success rates) which disproportionately target their members, police–community relations would improve, reporting behaviour would improve, and the flow of information about actual and potential offences could be beneficial both to communities whose members are blighted by crime and to the police who are in the business of preventing and detecting crime.

Conclusion

It is undeniable that the Stephen Lawrence murder and the inquiry that followed put race relations on the policy agenda and has had an impact on many other police–community relationships, especially those with lesbian, gay, bisexual and transgender communities, which will be explored in Chapter 5. Unfortunately, however, in some crucial respects, especially stop and search, the Stephen Lawrence Inquiry failed to deliver the new era in British race relations it promised. By failing to recommend that police stop and search policies be covered by the Race Relations Act, and by insisting that reasonable suspicion should be at police officers' discretion (although more tightly regulated and monitored) rather than being based on intelligence or evidence-related suspicions, the inquiry missed perhaps the greatest opportunity in the final year of the last millennium to eradicate the most persistent source of tension between police and ethnic minority communities. One is left wondering why this was the case, since (a) stop and search has been and still is a major source of police–community tension, and (b) there is little agreement among researchers that stop and search is an efficient policing mechanism. In the light of the latter, one could conclude that the desire to police 'street' criminality or, more accurately, 'black' street criminality, through the disproportionate stopping and searching of young African-Caribbean men on British streets has, in the end, overridden the desire to eradicate institutionalized racism from policing practices.

Many of the themes explored in this chapter will be taken up in subsequent chapters. Therefore, the chapter is an analysis of police–race relations in its own right but also acts as a springboard to the exploration of many of the themes to be examined in the chapters that follow in relation to a range of related 'social problems' that have emerged in increasingly multi-ethnic, multi-faith, multilingual and multicultural societies such as contemporary Britain. The importance of governing and policing with the consent and active participation of communities, so central to this chapter is a theme that recurs in Chapter 3 in relation to 'migrant' and 'host' communities in asylum and immigration policy, and in Chapter 5 in relation to the multi-agency response to the low reporting of homophobic crimes and in relation to the requirements and mechanisms relating to police–community consultation in the Crime and Disorder Act 1998. At the same time and interdependent with the latter themes, the chapter above signifies a discernible shift from race or difference as a social problem to racism, hatred and prejudice as *the* social problem, described in this chapter as a disease that must be eradicated from British society. In the next chapter, I turn from the analysis of police–African-Caribbean community relationships to focus instead on White and Pakistani community relationships in towns and cities in the north of England. The focus is on the institutional reflexivity associated with the examination of the lack of community cohesion in some of Britain's most culturally segregated areas, for example post-'riot' Bradford.

2 Trouble up north: building community cohesion in Bradford

> Globalism scours away distinctions at the surface of our identities and forces us back into ever more assertive defence of inner differences – language, mentality, myth, and fantasy – that escape the surface scouring. As it brings us closer together, makes us all neighbours, destroys the old boundaries of identity marked out by national or regional consumption styles, we react by clinging to the margins of difference that remain.
>
> (Ignatieff 1998: 58)

Introduction

In this chapter, the emphasis is again on the wider issue of 'race relations', but we move away from the African-Caribbean community to focus on the Asian community in Britain, in particular the Pakistani community. The focus also shifts from London to the North of England, to the towns of Oldham, Burnley and especially the city of Bradford. The 'Asian community' in Britain has until very recently confounded the theory of the correlation between crime and disorder and racial disadvantage as depicted in the Scarman Report. It was suggested by Lord Scarman that Asians, like African-Caribbeans, were subjected to high levels of disadvantage and that they experienced an even greater likelihood of becoming victims of racial attacks than African-Carribeans. However, unlike African-Caribbeans, Asians as a whole have a much lower arrest rate (Jefferson 1991). The explanation for this disparity between African-Caribbean and Asian criminality was usually located in cultural differences between these two communities; for example, the loose family and community structures of African-Caribbeans, as suggested by Lord Scarman in Chapter 1, were contrasted with the rather more tightly structured familial and religious cultures of Asian communities (Jefferson 1991). However, according to Alexander (2000), the representations of the social problem of race, 'which is so much assumed that it no longer needs to be overtly articulated' (p. 3), has increasingly,[1] shifted in emphasis from African-Caribbean to Asian youth. More recently, Oldham, Burnley and Bradford, and the Pakistani communities who live there (especially the young men of these communities), have become synonymous with violence and destruction. Alexander has suggested that before the riots and disturbances in the north of England in 2001, and leading on from the discussion of the social problem of 'race' in Chapter 1, Muslims have become the new 'black' with all its associations of cultural alienation, deprivation and danger that come with this position (Alexander 2000). Since the summer of 2001, these social problems associated with the Asian community in Britain have been overshadowed by the ongoing conflict between White and Pakistani-Muslim residents in these areas.

This chapter can be described as an examination of processes of counter-modernization in the form of the construction of defensive barriers between groups, as described by Beck (1997) in the Introduction to this book and lucidly depicted by Ignatieff (1998) in the quotation at the beginning of this chapter. In this chapter, as in Chapter 1, disturbances or 'riots' provide the initial context of the analysis. However, rather than focusing exclusively on the policing and legislative consequences of these events (this will be explored in the final section of the chapter), the main focus of the chapter will be on the unfolding institutional reflexivity in the form of central government (Home Office) and local government response to the disturbances and riots, in particular the segregation of White and Pakistani communities in these areas. At the very centre of this process is the problematization of Asian – particularly Pakistani-Muslim – 'culture' and community formations as being emblematic of failed integration at the heart of British immigration policy. Cities like Bradford and towns like Oldham and Burnley, and especially the way the Pakistani-Muslim residents live their lives in these areas, is increasingly being seen by the Home Office, Far Right groups and the tabloid media as *the* social problem to be addressed.

The 'riots' and disturbances that occurred in 2001, and especially the responses to them in the form of various Home Office and local race relations reports, are particularly rich sites of official discourses that illustrate the government's wider inclusive citizenship strategies which are being expressed through 'community cohesion' programmes. In these areas, the focus of community cohesion discourses and programmes is on the cultural aspects of exclusion. Thus, the mechanisms of cultural inclusion and cultural exclusion, rather than social inclusion and social exclusion, take precedence here. Cultural difference and the lack of inter-community communication, according to the official responses to these disturbances, are at the heart of the problems in theses areas.

In this chapter, alternative discourses are also examined that have been marginalized in (and by) the official discourses; these alternative discourses offer explanations other than cultural factors to explain why disorder broke out in these areas in 2001. These alternative discourses emphasize other factors, including: the role of British Far Right parties in these areas; the economic context in which the disturbances took place; and an appreciation of the centrality of 'second-generation malcontent' to the disturbances. The final section of the chapter explores the contradictions between official discourses that attempt to promote 'community cohesion' and improve inter-community relationships and the unfolding authoritarian backlash against Pakistani-Muslim 'rioters' in Bradford that is creating further tensions between White and Pakistani communities in this area.

Trouble in English mill towns

In the spring and summer of 2001, mill towns in the north of England were the setting of two seasons of unrest. Oldham, Burnley and the city of Bradford were at the epicentre of this disorder. These events, but in particular the events that occurred in Bradford on 7 July 2001, were the most serious 'riots' in Britain since the 1980s (Hussain and Bagguley 2003). These were also the first episodes of unrest to feature Pakistani-Muslim 'rioters' so exclusively. The disturbances in Oldham and Burnley and the riots in Bradford have prompted the publication of a number of high-profile reports in the form of 'race relations reviews' and 'community cohesion reports', which will be analysed below. However, before turning to the analysis of these reports, the events that occurred in the spring and summer of 2001 in these areas will first be described.

Oldham

It was the weekend of 26 and 27 May 2001 that violence erupted in flashpoints across the town of Oldham (Denham 2002). During these events, cars, houses, supermarkets and the offices of the *Oldham Evening Chronicle* were fire-bombed. On this weekend, riot police faced standoffs with groups of up to 200 Asian youths (Oldham Independent Review 2001). This weekend of violence was alleged to have been sparked by three factors: (1) National Front incursions, (2) the mugging of an elderly White pensioner and (3) an attack by a group of White men on a house in the predominantly Asian Glodwick area of the town (BBC News 2001). A few days later on 1 June 2001, the house of the Asian Deputy Mayor of Oldham was fire-bombed, one week later the British National Party (BNP) celebrated its highest election scores ever in a UK general election, taking over 6500 votes in Oldham West and Royton, 16 per cent of the vote, and over 5000 votes in Oldham East and Saddleworth, 11 per cent of the vote (Oldham Independent Review 2001).

Burnley

Similar episodes of disorder spread to the neighbouring town of Burnley during the weekend of 23 and 24 June 2001 (Denham 2002). These disturbances begun as violent clashes between Pakistani and White youths outside a night-club in the New Hall Street area of Burnley in the early hours of Saturday 24 June; during these disturbances, cars and property were damaged. Later, at 5.00 am on the 24th, an Asian taxi driver was attacked by a group of White men. Later that night at 10.30 pm, in response to rumours that gangs of White men were organizing (to attack Asian homes and businesses in the town), a group of Pakistani youths attacked the Duke of York public house. On Sunday 25 June, 'Asian' businesses were attacked across the town by groups of White men, in retaliation to Pakistani youths having previously fire-bombed the Duke of York. This disorder involved members of the Asian and White communities of Burnley. However, the Burnley Task Force Report observed that following the initial disturbances, White racist outsiders took advantage to exacerbate the situation to promote disharmony: 'it was said that some of these people came from out of town and appeared to have come just to cause trouble' (Burnley Task Force 2001: 36). By 2003, the BNP had won five more seats on Burnley Council, bringing the total number of BNP councillors to eight. The BNP were only 11 votes away from winning their ninth seat, which would have made them the official opposition to Labour on Burnley Council (Parker 2003).

Bradford

On the weekend of 7 and 8 July 2001, the city of Bradford also erupted in violence (Denham 2002). During this weekend, hundreds of Pakistani youths fought White extremists and police in the city. Trouble began to brew in advance of the weekend as a result of an announcement by the National Front that they planned to hold a march in Bradford on Saturday 7 July. In response, the Anti-Nazi League planned a counter-demonstration to be held in the city's Centenary Square. In an attempt to avoid disorder, the Home Secretary granted West Yorkshire Police special powers to ban marches and outdoor meetings in the area (BBC, Bradford and West Yorkshire, News 2001). However, on the afternoon of Saturday 7 July, a peaceful, racially mixed (with a large proportion of young 'Asian' men) rally of around 500 anti-fascists took place in Centenary Square, amidst a strong police presence including a number of mounted officers; at the same time, National Front supporters were also gathering at a pub near the square (Harris 2001). After the National Front supporters started shouting racial abuse, fights broke out in the surrounding streets. Just as in Burnley it was alleged that National Front supporters were prepared for this confrontation, many of whom had travelled to Bradford specifically to be involved in a confrontation (Harris 2001).

The fighting between Pakistanis and White racists rapidly spiralled out of control; the police intervened by pushing Pakistani youths and anti-fascist protestors away from the city centre towards the mainly Asian area of Manningham (Smith 2001). The worst of the violence took place on the White Abbey Road, which is the main thoroughfare into Manningham. It was here where the lines of 500 police officers in full riot gear were bombarded with stones and petrol bombs (Smith 2001). Many cars and business premises were damaged during these disturbances, which were classified as a 'riot' by the West Yorkshire Police Force. This 'rioting' went on for several hours and an extra 425 police officers were drafted in from forces in Greater Manchester, South and North Yorkshire, Merseyside, Humberside, Cleveland and Northumbria (Smith 2001). The disorder extended into the early hours of Sunday morning in the form of isolated incidents in which White youths attacked Asian business premises.

These disturbances, episodes of disorder and 'riots' have been the subject of several local reviews – The Independent Review in Oldham, the Task Force Review in Burnley and the District Race Review in Bradford – in which the causes of these events have been examined. In the next section, attention will turn to the response of the Home Office and Local Government Association to these disturbances, as well as a detailed examination of the programme for 'social renewal' advocated in the Bradford District Race Review and the Home Office's Community Cohesion Review.

The lack of community cohesion

The documents written and published in response to the disturbances in Oldham, Burnley and Bradford can be described as being significant in that the central objectives contained in their pages are an attempt to describe the problems that exist and to build community cohesion in some of Britain's most economically marginalized and culturally segregated areas. However, in relation to the wider themes of this book, these documents and the discourses included in them are also important Third Way artefacts in which citizens and communities are being encouraged to mobilize themselves and take responsibility for their own 'renewal'. At the same time, these documents are as much concerned with the larger questions of the crisis in British identity and British citizenship in a multi-ethnic, multi-faith, multilingual and multicultural society as they are with building community cohesion in specific areas.

The analysis of these documents will begin with the general findings and recommendations of the Community Cohesion Review Team (CCRT) Report. This will be followed by a more detailed analysis of the findings and recommendations of the Bradford District Race Review (BDRR) Report. However, before this analysis, the definitions of community cohesion that are presented in these documents will be examined. According to the CCRT, community cohesion has been the indirect focus of many of the government's policies and initiatives aimed principally at reducing social exclusion, for example:

> community cohesion is a term that has recently become increasingly popular in public policy debates. It is closely linked to other concepts such as inclusion and exclusion, social capital and differentiation, community and neighbourhood. In this way it has indirectly been the focus of a number of policies and initiatives aimed principally at reducing social exclusion.
>
> (Home Office 2001a: para. 3.1)

In the CCRT Report, it is stated that although community cohesion was initially defined in economic terms, along the lines of 'social exclusion', the achievement of community cohesion requires the consideration of a broader range of issues, including access to education and employment, poverty and social inequalities, social and cultural diversity, and even access to communication and information technologies (Home Office 2001a: Appendix C). The CCRT stipulates that there is no agreed upon definition of community cohesion. Instead, they offer a tabular representation of five domains of community cohesion with accompanying descriptions:

Domain	Description
Common values and civic culture	Common aims and objectives Common moral principles and codes of behaviour Support for political institutions and participation in politics
Social order and social control	Absence of general conflict and threats to the existing order Absence of incivility Effective informal social control Tolerance; respect for differences; inter-group cooperation
Social solidarity and reductions in wealth disparities	Harmonious economic and social development and common standards

	Redistribution of public finances and of opportunities Equal access to services and welfare benefits Ready acknowledgement of social obligations and willingness to assist others
Social networks and social capital	High degree of social interaction within communities and families Civic engagement and associational activities Easy resolution of collective action problems
Place attachment and identity	Strong attachment to place Intertwining of personal and place identity

Adapted from Home Office (2001a: para. 3.2).

A year later, the Guidance on Community Cohesion (GCC) Report produced by the Local Government Association (2002) offered a four-part definition of a 'cohesive society', which reflects the comprehensive nature of the CCRT's 'five domains' definition above, yet simplifies the definition relative to these domains in such a way as to clarify the specific focus of community cohesion initiatives. That is, in a 'cohesive society':

- There is a common vision and a sense of belonging for all communities;
- The diversity of people's different backgrounds and circumstances is appreciated and positively valued;
- Those from different backgrounds have similar life opportunities; and
- Strong and positive relationships are being developed between people from different backgrounds in the workplace, in schools and within neighbourhoods.

(Local Government Association 2002: 6)

The GCC Report definition removes many of the mixed messages encapsulated in the CCRT definition. For example, domain four – 'social networks and social capital' – as will become clear in the analysis below, is particularly problematic, as too much 'interaction' within communities is one of the main problems associated with bonding social capital. The GCC's definition focuses more directly on the difference, diversity and the building of stronger relationships between communities than the CCRT's 'domains' definition.[2] This particular approach (hidden in the detail of the CCRT's 'five-domain' definition) is actually central to the CCRT's primary concerns:

We believe that there is an urgent need to promote community cohesion, based upon a greater knowledge of, contact between, and respect for, the various cultures that now make Great Britain such a rich and diverse nation. It is also essential to establish a greater sense of citizenship, based on [a few] common principles which are shared and observed by all sections of the community. This concept of citizenship would also place a higher value on cultural differences.

(Home Office 2001a: paras. 2.12 and 2.13)

In many ways, the official reports and documents examined in this chapter are a problematization of the 'weakness' of British citizenship, especially among the members of migrant communities. The problems in Bradford, Oldham and Burnley, as will be demonstrated below, are presented as being the result of failed integration, where migrant communities become established in areas yet are not integrated with the 'host' community. According to the CCRT, White and Pakistani communities in these areas are united in their ignorance and hostility towards each other. Thus, non-integration of 'host' and established migrant communities, experienced as segregation, separation and a lack of 'contact' between these communities, is viewed by the CCRT as the root of the problems. The following factors were listed as being particularly problematic:

Separate: educational arrangements, community and voluntary bodies, employment, places of worship, language, social and cultural networks, means that many communities operate on the basis of a series of parallel lives. These lives often do not seem to touch at any point, let alone overlap and promote any meaningful interchanges.

(Home Office 2001a: para. 2.1)

In the BDRR Report (Bradford Vision 2001), specific details are provided concerning the social processes behind the tensions between communities in the city, especially in relation to the 'conflicting views' that the White and Asian communities are reported to hold about each other. These conflicting views are described in the following terms:

Many white people feel that their needs are neglected because they regard the minority ethnic communities as being prioritized for more favourable public assistance; some people assert that the Muslims and, in particular, the Pakistanis, get everything at their expense.

Simultaneously, the Asian communities, particularly the Muslim community, are concerned that racism and Islamophobia continue to blight their lives resulting in harassment, discrimination and exclusion. They argue that they do not receive favourable or equal treatment and that their needs are marginalized by decision-makers and public-service leaders.

(Bradford Vision 2001: 3.2)

According to the BDRR Report, the means of overcoming this 'community apartheid' in Bradford is to transform these entrenched and endemic views held by the local White and Pakistani communities by opening up the channels of communication between these self-segregating communities in an attempt to 'bust' the alleged 'myths' that foster the antagonism between them. According to the report, both of these polarized communities in Bradford feel they are 'hard done by' in slightly different ways, for example:

> Misinformation about and mismanagement of diverse community relations have fuelled White people's resentment about a perceived dominant presence of visible minorities with strong religious affiliations.
> Simultaneously, a fast growing Muslim community is, to an extent, resentful of perceived as well as actual unfair and unequal treatment. The Muslim community therefore tends to draw on the comfort and security derived from staying together, retaining its strong culture, religious affiliation and identity, to live in self-contained communities and maintain strong links with Pakistan.
>
> (Bradford Vision 2001: 3.5)

The BDRR solution to this problem of polarization and self-segregation is slightly different to the CCRT's solution, in that the emphasis of the CCRT Report was the renewal of citizenship through the recognition of core values shared by different communities. Instead, the BDRR Report suggests that the way forward is to focus on the identities of the city's diverse inhabitants. Commonality in Bradford is to be achieved through inventing a multicultural Bradfordian identity that all residents of the city can be proud of. This common identity is to be achieved through the 'Bradfordian People Programme' (Bradford Vision 2001: 24). This programme is to contain four interrelated features:

(i) citizenship education in schools;
(ii) the creation of a centre for diversity, learning and living;
(iii) the initiation of a behavioural competency framework for the workplace; and
(iv) equality and diversity contract conditions.

(Bradford Vision 2001: 4.7)

These components of the Bradfordian People Programme are designed to enable the people of the district to focus on their common interests and concerns and to be more mindful of the differences that do exist between different communities. By so doing, the intention of the programme is to break the habit of communities seeking to protect their identities, self-interests and cultures through self-segregation, especially through avoiding contact with other communities and institutions in the district. According to the review, the problem (and implicit solution) for all communities in the Bradford district is that:

> They have yet to be convinced about the benefits to be derived for themselves from a multi-cultural, multi-ethnic, multi-faith and multi-lingual society or community. That is the key for Bradfordians. It is to understand, believe in, see and share the benefits of its diversity.
>
> (Bradford Vision 2001: 3.9)

What can be observed here is an attempt to transform the forms of sociation in Bradford from exclusive bonding social capital to inclusive bridging social capital (Putnam 2000). This is a social programme whereby bonding social capital, which is not uncommon in 'ethnic enclaves' where it can provide crucial sources of social and psychological support 'for the less fortunate members of the community' (Putnam 2000: 22), is to be transformed into the bridging social capital necessary for generating and maintaining inter-community networks, and inter-community toleration and mutual understanding. However, is the focus on segregation merely a drastic simplification of the problems being experienced in towns like Oldham and Burnley and in the city of Bradford? According to Karla (2002), the emphasis of much of what has been said in the popular press and in various policy reviews about the problems in these areas is tantamount to the 'comically simple' thesis that 'these people do not live together and therefore this is the reason they do not get on and therefore riot' (p. 25). Other commentators such as Kundnani (2001a,b) and Amin (2002) have also noted that in local reports (for example, the BDRR Report) and in national reports (for example, the CCRT Report) that 'segregation discourse' has focused too much on 'Asians' as segregated from Whites, rather than the process of Whites segregating from racialized groups (Karla 2002). 'White flight' and the fear of racial harassment (Kundnani 2001a) are two dynamics in the 'segregation discourse' that are de-emphasized in these policy reviews (alongside others including material deprivation; see below) in favour of what will be the focus of the next section: facilitating community cohesion through opening the channels of communication between different groups.

The facilitation of community cohesion

The Local Government Association's Guidance on Community Cohesion Report (GCC) published in 2002 puts forward a three-part model for achieving bridging social capital networks between diverse and polarized communities in local areas. The three components of this model are: (i) developing a shared vision; (ii) turning the vision into action; and (iii) reaping the benefits of an agreed vision. According to this document, when attempting to facilitate community cohesion in local areas, the message must be that cultural pluralism and integration are compatible. And 'unity in diversity' should be the theme when developing a shared vision. Following on from the BDRR's attempt to persuade the population of Bradford to re-brand themselves as 'multicultural Bradfordians', the GCC model for achieving community cohesion can be described as a project dedicated to 'making' diversity an attractive characteristic in culturally segregated areas. The GCC message is that: 'A shared vision should be challenging, inspirational and inclusive, grounded in respect for our common humanity and recognition of our shared responsibility for the future of society' (Local Government Association 2002: 13).

The development of this commonality and 'future-orientated' shared vision between communities is to be achieved, according to the GCC Report, through open discussion involving the whole community – that is, open and honest dialogue and consultation involving all sections of, and organizations involved with, the community. The GCC Report is suggesting a programme of political engagement and deliberation similar to that advocated in Hannah Arendt's political theory of judgement, where 'public conversations' result in the cultivation of the faculty of judgement and the formation of an 'enlarged mentality' (Benhabib 1992: 121). In Arendt's political theory, it is through public debate that individual, private opinions are tested; it is through public dialogue that opinions and ideas are purified (Passerin d'Entréves 1994: 164). According to Arendt:

> this enlarged way of thinking ... [to] ... transcend its individual limitations, cannot function in strict isolation; it needs the presence of others 'in whose place' it must think, whose perspective it must take into consideration, and without whom it never has the opportunity to operate at all. As logic, to be sound, depends on the presence of the self, so judgement, to be valid, depends on the presence of others.
>
> (Arendt 1968: 220–1)

The recognition (and negotiation) of common values and shared principles are only possible in Arendtian political theory through open public debate. According to Benhabib (1992), the ability to think from the perspective of everyone else is founded upon the ability to listen to what the other is saying, even when the voice of the other is absent – one must imagine oneself in conversation with the other as a dialogue partner. What Arendt's theory of political judgement amounts to, therefore, is enlarged thought through a dialogic ethics (Benhabib 1992). Dialogism here amounts to the rejection of one stance (a monologic position) through trying to foster a 'mutuality of voices' (Plummer 2003: 46). Politically, this ethics is implemented through the creation of institutions and practices whereby the voice and the perspective of others, often unknown to us, can be expressed in their own right; this entails the creation of a 'shared public culture' which challenges the self-centred perspective of the individual (or, in this case, insular community) (Benhabib 1992). The second stage of the GCC model attempts to implement such a 'shared public culture' where the newly de-polarized and 'other-aware' communities proceed to collectively design a programme of work that will outline what needs to be done to make the shared vision of, for example, the new Bradford a reality. The following objectives are suggested in the guidance:

- The development of conflict resolution strategies;
- The development of a programme of 'myth-busting' to counter traditional stereotypes;
- An ongoing series of events and programmes to foster openness and cross-cultural contact;
- Developing festivals and celebrations that involve all communities.

(Local Government Association 2002: 13)

The third and final stage of the model consists not of facilitating but encouraging local areas to celebrate the culture of 'diversity appreciation' they have forged and implemented in stages one and two of the programme. This is encapsulated in the following outcomes:

- An improvement in community cohesion for the local area;
- A reduction in inter-racial tension and conflict;
- A reduction in perceived or actual inequalities for all sections of the local community;
- Creating value from the diversity of the local community;
- Adding to the quality of life and sense of well-being; and
- Greater participation and involvement in civic life from all sectors of the community.

(Local Government Association 2002: 14)

The Bradfordian People Programme and the GCC programme for achiev-ing community cohesion can be described as attempting to transform the perception of 'diversity' from a 'social bad' from the perspective of the local social groups in some of Britain's poorest multi-ethnic and multi-faith areas into a 'social good' – that is, as a resource that can be valued by the diverse communities living and working in these areas. However, the objectives and outcomes listed by the GCC Report above are heavy on 'process' (dialogue, communication) but light on 'content'. That is, there is no operational conception of the 'new' model of citizenship that is being encouraged here. However, there is an assumption that it will emerge as a result of local com-munities participating in these activities and that local community dynamics will be transformed through the process of finding the broader common ground of mutual understanding associated with bridging social capital. This distinction between bonding and bridging forms of social capital is useful for describing the problems in areas such as Bradford. However, in his book *Bowling Alone*, Putnam (2000) does not adequately describe how the process of trans-forming community orientation from bonding to bridging is to be achieved. Putnam describes the forms of bonding and bridging, yet does not suggest the process by which the defensive and often antagonistic identification pro-cedure associated with communal identities is to be disrupted.

According to Fuss (1995), the process of identification occurs through the interaction of difference and similitude in self–other relationships. Fuss suggests that it is through the detour of the other that the self often defines itself. This interplay between the self and the other in the identification pro-cess is similarly described by Hall (1996) as a process of articulation, a suturing, an over-determination not a subsumption; it requires what is left outside, its constitutive outside, to consolidate the process. The constitutional aspect of 'the other' in the self's identity here, especially the projection of negative characteristics onto the other, is a significant component of inter-group hos-tilities. It is the close proximity to the other which in many cases fuels the obsessive comparisons of the self with the other in relation to perceived or actual access to resources and 'special treatment', as reflected in the BDRR Report's depiction of the root causes of polarization in Bradford above. What is clear is that these processes of identification play an important role in the self-segregation and polarization of antagonized communities; and perhaps also play a significant role (absent in Putnam) in the transformation of bonding social capital into bridging social capital.

But how is this programme for transforming the social capital and the accompanying constitutive identification processes between communities in these areas to be achieved? Are these local communities simply to get on with this process of transformation from segregation, polarization and non-communication to the Arendtian-Putnamesque ideal of a dialogic civic social capital all by themselves? This is certainly not the case. According to the GCC

Report, these processes of community facilitation are to be led by the Neighbourhood Renewal Unit primarily working through regional government offices, which, in turn, are to work in close partnership with local authorities to provide community facilitators in local areas (Local Government Association 2002). The emphasis of this central, regional and local governmental intervention, according to the GCC Report, is the development of a long-term strategic approach to capacity-building and conflict-resolution in local areas with an emphasis on developing skills and knowledge and putting in place processes at local level so that communities themselves are better equipped to resolve conflict themselves.

What is interesting about these recommendations is the government's attempt to secure order in segregated local areas through interventions that seek to target (1) the 'cultures' of local neighbourhoods and communities and (2) the affiliations, allegiances and attachments forged within them in civil society. In terms of governmentality theory, what can be observed here is a further extension of government in and through the sign of 'community'. However, in this instance, the focus is on desirable or undesirable forms of sociation in communities. In governmentality theory, government is conceptualized as 'working' through its power to put others into action, to stir up the desire, the interest and the will to participate or to act 'politically' (Cruickshank 1994). This is instrumentalized in community cohesion discourses through encouraging local people to alter their ways of thinking about, doing and being communities. What this programme seems to be approaching can be described as a problematization of habitus. According to Bourdieu (1977), habitus can be defined as a system of dispositions that designate ways of being – habitual states – in particular predispositions, tendencies, propensities and inclinations. Habitus, it can be argued, alongside the problematization of the processes of identification, is central to the Putnamesque social capital reorientation process being advocated in the name of building community cohesion because:

> Habitus is precisely this immanent law, *lex insitia*, laid down in each agent by his earliest upbringing which is the precondition not only for the co-ordination of practices but also for practices of co-ordination, since the corrections and adjustments the agents themselves consciously carry out presuppose their mastery of a common code.
>
> (Bourdieu 1977: 81)

Thus, Bourdieu's concept of habitus facilitates a deeper analysis of the structures of sociation. In relation to 'undesirable' social capital, habitus offers particular insights into what is to be modified in relation to a group's internal organization in the form of its internalized structures, schemes of perception and action common to all members of the same group or class (Bourdieu 1977). These insights into the internalization of habitus and the socialization process, in relation to social capital, will be returned to below. Bourdieu, Arendt and Fuss have been particularly useful here in attempting to break into and break down the 'deeper' social processes which are the absent presences that haunt the application of social capital theory to areas such as Bradford, especially when attempting to develop a deeper analysis of precisely what is being problematized and proposed for modification in the name of community cohesion.

However, is it enough to inspire communication and representative thinking, to refurbish order through manipulating (governmentalizing) identities (or more accurately identification processes) and re-orientating the internalized structures of habitus in these areas? What are the factors that fall outside of these programmes for facilitating community cohesion through encouraging bridging social capital?

Deprivation, citizenship and 'the second generation'

> Segregation is in itself an odd idea with an odder policy solution: cohesion. So basically by people mixing more with each other, the issue of poor housing, unemployment and lack of qualifications will somehow go away and perhaps more specifically the issue of poor policing and intrusions by right-wing groups will suddenly vanish.
>
> (Karla 2002: 27)

In this section, I explore the de-emphasized aspects of the troubles in Oldham, Burnley and Bradford in the community cohesion reports, including: (1) the neglect of socio-economic inequalities; (2) the centrality of 'second-generation' malcontent in these areas; (3) the role of Far Right groups; and (4) the authoritarian backlash in Bradford in response to the riots.

In the CCRT, BDRR and the GCC reports, the emphasis is on cultural factors related to the lack of contact between communities in these culturally disharmonious areas. What is not emphasized enough in these reports are the contributory factors, such as poverty, exclusion from the workforce and exclusion from consumption patterns,[3] in which these cultural problems are contextualized. Perceived and actual material deprivation was acknowledged in places, especially in the CCRT Report. For example:

> we recognise that some communities felt particularly disadvantaged and the lack of hope and the frustration borne out of the poverty and

deprivation all around them, meant that disaffection would grow. Yet they were not always well targeted, nor even identified.

(Home Office 2001a: 2.10)

However, the overwhelming emphasis is firmly focused on 'cultural recognition', 'cultural respect' and the opening up of the channels of communication between 'cultural groups' rather than dealing with perceived and actual material deprivation. In relation to the 'five domains' definition of community cohesion (see above), 'social solidarity and reductions in wealth disparities' is the only domain dedicated to material disadvantage and redistribution; the other four domains are on the whole dedicated to intra- and inter-community relationships.

The central goal presented in community cohesion discourses and programmes can be described as being similar to Iris Marion Young's model of cosmopolitan 'city life', through attempting to achieve the unproblematic 'being together of strangers' (Young 1990: 237). However, this model of sociation (associated with the political dream of pluralist multiculturalism), in which diverse communities co-exist harmoniously in close proximity, is not without its critics (e.g. Bhabha 1990; Lemert 1997; Escoffier 1998). One of its most notable critics is Nancy Fraser, whose main criticism is that pluralist multicultural politics fights only half the battle, as injustices of distribution are often neglected. That is:

> The multicultural view of a multiplicity of cultural forms represents an unsurpassable gain, but this does not mean that we should subscribe to the pluralist version of multiculturalism. Rather, we should develop an alternative version that permits us to make normative judgments about the value of different differences by interrogating their relation to inequality.
>
> (Fraser 1997: 187)

What is needed here is what Fraser (1997) describes as the integration of the egalitarian ideals of the redistribution paradigm with whatever is genuinely emancipatory in the paradigm of recognition in multiculturalism. That is, to fuse what in many cases are seen as two separate areas of injustice, where one is concerned with socio-economic inequalities and the other with cultural injustices, for example discrimination and intolerance (Young 1999a). By focusing in the main on opening up channels of communication, on generating a culture of respect of difference through attempting to encourage commonality – in place of division – what is observable in community cohesion discourses and programmes is a partial repression of 'conflict' achieved through discursively placing unwanted characteristics (such as material deprivation) outside of debate. Oldham, Burnley and Bradford are not only cities and towns that suffer from actual and perceived cultural injustices and the associated cultural disharmony, they are also places characterized by deprivation and perceived and actual socio-economic inequalities. The de-emphasis of these factors associated with the injustices of redistribution are similar to Levitas's (1998) observations concerning the 'discursive containment' in New Labour social exclusion discourse, where conflict is constructed as a problem of the pathologized few, which diverts attention away from the essentially class-divided character of society and allows a view of society as basically benign to co-exist with the visible reality of poverty. Fairclough (2000) takes Levitas's observations further, by suggesting that by focusing on those who are excluded from society and coming up with ways of including them, the government's 'social inclusion strategies' shift away from inequalities and conflicts of interests among those who are included, and presupposes that there is nothing inherently wrong with contemporary society as long as it is made more 'inclusive' through government policies. For the purposes of this chapter, one could replace 'inclusive' with 'cohesive' in the last sentence to hammer home the point that by merely attempting to transform an area's social capital from bonding to bridging might, as Fraser suggests in relation to the politics of pluralist multiculturalism, be only half the battle. All the wards affected in the disturbances that stretched from Oldham to Bradford are among the 20 per cent most deprived in the country and parts of Oldham and Burnley rank in the most deprived 1 per cent; all have average incomes that are among the lowest in the country and many of the wards in these areas also have low educational attainment standards in schools (Denham 2002). The other demographic factor that is particularly relevant is that the participants in the disturbances were overwhelmingly men; those arrested were predominantly between 17 and 26 years of age. In Bradford, the latter demographic is significant, as unlike the wider demographic picture that emerges from the UK, Bradford has a very young population, with over 50 per cent of its ethnic minority communities aged under 18 (Allen 2003). One of the problems in Bradford, according to Allen (2003), is that a significant number of young ethnic minority people are entering the labour market at precisely the moment that there are significantly fewer jobs available. The result of this is that second-generation ethnic minority young people in Bradford are experiencing persistent unemployment. Six wards in Bradford have long-term (over 1 year) unemployment rates of over 25 per cent. High rates of youth unemployment exist in many parts; for example, in the Little Horton ward it is over 20 per cent (Allen 2003).

Hussain and Bagguley (2003) and Young (2003) take issue with the assimilationist and integrationist emphasis of the prevalent community cohesion discourses in their attempt to explore alternative explanations as to why the young men of Burnley, Bradford and Oldham took to the streets in the summer of 2001. According to Young, these events cannot simply be reduced to a lack of integration with other cultures, or a crisis in citizenship. Young describes the disturbances as being motivated instead by a lack of citizenship, of 'citizenship thwarted' (Young 2003: 449). For Hussain and Bagguley, what the discourses of community cohesion fail to realize is that the identities of the second generation are hybribized identities, combining as they do elements of South Asian culture, Islam and Western culture within their identities as British citizens. These young people do not lack a sense of citizenship. They actively create a sense of British citizenship in fusion with other cultures and nations. However, and here is the rub, they expect the natural rights of a 'British born citizen' (Hussain and Bagguley 2003: 1) and incorporate notions of citizenship in all its economic, social and political aspects. This, according to Young (2003), is why discontent is highest among second-generation immigrants. The paradox that can be observed here is that as the second generation become culturally closer to the 'host' population and their economic and political aspirations concur with the wider society, they face both cultural exclusion because of racism and prejudice and become aware of the limits of their economic opportunities in the deprived areas in which they often live (Young 2003).

Back *et al.* (2002) also try and tease out some of the issues de-emphasized in the community cohesion discourses. According to Back *et al.*, and echoing Young and Hussain and Bagguley, the 2001 disturbances should be seen as highly complex phenomena that should not be reduced to the problem of segregation – that is, the 'lack of integration/not assimilated enough' explanations focusing on 'Asian' communities emanating from the Home Office. These disturbances must be placed in their context, 'in which cultural dialogue, the sharing of standard forms of communication and local vernaculars and divisions exist simultaneously' (Back *et al.* 2002: 10). These are young people who are all too well assimilated into a society divided by racism and discrimination, who:

> had the same accents and expectations as the white youths who rioted on the other side of the ethnic line. They scarcely needed teaching citizenship or English – they knew full well that bad policing was a violation of their citizenship just as was a drastic exclusion from the national job markets.
>
> (Young 2003: 458)

'Community' defence and authoritarian populism in Bradford

> The maniacs who were engaging in this are now whining about sentences they have been given. The police have done a really good

job in following this through and at last the courts are handing out sentences that are a genuine reprisal but also a message to the community. For every sentence, for every tough new law, for every sensible measure, there's some bleeding heart liberals who are there wanting to get them off, get them out and reduce their sentence. These maniacs actually burned down their own businesses, their own job opportunities.

(Blunkett, in Travis 2002)[4]

This particular bleeding heart liberal does actually take on board that the disturbances that took place in July 2001 in Bradford were not a storm in a teacup. These disturbances resulted in damage estimated at £27 million and caused injuries to 300 police officers (Travis 2002). However, there are some inconsistencies that should be examined here. In particular, the sentencing policy in the aftermath of the disturbances, under Judge Stephen Gullick (celebrated by the former Home Secretary above), does not square with the Home Office's commitment to building community cohesion in this area. Since the summer of 2001, 282 individuals have been arrested in Bradford in relation to the disturbances; 134 individuals, the vast majority of them Asian males, have been given sentences of between 18 months and 5 years under the charge of 'rioting' (BBC2 2002). The disturbances in Bradford were classified as a riot[5] rather than as a violent disorder, which is how the previous disturbances in Oldham and Burnley in the spring and summer of 2001 were classified. The charge of violent disorder carries a maximum sentence of 5 years; in fact, sentences of 2–3 years were the maximum handed down to those so charged in Oldham and Burnley (BBC2 2002). However, the charge of riot under the Public Order Act 1986 carries with it a maximum sentence of 10 years; the average sentence incurred by those so charged in Bradford was 5 years (Travis 2002). It is this issue of harsh 'scorched-earth sentencing' that has prompted the Fair Justice For All campaign that is actively organized by the families of the charged or sentenced 'rioters' and other members of the local Asian community to mobilize in Bradford.

Judge Gullick does seem to be working to a particularly harsh sentencing regime in response to the 'rioting' in Bradford; he seems intent on sending a clear message to the community by making an example of the 'rioters'. For example, Gullick is allowing no discount for first-time offenders and is largely ignoring the situation of these young men, who are the breadwinners in a significant number of local families and many of whom are academically capable young people, in some cases preparing to take up university places (Fair Justice For All 2003). The Fair Justice For All campaigners organized a weekly protest outside Bradford Crown Court, which attracted support from across the city. They presented a petition containing 3000 local signatures to the Home Office during a demonstration held outside the Home Office on

17 September 2002, in response to David Blunkett's 'whining maniacs' comments and his support of Judge Gullick's sentencing policy. The campaign is also gathering political support from the Conservative candidate for Bradford North and the Liberal Democrats in Bradford. Lord Ouseley (ex-chairman of the Commission for Racial Equality and chair of the BDRR) has himself called for an inquiry by the Lord Chancellor into the severity of the sentences and warned they could produce lasting resentment (Travis 2002).

In cities such as Bradford after the 'troubles' of the spring and summer of 2001, there appears to be an unresolved tension between punishing 'criminal actions' (rioting) and ameliorating the cultural tensions that exist in these areas, between communities and between communities and the police. The criminal justice system is sending out a clear message here (supported by Mr Blunkett), not of reconciliation and conflict-resolution, but rather of social defence through an 'other-directed' project of criminalization focused on the young men of Bradford's Pakistani community. Judge Gullick's sentencing policy has all the hallmarks of a social reaction to a so-called 'dangerous other' or 'folk devil', in this case 'the rioter', with the required social necessity of defending society against a dangerous enemy (Garland 2001). At the same time in moral panic tradition, appeals to the moral consensus of the majority were made by Judge Gullick as well as throughout the reports that make up the community cohesion archive. For example, the following was stated in the Denham Report:

> nothing can excuse this kind of violence and wanton destruction of property inflicted on the communities caught up in last summer's disorders. The police – of whom over 300 were injured – did a difficult job well in protecting the public. The damage done to local businesses, and to the image of, and relations between, those communities will not be made good quickly. It is the ordinary, decent law-abiding majority affected who have suffered the most.
>
> (Denham 2002: 10)

Ordinary decent people following Denham and Blunkett are not in the business of irrational (burning down their own businesses), wanton, maniacal acts of violence and destruction. Here the disturbances were reduced to 'simple criminality' as deviant and anti-social behaviour rather than legitimate protest (Alexander, in press). This criminalization of the rioters was further confirmed by the essential characteristic of visibility (Valier 2002) through the posting of 'wanted' posters containing the photographs of 212 young Asian men (Alexander, in press) who were filmed by closed-circuit TV cameras (during the Bradford 'riots') as part of Operation Wheel, which, to date, is Britiain's largest scale criminal investigation (Allen 2003). The hallmarks of a moral panic are traceable backwards from the authoritarian flavour of the Gullick sentencing strategy, to the media reporting and the Home Secretary's interpretation of the events as a catastrophic disaster involving unprecedented urban violence. Valier (2002) reminds us that Stan Cohen's theory of moral panics 'conveyed a sense of an unusual and brief flare-up of alarm. In his theory, anxiety is spatio-temporally circumscribed, and panic originates in locally defined interests' (p. 324). Thus, moral panics are a temporary and aberrational over-reaction; these qualities are associated with the immediacy and rapidity of the escalation of the events. Like the original Mods and Rockers moral panic, the disturbances in Oldham, Burnley and Bradford were also 'weekend' events that were localized to specific areas, often to specific streets in these areas. The high-profile televisual and print media representation of the rioters publicized the visible face of the folk-devil responsible, which was further confirmed in the arrest figures in post-riot Bradford, as 90 per cent of those arrested were young men of Asian Muslim descent (Allen 2003). Alexander summarizes this particularly second-generation moral panic succinctly in the following passage:

> the 'riots' were represented and understood as the result of a triple alienation – culture, masculinity and youth – and the harsh levels of social control enacted in their wake can be seen to reflect an extreme reaction to the personification of a national nightmare.
>
> (Alexander 2003: 30)

The unfolding long-term repercussions of this moral panic are legion. Not only are literally hundreds of young Muslim-Pakistani men being sent to prison for extended periods of time, the complexity of the causes behind the disturbances are not being addressed. A number of crucial issues and problems are being ignored in the judicial aftermath in response to the riots: First, the role of British Far Right organizations in provoking the disturbances in Burnley and Oldham, in the weeks and months before the Bradford 'riot', and second, the role played by the West Yorkshire Police Force in fanning the flames of discord. The Fair Justice For All campaigners have noted that the provocations from right-wing groups such as the National Front and Combat 18 on the day of the disturbances in Bradford have been continuously omitted from Judge Gullick's proceedings. As noted above, a planned National Front rally was held in Bradford city centre on the day the 'riot' began. The Fair Justice For All campaigners view this rally as the last straw that caused the city to erupt in violent disturbances. The Pakistani community in Bradford also disagrees with the Home Secretary's description of West Yorkshire police as 'doing a very good job'. From the Bradford Pakistani community's perspective, the police's handling of the disturbances was a continuation of a history of heavy-handedness and targeting of the Pakistani community[6] akin to the oppressive policing of Black communities in London in the run up to the riots in Brixton in 1981 (see Chapter 1):

> For many years the predominantly Pakistani community has been complaining of targeted policing and racism on the part of police officers. Instead of keeping out National Front activists bent on stirring up racial violence, the police instead engaged in heavy-handed tactics against the community. This inevitably fuelled built up resentment and anger on the part of the local community.
>
> (Fair Justice For All 2003)

In the towns of Oldham and Burnley and the city of Bradford, ethnic and religious minority and working-class White communities, as noted above, are often at each other's throats in competition for scare resources. These areas are particularly fertile ground for the emergence of emotionally charged counter-modern mobilizations (Beck 1997). The susceptibility of this area to counter-modern mobilizations is evident in the success of Far-Right councillors in the local elections in Burnley in 2002. In the summer of 2001, the BNP's intervention was running in high gear for the general election. The Pakistani communities of Oldham, Burnley and subsequently Bradford clearly did not trust the West Yorkshire police to protect them from the provocation and agitation of hatred and intolerance that was being inspired by these Far Right groups.

In the light of the latter, the actions of the Pakistani young men of Oldham, Burnley and Bradford need to be reinterpreted not in terms of the scale of damage and injuries caused, but rather as a revolt against racism and militarized police oppression (*Weekly Worker* 2002); as a collective display of 'hostility to hatred' and prejudice; as a defence of racial and religious tolerance; as a refusal to be imprisoned by fear. According to Hussain and Bagguley's research conducted in Bradford after the disturbances, this seems to be the case for the second generation of young Muslim men in the area:

> for the younger generation their British citizenship is central to their self-understandings and assertions of who they are, and for them the threat of the NF [National Front] and BNP is just as much a threat to their Britishness as citizens as it is to their ethnic identities. However, their accounts of this threat are not in terms of a British or English national identity, but in terms of their rights as British born citizens. They are expressing and defending a British multicultural, multi-ethnic citizenship.
>
> (Hussain and Bagguley 2003: 4)

From this perspective, the motivations of the British-Asian 'rioters' can be seen not as the activities of 'maniacs', but as a group of people who had had enough, who could not depend on the police or the government to do anything about their situation, who had to take matters into their own hands. In this case – in relation to how British justice deals with the individuals and groups who take matters into their own hands – one is reminded of the saying: *fiat justitia, pereat mundus* (justice be done, even if the world perish) (Simmel 1950: 42). One of the most perplexing aspects of this judicial intervention in Bradford is that only one of the many and competing interpretations of how justice should be carried out is actually being applied in this city. This is not the only route to justice, punishment and reconciliation that could have been taken in Bradford. It seems that the sentencing policy not only runs against the grain of community cohesion discourse, it is also out of step with what Garland (2001) refers to as the 'responsibilization strategy' in contemporary criminal justice practices. Garland has the following to say about the significance of bottom-up social processes in the institutions of civil society as the state's 'new strategy':

> For the first time since the formation of the modern criminal justice state, governments have begun to acknowledge a basic sociological truth: that the most important processes producing order and con-formity are mainstream social processes, located within the institu-tions of civil society, not the uncertain threat of legal sanctions . . . the state's new strategy is not to command and control but rather to persuade and align, to organize, to ensure that other actors play their part.
>
> (Garland 2001: 126)

What the sentencing policy in Bradford amounts to is a highly selective, top-down (and therefore uncertain) programme of order maintenance that marginalizes alternative, and more suitable (given the context), bottom-up, long-term processes for restoring order in the city.

Conclusion

There are clearly two major strategies unfolding in Bradford in response to the disturbances and both are associated with 'cultural' difficulty. The first takes the form of a declaratory technology whereby the harsh sentencing regime so celebrated by David Blunkett is being used to send a clear message to all those who have or have the capacity to indulge in such violence that their actions will, regardless of circumstances, be subjected to the full weight of the law. The second strategy that is being rolled out in these areas is associated with the building of community cohesion. This second strategy, as noted above, is antithetical to the latter, as the perception of injustice on the part of the Pakistani community as a result of the scorched earth sentencing, espe-cially in Bradford, is now one of the major stumbling blocks in the way of building community cohesion. Despite the main limitations, especially the de-emphasis of material deprivation and the harsh sentencing regime in Bradford, the local and national reviews associated with building community cohesion open up a rich discursive vein for academic scrutiny in relation to the Labour government's strategies associated with integration, migration and citizenship.

Although the issues and problems examined here are based in specific locations in the UK, they are part of a larger and ongoing problematization of British national identity and British citizenship in general under the New Labour government, which I will continue to explore in subsequent chapters. This larger project is associated with the wider project whereby British national identity and British citizenship are currently in the process of being re-imagined. Active citizens in active communities are the foot soldiers of this attempted re-branding of Britishness.

As will be revealed in the next chapter, established migrant communities in Bradford, Oldham and Burnley are seen as posing particular problems for Britain, in that they are viewed as inactive, non-participating communities isolated from political processes and whose loyalty and commitment to Britain and Britishness is questionable (this will be taken further in Chapter 4 in relation to the crisis of loyalty associated with Muslim extremists). The lesson the Labour government has learned from the disturbances in these areas, as will be revealed in the next chapter, is not that the experience of multiple forms of deprivation leads to geographically proximate yet culturally distant communities becoming antagonized in the competition for scarce resources in local areas. Rather, the central lesson that the Labour government is taking from the disturbances in 2001 is that Britain cannot allow 'migrant communities' in the UK to establish themselves as separate and distinct cultural groupings that proceed to live in isolated enclaves segregated from 'mainstream British culture'. The disturbances of 2001 in Bradford, Oldham and Burnley are directly cited as part of the government's justification for proposing compulsory post-entry integration strategies, wherein migrant communities will be instructed in 'Britishness' through citizenship classes and English lessons to ensure that all new arrivals in Britain have the capacity to be active and participating citizens. These initiatives are designed explicitly to disrupt the processes whereby the 'cultural apartheid' between communities that exists in, for example, Bradford, is avoided.

3   Asylum hysteria: insecure borders, anxious havens

Introduction

Overt, explicit racism, according to Malik (1996), is an outlook foreign to the British political traditions of tolerance and moderation. However, in relation to asylum and immigration, there have been key moments in British history during the twentieth century when racism, nationalism and immigration policy have taken centre stage. In this introduction, I will reflect on these moments, before proceeding to focus on asylum and immigration policy under the New Labour government.

British immigration and asylum policy was formalized in 1905 (the Aliens Act), when limits were set to prevent unwanted immigration in response to an influx of 120 Jews from Eastern Europe (Cohen 1994). It was, however, the threat of post-colonial immigration from former African colonies, India, Pakistan and Hong Kong in the post-war period when the relationship between national decline, national identity and the threat of unmanaged immigration came to the fore in Britain. It was this alleged threat that was referred to in Enoch Powell's now famous 'rivers of blood speech' made in April 1968, wherein he suggested that the horror (race riots, civil riots protests, etc.) that was unfolding in the USA 'is coming upon us here by our own volition and our own neglect' (Powell, in Solomos 1993b: 67). Powell's long-term solution went beyond immigration controls in that he suggested the repatriation of immigrants already settled in Britain (Solomos 1993b). Although Powellian nationalism broke with the political consensus, in that its fervent anti-immigration message was explicitly constructed around the internal battle against a specifically post-colonial 'enemy within', the Black immigrant, its influence has resurfaced since. For example, Smith (1994) suggested that it laid much of the groundwork for the jingoistic 'Falklands war spirit' of Thatcherism. According to Smith, the Thatcherite deployment of nationalism in the 1980s was a significant site for the re-coding of race in post-colonial nationalist discourse. While in power, the Conservatives under Margaret Thatcher, and later under John Major, introduced harsh new immigration and nationality laws such as the 1981 Nationality Act, the 1987 Carriers Liability Act, the 1992 Asylum Act, the 1993 Immigration Appeals Act and the 1996 Asylum and Immigration Act. However, despite the harshness and defensiveness of these laws, the Conservatives, according to Malik (1996), trod a fine line between anti-racism and racism with regard to asylum and immigration policy, in which Powellian extremism was influential and manipulated in populist discourses, yet also characterized as alien to 'the culture of moderation, compromise and consensus that supposedly characterizes the British polity' (p. 191). However, Malik suggests that the debate opened up by Powell on immigration in the context of national decline set the themes of the subsequent discussion of British national identity.

In the previous chapter, this chapter and the next, I examine the current relationship with those individuals and groups who have migrated to British shores. At the same time, these chapters continue the examination of British national identity (and more finely calibrated, locally based forms of nationalisms) in the contemporary context in which 'we' live now. Rather than Thatcherite (and Powellian) conceptions of defensive British nationalism, New Labour is very keen to promote the idea of a new Britain, a future-oriented Britain that is not only comfortable with diversity but actually celebrates all the benefits that this diversity can bring. In this context, asylum and immigration policy has yet again surfaced as a highly emotive site. In this chapter, I show that the source of this particular wave of asylophobia has shifted in emphasis from the African-Caribbean immigrant as 'inner enemy' in the post-war, post-colonial period, to a general xeno-racism at the turn of the twenty-first century associated with all poor migrants. At the same time, the crisis in community cohesion in Bradford, Oldham and Burnley associated with the lack of integration of established migrant (Pakistani-Muslim) communities with the 'host' community, and the inter-community tensions that exist between Pakistani and White communities in these areas, is at the epi-centre of the Labour government's institutional reflexivity in terms of the 'integration with diversity' asylum and immigration policy.

Thus, whereas immigration has been linked to the construction of the 'social problem' of race in Britain for a number of decades, and there have been numerous examples of the use of state intervention to halt the 'gathering momentum' of Black (African-Caribbean) immigration and to resolve the social 'problems' perceived to be linked to it (Solomos 1993b), these recent developments, although characterized by some modifications and shifts (especially the emphasis on Pakistani-Muslim rather than African-Caribbean immigrants), should be mapped against this longer history. Therefore, this chapter explores the Labour government's 'tough' stance on immigration and asylum (which is mirrored by sections of the tabloid media) in relation to contemporary modifications on established themes. The chapter also examines the evolution of policy under the Labour government in relation to asylum and immigration from a 'politics of deterrence' to a 'politics of managed integration' in direct response to the crisis in community cohesion between 'host' and established migrant communities in Bradford, Oldham and Burnley, and the risk of similar types of segregation and social disorder developing in other parts of the country. It is in this context that attention will turn to the emergent technologies of integration under New Labour, in which migrants will be subjected to programmes dedicated to the promotion of a particular type of British citizenship, which suggests that these particular social problems should be ameliorated through strategies dedicated to promoting active citizenship, responsibility and participation in new migrant communities.

The chapter will close by looking at the impact of UK asylum and immigration policy on asylum seeker communities, with a view to examining in particular the unintended consequences of the government's policy for dispersing asylum seekers from the south-east of England to often far-flung and already socially deprived areas of the country, including Sighthill in Glasgow and the Caia Park Estate in Wrexham in North Wales. Here the narcissism of minor differences, and the assertion of the 'Whiteness' of 'the not very privileged', will be explored as an example of a 'nationalization' or 'nationalism' of 'the neighbourhood' (Cohen 1996; Knowles 2003) in the context of the convergence of asylophobia with Islamophobia in the aftermath of 9/11.

New Labour: the politics of deterrence

The 1998 White Paper *Fairer, Faster and Firmer* (Home Office 1998c) and the eventual Immigration and Asylum Act 1999 are important milestones marking the development of the Labour government's asylum and immigration policy. The major impact of this policy was the introduction of deterrence as the organizing principle of immigration and asylum policy. The result of this was the formalization of the British component of a Western European culture of suspicion in relation to asylum seekers, which has had far-reaching implications for the way the British public and the British media portray 'the asylum problem'. In this culture, all asylum seekers are portrayed as potential illegal immigrants and/or economic migrants. A central component of the Immigration and Asylum Act was the government's attempt to make Britain an unattractive destination for prospective economic migrants who could be posing as asylum seekers (this policy will be more fully examined below). Britain is not alone in this strategy. The institutionalization of policies of deterrence has led to the emergence of what Sivanandan (2001) has referred to as xeno-racism in European-wide immigration and asylum policy. According to Sivanandan, xeno-racism combines racist prejudice with xenophobia: 'the (natural) fear of strangers' (p. 2). This is a form of racism that is not colour-coded, that is not only targeted at those with darker skins from a different race, but is also directed at White asylum seekers from Eastern European countries.[1] Xeno-racism is not only associated with fear and/or hatred of strangers, but is also concerned with counter-modern defensiveness (Beck 1997) in which 'host' peoples attempt to preserve their way of life, standard of living and/or identity (Sivanandan 2001). Xeno-racism is thus 'racism in substance but xeno in form – a racism that is meted out to impoverished strangers even if they are White' (Sivanandan 2001: 2). Thus, xeno-racism is most closely associated with the deterrence of 'poor' economic migrants from coming to 'Fortress Europe'. According to Fekete (2001a), with the election of the Labour government in 1997, xeno-racism was incorporated into British immigration and asylum policy.

At the centre of the Labour government's immigration and asylum policy in the 1999 Act is an attempt to project an image to would-be asylum seekers, that Britain is not a 'soft touch' (Crawley 2003: 2). A balance was sought in the 1999 Act whereby the government attempted to fulfil two main requirements: (1) its international commitments; and (2) introduce measures that would make the UK a less attractive prospect for 'economic migration'. The result of this policy, and especially the tabloid media's interpretation of it, was that increasingly all asylum seekers to Britain were being portrayed as 'bogus' – that is, motivated by economic gain rather than motivated by the 'genuine' circumstances of displaced peoples and groups, such as persecution, genocide and civil war. According to Fekete (2001a), by making the 'philosophy of deterrence' the organizing principle of asylum and immigration policy, the government is sending out a signal to society that anti-asylum prejudice is socially acceptable. This anti-asylum prejudice in government and tabloid discourses came to crystallize around a particular issue: 'asylum shopping'. Asylum shopping is associated with the belief that would-be asylum seekers 'shop around' for the European country with the best and most easily obtained social security benefits (Fekete 2001a). Thus, the social security benefits asylum seekers could claim became the focus of the Labour government's reforms in the 1999 Act. The government proceeded, following the lead of schemes already introduced in Germany and Switzerland, to introduce a voucher system of basic support for asylum seekers, which replaced the cash-benefit system (Fekete 2001a). The government also introduced a 'no-choice' national dispersal scheme. Both of these schemes were to be coordinated by the National Asylum Support Service (Audit Commission 2000). The voucher system is an explicit institutionalization of a culture of suspicion in UK immigration and asylum policy, in that it is an anti-fraud measure, which by default labels all asylum seekers as potential benefit fraudsters. Jack Straw, a former Home Secretary, justified the voucher 'social security' system in the following statement in the House of Commons with regards to deterring would-be asylum seekers: 'cash benefits in the social security system is a major pull factor that encourages fraudulent claims' (Straw, in Fekete 2001a: 35). By removing access to social benefits and making cash benefits as small as possible, the state was implying that protection from absolute destitution was the only obligation it had towards asylum seekers, which is implicit in a regime that denies them access to the welfare state. Fekete is concerned with the punitive message being sent out to all asylum seekers:

> The overall message – that asylum seekers, in the future, will be treated as a suspect group – is one that justifies popular resentment and fuels prejudice. Held under suspicion of being illegal entrants and economic migrants and guilty until proved innocent – of lodging false claims, asylum seekers were, henceforth, to be subjected to policies designed not to protect their human rights but to protect the public from them.
>
> (Fekete 2001a: 31)

According to a report published in 2001 by the European Commission Against Racism and Intolerance (ECRI), many UK organizations working with asylum seekers and refugees were concerned that separating the system of support from the benefits system in the Immigration and Asylum Act 1999 introduced not only a 'destitution criterion', but also a system whereby asylum seekers were expected to live in the UK on a support package equivalent to 70 per cent of income support rates. Moreover, asylum and refugee organizations reported to the ECRI that many asylum seekers in the UK found queuing for food parcels degrading and that using food vouchers at supermarket checkouts was a stigmatizing experience for many asylum seekers. In the 2002 White Paper *Secure Borders, Safe Haven*, it was suggested by the Home Office (2002b) that the voucher system for asylum seekers would be phased out. The main reasons cited were that this system was associated with suspicion of asylum seekers at state level, which was being translated into a source of stigma marking asylum seekers as an inferior social group.

However, it is the national dispersal policy proposed in the White Paper in 1998 and implemented in the Immigration and Asylum Act 1999 that will be the focus of much of this chapter. The intention of the dispersal system was to relieve pressure from the south-east of England, especially London and Kent, of excessive numbers of asylum seekers (Audit Commission 2000). Part of the would-be 'asylum shopper's' perception of the attractiveness of 'soft touch Britain', according to the Home Office, was that asylum seekers could choose to join established friends, family and/or communities in the south-east of England after entering the country. The government decided to kill two birds with one stone by introducing the no-choice national dispersal policy thus reducing the pressure on the south-east by dispersing asylum seekers nation-ally and at the same time the UK could discourage potential asylum shoppers who might view the dispersal policy as being less attractive than choosing to settle in established 'asylum communities' in London and Kent. The dispersal arrangements commenced in April 2000. The rationale for selecting dispersal sites was that these areas would have available accommodation, existing multi-ethnic populations and the scope to develop voluntary and community support services (Audit Commission 2000). These criteria were not always evenly balanced in these sites, as will be observed below. Often it was the availability of housing stock that was the overriding reason for the selection of a dispersal site. The ECRI Report suggested that refugee and asylum organiza-tions in the UK had voiced concerns about asylum seekers being accom-modated in areas of the country where there were no other members of their community of origin or where refugee support organizations were not well established (ECRI 2001). Further problems associated with the dispersal policy will be explored below in relation to Sighthill in Glasgow and the Caia Park Estate in Wrexham.

Taken as a whole, the Immigration and Asylum Act 1999 is a xeno-racist political strategy justified by a particular set of discourses that construct asy-lum seekers as a social problem which the government is attempting to control or at least manage. In this context, the UK's international commitments and the plight of genuine asylum seekers faded into the background as the gov-ernment demonstrated that it was prepared to introduce policies in which suspicion and deterrence were the organizing principles. The ECRI Report acknowledges the role of the media in the construction of this particular problem. However, final responsibility rests with the Home Office:

> The ECRI is concerned with the general negative climate concern-ing asylum seekers and refugees in the UK. Opinion polls suggest that asylum and immigration issues feature increasingly high in the lists of concerns of the British electorate . . . the printed media par-ticularly contribute to creating such a climate. However, the ECRI considers that the frequent changes in immigration and asylum policies designed to increasingly deter these categories of persons from coming to the UK have played a fundamental role in this respect.
>
> (ECRI 2001: 18)

With the publication of the White Paper *Secure Borders, Safe Havens*, the Home Office (2002b), under the former Home Secretary David Blunkett, has been accused of attempting to introduce yet another wave of asylum and immigration policy that has perpetuated a political context in which anti-immigration agendas thrive (Crawley 2003). Since 1998, the government has been implicated in the creation of an anti-asylum-seeker climate. However, in the 2002 White Paper, the Home Office is pandering to this climate. The emphasis of this White Paper is on integration or, more accurately, remedying the failure of integration in previous UK immigration and asylum policy.

Secure borders, safe havens: the politics of managed integration

In response to the 2002 White Paper *Secure Borders, Safe Havens*, Young (2003) has suggested that three events have shaped recent UK immigration policy: (i) media coverage of illegal immigrants entering Britain, usually associated with the Sangatte detention centre in France; (ii) the disturbances in Bradford, Oldham and Burnley in the summer of 2001; and (iii) the hostile reception of the national asylum dispersal policy (including disturbances and local communities demonstrating against plans to disperse asylum seekers in their areas[2]). According to Young, the disturbances in Oldham and Burnley and especially the riots in Bradford in 2001 (examined in Chapter 2) are the most pivotal events leading to the Home Office regarding 'integration' as the key issue in their immigration and asylum strategy. Here, I explore Young's contention by examining the provisions suggested in the White Paper.

The 2002 White Paper suggested an array of practical measures to ease the integration of immigrant communities and asylum seekers. These include strategies devised to 'prepare the host'[3] and strategies devised to 'prepare the migrant'. A central element of both of these 'preparation' processes was the renewal of 'the social fabric' through the re-creation of a 'common sense of citizenship' between 'host' and migrant communities, which are also central to the community cohesion initiatives examined in Chapter 2. In relation to 'host' communities, the problems experienced in Oldham, Burnley and Bradford were presented as emblematic of the failure of integration in previous policies:

> in other areas we have failed. The reports into last summer's disturbances in Bradford, Oldham and Burnley painted a vivid picture of fractured and divided communities, lacking a sense of common values or shared civic identity to unite around. The reports signalled the need for us to foster and renew the social fabric of our communities, and rebuild a sense of common citizenship, which embraces the different and diverse experiences of today's Britain.
>
> (Home Office 2002b: 10)

At the same time, the more overt 'anti-asylum' climate among the British electorate fuelled by sections of the tabloid media were also cited in the White Paper as evidence that the host community's fears concerning immigration and asylum need to be part of policy consideration. For example:

> One of the issues which troubles the public most in relation to nationality and immigration is a belief that entry into this country and residence here is subject to abuse. The amount of column inches devoted to those trying to reach our shores through clandestine routes illustrates that the issue of asylum out-weighs the much broader debate about migration, nationality and integration.
>
> (Home Office 2002b: 22)

The public's concern over economic migration is hardly surprising, since the Home Office itself, especially in the 1998 White Paper *Fairer, Faster and Firmer* and in the provisions of the Immigration and Asylum Act 1999 helped to transform all asylum seekers into a suspect class of potential benefit shoppers and benefit fraudsters. The 2002 White Paper *Secure Borders, Safe Havens* is a key artefact in which the Home Office's (institutional) reflexivity in relation to 'the problem of asylum' is found. The result is a carefully constructed confection of discourses in which British identity and British citizenship are being subtly re-imagined (in relation to processes of renewal); however, at the same time, 'host' community counter-modern tendencies are also being pandered to, especially in relation to assuring 'host' communities that the asylum system will not be subjected to abuse. Thus, in the 2002 White Paper the Home Office is at pains to re-focus the agenda away from asylum as a social problem to asylum and immigration as an opportunity for enhancing the integration of diverse communities with the 'host communities' in local areas. This strategy works in tandem with community cohesion initiatives that aim to enhance the integration between 'host' and established migrant communities, as examined in Chapter 2.

Confidence, security and trust, according to Mr Blunkett in the foreword to the White Paper, makes all the difference in enabling a safe haven to be offered to those coming to the UK (in Home Office 2002b). 'Security' here comes from the 'host' community being secure about its sense of belonging and identity; that is, a 'host' community secure in its own identity will 'be able to reach out and embrace those who come to the UK' (Blunkett, in Home Office 2002b). At the same time, trust and confidence also refers to trust and confidence in the government to minimize risk or at least manage risk to transform them into 'acceptable risks' (Giddens 1990). Therefore, the 'host' community's trust and confidence in government regarding immigration and asylum is to be achieved through the government persuading them that some (acceptable) risks of migration are to be expected, but to assure them that they should be confident that government will protect and sustain the continuity of their self-identity and the constancy of the surrounding social and material environments of action, that is, their ontological security (Giddens 1990) as much as possible.[4] The following was suggested in the White Paper for better preparing and integrating new migrants:

- Speeding up the process of acquisition.
- Preparing people for citizenship by promoting language training and education for citizenship.
- Celebrating the acquisition of citizenship.[5]

(Home Office 2002b: 31)

The intention here is to transform the process of 'becoming British', of gaining British citizenship, from a bureaucratic process into 'an act of commitment to Britain and an important step in the process of achieving integration into our society' (Home Office 2002b: 32). The acquisition of English language and knowledge of 'British life' are seen as key to successful integration. Without them, according to the Home Office, migrant communities are vulnerable and ill-equipped to take an active role in society. What this means is that the process of becoming British will take the form of a *rites of passage*, whereby migrant communities will be first orientated to British life and then be given the practical tools to contribute to British life. This integration philosophy is directly related to the crisis in community cohesion examined in Chapter 2. In both the 2002 White Paper and the community cohesion reports, inter-community apartheid, segregation and conflict in relation to cultural difference in areas such as Bradford, Oldham and Burnley, are presented as symptoms of a failed strategy of integration. The strategy for improving the integration of 'host' and migrant communities that has emerged out of the recognition of this failure is, like initiatives dedicated to increasing community cohesion, focused on increasing the opportunities for, and improving the quality of, dialogue between 'host', established migrant and new migrant communities. The ability of speaking English is central to this process. That is, the ability to speak English becomes, by extension, a practical and reasonable suggestion in relation to the goal of facilitating 'face-to-face' dialogue between culturally different groups, thus ensuring that 'every individual has the wherewithal . . . to enable them to engage as active citizens in economic, social and political life' (Denham 2002: 20).

One could say that this pedagogical approach to integrating migrant communities could also be interpreted as a racialization of 'lack' (Van Loon 2002). The 2002 White Paper can be described as just one component of an archive of reports/inquiries (the Scarman Inquiry, for instance; see Chapter 1), where 'lack' is an organizing theme in relation to the discussion of social problems associated with established and inwardly migrating social groups, especially ethnic minority groups. The assumption in the White Paper is that without these programmes of induction, reorientation and education, migrant communities will not be civilized, loyal or committed enough to be part of Britain, and that what they lack (Britishness) could be the source of future social risk. Thus, one of the fundamental assumptions that organizes the Home Office's proposed management-preparation of migrant communities is that difference, especially racial difference, = lack = risk of future violence (Van Loon 2002). This is evident in the Home Office's (2002b) suggestion that 'failure to ensure the successful integration of those settling in the UK today will store up problems for future generations' (p. 28). This is an acknowledgement of the second-generation backlash, as depicted in Chapter 2 in relation to the 'riots' in Bradford. Just as in the community cohesion reports analysed in Chapter 2 which attempted to isolate the 'problem' in cities such as Bradford, the 'social problem' of integration in the 2002 White Paper is similarly reduced to 'cultural difficulty' portrayed as cultural lack in relation to the capacity for integration. However, just as in community cohesion discourses, this is only half of the problem, as 'the cultural' is once again prioritized over 'the material' in the White Paper.

The overriding principles of the multicultural project of 'inclusion through respecting diversity' are not the central principles of 'the integration with diversity project' that is emerging out of both the community cohesion programme explored in Chapter 2 and the emergent immigration and asylum policy in the 2002 White Paper. This is evident in the logic of equivalence identified in Chapter 2 that cultural differences, if too respected (that is, left alone as a component of the British multicultural mosaic), could result in non-integration in the form of cultural polarization, excessive intra-community bonding and antagonism with physically proximate yet culturally distant neighbouring communities. This is also evident in the Home Office's 'politics of reassurance' (for the benefit of Middle England) in which toughness at the point of entry is central. However, it is the promise to better manage post-entry integration of migrant communities where the government's assimilationist strategy is revealed. This is a strategy dedicated to scouring away the surface of cultural distinctiveness in migrant communities to break down the cultural barriers to their fuller integration that is antithetical to a multicultural project dedicated to respecting diversity (the New Labour immigration–multicultural paradox will be examined further in Chapter 7).

To a certain extent, the respect of different cultures here is being overtaken by the principle that 'host', established migrant and new migrant communities must be engaged in the process of renewing the social fabric of the areas in which they live. According to Mr Blunkett, this is to be achieved through encouraging 'commitment and action from the host community, asylum seekers and long-term migrants alike' (in Home Office 2002b). Active or participatory citizenship, therefore, emerges as the key mechanism for achieving integration with diversity in the White Paper; in fact, active citizenship is fast becoming an all-round policy solution to many different 'social problems' relating to overcoming the barriers between minority communities and dominant social groups and between minority communities and organizations such as the police. Although active citizenship is key to the preparation of both 'host' communities and the migrant communities in the White Paper, the emphasis of the programmes for creating active citizens is on the migrant communities. For example, the White Paper stipulates that the proposed process through which migrant communities are to be 'naturalized' as British citizens will no longer emphasize the 'theoretical entitlements' of their newly acquired British citizenship; instead, the emphasis will be on the contribution migrant communities can and must make in their new country (Home Office 2002b).

The 2002 White Paper is a significant component in an emergent discursive formation emanating from the Home Office, whereby British citizenship and British national identity are being re-imagined through the technologies of active citizenship in a context of participatory dialogic democracy which could have profound effects on 'host', new migrant and established migrant communities. These themes will be developed further in Chapter 7. In the next section, attention turns to the conflation of asylophobia with Islamophobia in Britain in the aftermath of 9/11.

Border trouble – global horror

It is important to acknowledge the impact the 9/11 attacks of 2001 on America have had in relation to how migrant groups, such as asylum seekers, are perceived by the government, the media and the general public in Britain. According to Weber and Bowling:

> As recently as July 2001, an article in the Amnesty International newsletter noted a positive tone in government rhetoric about immigration, spoke with cautious optimism of a possible 'brighter outlook', and called on the UK Government to stop treating asylum seekers as a 'problem'. Just a short time later, that hope seems to have collapsed along with the twin towers in New York. We are now faced with a renewed moral panic about global terrorism that threatens to further undermine the rights of immigrants, asylum seekers and refugees, and to promote hostility towards established minority communities.
>
> (Weber and Bowling 2002: 129)

I would suggest that moral panic theory is an inadequate tool to capture the converging sites of panic and anxiety that have been played out in advanced Western societies since the 9/11 attacks in relation to the imagined and potential threat of terrorism. With specific reference to the UK, this convergence can be more readily understood through Valier's (2002) depiction of the 'gothic' nature of many contemporary social risks, from child killers to unremarkable 'inner terrorists' who turn everyday events such as flying on a domestic plane into catastrophic acts of terror. The gothic nature of social risks comes from their fundamental threat to security: national security and personal ontological security. Van Loon (2002) understood the implication of the 9/11 attacks all too well: 'if anything, the shocking events of 11 September 2001 show that security is a deeply suspect concept' (p. 1). Security is often associated with boundaries and the protection of borders; insecurity comes from the violation of the boundaries, symbolic and real, that individuals and groups think protect them. In her 2002 article, it was Valier's intention to wrestle theorization about populist and catastrophic social problems away from the habitual reference to moral panic theory. In so doing, she opened up a new theoretical vocabulary for exploring the nature of contemporary social problems that are directly applicable to post 9/11 'race relations' and concerns over asylum and immigration. As Weber and Bowling suggest, in relation to UK immigration and asylum policy, hope collapsed with the twin towers; what has risen in the dust of the 9/11 attacks is a Gothic populism in the form of a particularly anxious strain of asylophobia associated with the threat of 'terrorist' violence perpetrated by unremarkable (unmarked, invisible and ordinary) perpetrators[6] that could enter the UK through our 'insecure borders'.

As depicted in Chapter 2 in relation to the Bradford 'riots', moral panics are often associated with local, short-lived events involving readily identifiable 'types'. These are ultimately resolved through law and order strategies fed by populist law and order discourses which manufacture a wide consensus and in turn justify long-lasting repercussions (see Valier 2002). The events surrounding the converging sites of anxiety that have emerged in the form of post-9/11 paranoia tend to include terrorists, young Muslim males and asylum seekers in chains of articulation that seem to be of another 'order' of panic. Here the problems are not local but global (for example, the threat of, and war on, global terrorism) and the 'folk-devils' are often identifiable, yet also unquantifiable in the faceless mass of migrant communities including illegal immigrants dispersed among established ethnic minority communities. Valier points out that in a moral panic narrative (often depicted in story board diagrammatic forms), local, short-lived 'catastrophes' are usually followed by a phase of rescue and recovery, including the restoration of law and order. In scenarios characteristic of Gothic populism, 'rather than recovery, the gothic attains its formidable effects through repetitive themes of haunting and dereliction . . . it is a convention of the Gothic that there can be neither rescue nor escape from a besieging horror' (Valier 2002: 323) in which an 'us' is threatened by a 'them'. This antagonism between a 'them' and an 'us', when articulated in, for example, the Gothic populist discourses in tabloid newspapers, is constructed through appeals to 'common sense' which are articulated through attempting to adopt 'the people's voice' to objectify a consensual antagonism between an 'us' who are afraid and a 'them' who threaten 'us' (Erjavec 2003: 94). Pronouns – for example, 'them', 'us', 'we' and 'they' – are essential to the generation and complicity of consensual antagonisms in these discourses, in which unity is created through presenting the one true perspective on events, the one 'reasonable point of view' (Erjavec 2003). In terms of the media, this is achieved by agenda setting, through focusing on a narrow range of topics in a repetitive fashion. By employing this strategy, journalists can constitute 'social problems as political problems'. This is not to suggest that the media, whether televisual or print-tabloid media, are 'all powerful' and their audience are 'media-dupes', but to recognize that influencing what people think is related to precisely what they think about (Entman, in Erjavec 2003). Kushner (2003) suggests that in relation to asylum seekers the populist media's role is that of keeping the subject prominent in the public mind and focusing attention on specific allegations – for example, illegal immigration, fraudulent claims, abuse of the system – and, as will be examined in the next chapter, connecting asylum seeker communities and established migrant communities with the post-9/11 terrorist threat.

Even the Home Office (2002b) is concerned with the amount of tabloid 'column inches' dedicated to asylum seekers, especially stowaways and all 'those entering our shores through clandestine routes' (p. 22), which is prioritized by the media over the other issues facing asylum seekers and the challenges to asylum and immigration policy. Yet the Home Office's role in constructing asylum seekers as a social problem to be managed in the first place is, according to Kundnani (2001b), an example of a state-generated mindset of popular racism that creates an interface with the tabloid media. The result of this hostility to asylum seekers in the media is unprecedented in its intensity (Kushner 2003). In this context, the New Labour government's attempts to get 'tough seems to be a matter of placating the delirium of racist scare mongering' (Back et al. 2002: 8). Back et al. describe the interface between the Home Office's 'getting tough' on asylum discourses and the popular racism of the tabloid media as being tantamount to creating a tidal wave of xenophobia that fans the flames of the general public's fear of asylum seekers and their outrage against asylum seekers, which is the context of the emergence of a virulent strand of asylophobia in Britain.

According to Van Loon (2002), racism's appeal to common sense is always heavily endowed with a risk sensibility. The common sense risk sensibility currently rampaging in 'Middle England' in relation to migrant communities is clearly one in which the following sentiments are increasingly common:

'things have gone too far', 'there are too many of them', 'who is going to pick up the bill for all of these people?' At the same time, these general xeno-racist sentiments have become the fertile ground for the flourishing of a convergence of asylophobia with Islamophobia in the post-9/11 political context in the UK, which will be explored below and in the next chapter.

Asylum dispersal – the mobilization of virulent hostility

> No human difference matters much until it becomes a privilege, until it becomes the basis of oppression. Power is the vector that turns minor into major.
>
> (Ignatieff 1998: 50)

In this section, the emphasis will be on the relationship between 'host' communities and asylum seeker communities. Previously in this chapter it was suggested that 'preparing host communities' was (as well as encouraging 'active citizenship') a matter of shoring up their ontological security – that is, the array of emotional and subjective factors relating an individual's sense of confidence in the constancy and continuation of their self-identity and their social and material environments of action and influence (Lupton 1999–8). Giddens's theory of ontological security has much in common with Sivanandan's theory of the emergence of xeno-racism in relation to asylum seekers, also explored earlier in this chapter, where the racist elements of this phenomenon are also concerned with the protection of privilege, status, ways of life and standards of living; and both of these theories can in turn be related to Freud's theory of 'the narcissism of minor differences'[7] which has been popularized in recent years by Ignatieff in relation to his work on the conflicts in the former Yugoslavia. In this theory, it is the preservation of identity and privilege (the narcissistic aspects) with xenophobia (fear and hatred of strangers) which is expressed through the exaggeration of difference (e.g. cultural, religious and ethnic differences):

> In the undisguised antipathies and aversion which people feel towards strangers with whom they have to do we may recognize the expression of self-love – of narcissism. This self-love works for the preservation of the individual, and behaves as though the occurrence of any divergence from its own particular lines of development involved a criticism of them and a demand for their alteration.
>
> (Freud, in Ignatieff 1998: 50)

The last sentence of this quote is particularly telling with regard to 'host' and asylum seeker community relationships – that is, not only will an influx of strangers become a burden on the tax-paying 'host community', their strangeness might also be perceived as a threat to the continuation (development) of 'host' self-identity and status, and cause their way of life to change. Freud's theory places this form of antagonism where it belongs at the level of group psychology, of the collective projection of one community's hostility onto another community. In Chapter 2, this type of hostility was explored through psychodynamic theory, where the Muslim and 'White' communities in, for example, Bradford shored up their identity by the process of projecting onto the other negative characteristics. However, Freud's theory facilitates a deeper understanding of inter-community hostility than the latter. Freud's theory allows for the examination of the nature of the projection of the expression of the hostility. According to Freud, when it comes to negative or hostile group dynamics, it is always the minor differences between groups that are exaggerated. Freud suggests that by focusing on difference, the major similarities between people, communities and nations are ignored. Apart from a few differences – for example, skin tone, religious beliefs and culture – humans according to Freud are 'otherwise alike'; these are superficial differences compared to what all humans have in common in terms of biology and similarities in culture cross-culturally (religion, family formation, commerce, etc). However, 'it is precisely the minor differences in people who are otherwise alike that form the basis of feelings of strangeness and hostility between them' (Freud, in Ignatieff 1998: 48). Freud's theory of the narcissism of minor differences and other examples of psychodynamic theory, including Kristeva's theory of abjection, are useful analytical tools for exploring the tensions between asylum seeker and 'host' communities. However, as in Chapter 2, it is important to point out that these theoretical devices for exploring inter-community dynamics must not be abstracted from the context of their emergence. Material deprivation is the stage on which these examples of counter-modern hostility fester, in that it is in the competition for scarce resources where the minor differences between competing communities are at their most exaggerated. When these theories are employed to explore the current hostility towards asylum seekers, it is evident that host communities in the UK resort to defensive tactics which begin with the process whereby 'real individuals in all their specificity are depersonalized and turned into ciphers or carriers of hate group characteristics' (Ignatieff 1996: 228). However, in relation to the British general public's relationship with asylum seekers, this process of abstraction was undoubtedly fuelled and informed by both government and media discourses that present asylum seekers in general as a suspect class. In these discourses, the term 'asylum seeker' had already become a term of abuse (Kundnani 2001b) as the 'enemy within' (Fekete 2001a: 38–9).

Within this climate, it might be difficult for 'host' communities to 'reach out and to embrace those who come to the UK' (Blunkett, in Home Office 2002b) when, for example, the tabloid press (in this case *The Sun*) are bombarding the British public with the following headlines and by-lines dedicated to asylum seekers: 'a sea of humanity . . . polluted with terrorism and disease', 'read this and get angry' and 'Britain is now a Trojan horse for terrorism' (Renton 2003: 81). The metaphors of threat are everywhere in the tabloid press, where asylum seekers are presented as an invasion, a river, an unstoppable flood (Erjavec 2003).

These metaphors depict a specific anxiety related to the insecurity associated with the failure of the defensive rituals of setting boundaries and of attempting to secure borders. Kristeva's (1982) theory of abjection is particularly useful here because it focuses on the permeability of boundaries and on the persistence of abject (or waste) materials (e.g. blood, excrement and urine) that can never be fully eliminated from the body, from identity, from the social body of the nation. Abjection – the failure of insecure boundaries arises from that which 'disturbs identity, system, order', that which 'does not respect borders, positions, rules' (Kristeva 1982: 4). The asylum seeker in this scenario is a body out of place, is dirty and contaminating (Douglas 1966) and above all dangerous. The abject according to Lupton is a:

> psycho-dynamic phenomenon that is constructed through social and cultural processes but is experienced as a series of emotions arising from within, this provides some explanation for the 'irrational' virulent feelings to which some individuals and social groups are exposed.
> (Lupton 1999: 139)

When the latter is taken into consideration, it is not surprising that host community anxiety in the form of 'hot' emotions and defensive impulses was already heightened before the first group of asylum seekers arrived at Sighthill in Glasgow and on the Caia Park Estate in Wrexham in North Wales as part of the national asylum dispersal strategy. However, it was not only xeno-racism that characterized the host and asylum seeker community relationships in these dispersal areas. In the post-9/11 context, Islamophobia also infused these inter-community relations. It is not insignificant that asylum seeker–host community hostilities since the inauguration of the national asylum dispersal system have predominantly involved Muslim asylum seekers.

The national asylum dispersal policy introduced in the Immigration and Asylum Act 1999 has been described as creating a 'geography of fear' throughout the UK (Kundnani 2001b: 44). Before the dispersal system was introduced, 90 per cent of asylum seekers were housed in London, usually in neighbourhoods where fellow nationals were concentrated. However, increasingly asylum seekers were claiming asylum and being settled in cheap accommodation in coastal towns in Kent away from London's booming property market. Many of these towns, including Dover, were 99 per cent White. In London, according to Kundnani (2001b), local networks of community support provided some in-built protection against racism and in the multi-racial capital asylum seekers went relatively unnoticed. This was not the case in Dover, with incoming groups of asylum seekers being seen as an invading outside force. For example, local newspapers the *Dover Express* and the *Folkestone Herald* described towns in Kent as becoming besieged by floods of asylum seekers (Kundnani 2001b). Dilley (2000) describes the simmering discontent in Dover among local people who had expressed concern over the numbers of refugees housed in the town. In this climate, violence against asylum seekers became an almost daily occurrence. Dilley describes how the simmering discontent turned to verbal and then physical abuse between asylum seekers and members of the local community, resulting in the Kent police asking the local press to stop 'inflaming emotions' with respect to asylum seekers. However, it was not until August 1999 when fighting broke out between asylum seekers and local youths at a fairground in the town that the asylum issue in Kent hit the national newspapers. For example, the *Daily Mail* proceeded to publish its own 'investigation into Britain's immigration crisis' with the headline 'The good life on asylum Alley' (Kundnani 2001b: 46), referring to the Folkestone Road in Dover, which is referred to locally as 'asylum alley' (Dilley 2000).

The government's solution to the burden on local authorities in the south-east of England and the increasing hostilities between 'host' and asylum communities in south coast towns was to introduce the National Asylum Dispersal System (Audit Commission 2000). One criterion under which the dispersal system worked was the availability of housing stock in areas with established migrant communities with existing 'support' organizations. However, another criterion was in operation in the dispersal system, that of dispersing asylum seekers in 'language clusters' (Audit Commission 2000: 12). It will be argued below that this is a crucial factor leading to a reaction directed at Muslim asylum seekers in particular in specific dispersal sites, rather than a xeno-phobic reaction directed at all asylum seekers. The Audit Commission noted that the location of dispersal sites was in practice problematic:

> Ideally, a broad range of criteria should be taken into account when identifying suitable locations for asylum seekers, but realistically few areas will meet all (or even a majority) of these criteria in the short term. Different problems could emerge in different locations. While multi-cultural areas offer better community networks and minimize racial tensions, accommodation may be concentrated on run-down housing estates with few employment opportunities and over-stretched public services. Placement in such areas would risk compounding the exclusion of asylum services and may heighten deprivation in the host community. And yet placing asylum seekers in areas that are not multi-racial can also create problems. One local authority housed 30 Somalian families on an outlying, predominantly

> White, estate. Within a few years, all but three families had left because
> of harassment from other residents and isolation from their own
> community groups, which were concentrated in the town centre.
>
> (Audit Commission 2000: 48–9)

What the national dispersal system seems to be achieving, according to
Kundnani (2001b), is the dispersal of violence across the country through
dispersing asylum seekers to already deprived areas with surplus housing stock
and which are predominantly mono- rather than multi-racial areas. This policy is focusing 'White hate' on migrant communities, and when these asylum
seekers are dispersed in the post-9/11 climate within Islamic-speaking 'language
clusters', the hostility towards them is further exacerbated.

Case study 1: Sighthill, Glasgow

On 5 August 2001, a few weeks before the 9/11 attacks on the USA, Firsat Dag
was killed by a single stab wound to the chest from a pair of scissors. Mr Dag
was a 22-year-old Kurd from Turkey; he was left to die on the street in the
Sighthill area of Glasgow. Within hours of his death, the Sighthill area was in
uproar. Sighthill is one of Scotland's 'sink estates', it is the poorest constitu-
ency in Scotland, the second most unhealthy in Britain (with a lung cancer
rate twice the national average), and it has the highest male unemployment
rate in Britain (Hill 2001). The only dispersal location criterion matching the
selection of Sighthill was the abundance of housing stock. According to Hill,
Glasgow City Council had long been unable to persuade local council tenants
to move into the tower blocks that dominate Sighthill. However, these flats
seemed ideal to the National Asylum Support Service for housing asylum
seekers (Hill 2001). When the Home Office announced its dispersal policy,
Glasgow (which has the largest housing authority in Britain) was the only
Scottish city that agreed to accept asylum seekers under the scheme. The 2000
family flats and 500 single apartments set aside to house asylum seekers under
the dispersal scheme represented a quarter of the city's annual lettings (Fekete
2001b). It is estimated that almost half of Glasgow's 500 asylum seekers have
been housed in the Sighthill and Springburn areas. Glasgow will receive £20
million a year from the National Asylum Support Service over the next 5 years
of its contract (Fekete 2001b).

The main source of tension in the area between locals and asylum
seekers is the competition for scarce resources. Fekete (2001b) reports that
from the moment new asylum seekers arrived on the estate they were the
victims of envy, racism and resentment, in that local residents complained
that 'refugees' were getting preferential treatment over them. According to
Hill (2001), the local population could not help but resent the sight of the

lines of vans turning up on the estate delivering thousands of brand new appliances (washing machines, cookers, televisions and fridges) and furniture (beds and couches) to asylum seekers. Locals complained that while asylum seekers were receiving preferential treatment, they had to wait months for repairs to their dilapidated homes (Fekete 2001b). What can be observed here is resentment originating from the threat to the ontological security of the local Glaswegians through the perception that their status was slipping below that of 'the lowest of the low': the asylum seeker. Far Right groups, for example Combat 18 and the BNP, were in turn eager to exploit[8] the great emotional importance that is attached to very small differences between groups in close physical, social and economic proximity to one another (Bocock 1980).

Three days after the murder of Mr Dag, a second asylum seeker, 22-year-old Iranian Davoud Rasui Naseri, was stabbed outside his front door by a group of White teenagers, who are said to have ambushed him shouting racist taunts (Fekete 2001b). After his attack, Mr Naseri said that he did not feel safe in Glasgow and that it would be better to be in Iran, as 'it would be better for me because I would be killed [in Iran] because of my aims, not because of nothing' (Fekete 2001b: 4). 'Nothing' here refers to the 'host' community's jealousy over a new fridge or a sofa, his aims being political or religious aims counter to the Iranian regime. According to Elspeth Jones, one of the local residents of Sighthill, it was all a matter of the 'host' community being unprepared:

> If the council had explained to the community what was happening, the asylum seekers would have been greeted with open arms because the majority of people here are typical Glaswegians: warm-hearted and friendly . . . But these scared and vulnerable people arrived fleeing countries and conflicts local people had never heard of into an atmosphere already heavy with images of bogus asylum seekers thanks to the rhetoric and the media.
>
> (Hill 2001: 3)

Immediately after Mr Dag's death, around 400 asylum seekers and campaigners marched to the town hall only to be taunted with racial abuse and pelted with stones by groups of local youths, which resulted in retaliation by young male asylum seekers culminating in the arrest of one 16-year-old asylum seeker, which in turn resulted in groups of local asylum seekers holding a sit down protest and agreeing to move on only when he was released (Fekete 2001b). The day after, riot police had to be called to the estate to stop clashes between hundreds of asylum seekers and hundreds of local residents. Locals then announced their own protest to be held against asylum seeker violence and 'the preferential treatment given to refugees'; around 200 local people staged a protest outside the block of flats where the murdered man had resided (Fekete 2001b).

There were some problems in relation to the dispersion of asylum seekers to Sighthill. For example, the language cluster policy under which the National Asylum Support Service operated caused some intra-asylum community tensions through housing Iraqis and Iranians as neighbours in the same tower blocks. However, perhaps the main problem in this area was that there was no extra funding for police, health or leisure provision on the estate to cater for the large numbers of new arrivals, causing local resources to be stretched and resulting in increased tension between the 'host' and asylum communities.

Complaints by asylum seekers of abuse and harassment against them steadily increased throughout 2001. The murder of Mr Dag resulted in marches by groups of asylum seekers in the estate, which further strained relations with the 'host' community. Two further events brought the Sighthill Estate to boiling point: *The Daily Record* (Scotland's best-selling tabloid) claimed a few days after his killing that Mr Dag was a bogus asylum seeker; and a few days after the attack the Turkish football team Fenerbahce played Glasgow Rangers at the Ibrox Stadium in a qualifying tie for the Champions League. During this match racial chants were directed at asylum seekers, especially Kurds from Iraq and Turkey (Hill 2001). The result of these events was that Arabic-speaking asylum seekers were sent into panic; 14 asylum families fled the city on trains to London only to be returned by bus to Scotland by the National Asylum Support Service (Dodd and Seenan 2001). Sighthill has been described by Chief Inspector Irvine of the Strathclyde police as having a proud history of welcoming refugees; however, he suggests that the National Asylum Support Service intake was different in the sheer scale of asylum seekers and in the depiction of them by the media and politicians:

> They took Chileans into their homes in the Seventies and warmly welcomed the Kosovans last year. The difference here is that they're being expected to accept thousands of people from countries and conflicts they've never heard of in an environment where politicians and the media present them as spongers and cheats.
>
> (Hill 2001: 2)

It is difficult to believe that the plight of both Turkish and Iraqi Kurds, and other groups displaced by conflicts in the Middle East, especially associated with the regime of Saddam Hussein, was unknown to the population of Sighthill. What is being edited out of Elspeth Jones's and Chief Inspector Irvine's statements above is a recognition of the context of the conflicts that have caused many of the asylum seekers to be displaced from their countries of origin and ending up in Sighthill in the first place. Virulent Islamophobia combined with asylophobia is the absent presence that haunts the depiction of warm-hearted Glaswegians with their history of welcoming asylum seekers.

Since Mr Dag's murder, the Home Office has suspended sending asylum seekers to Sighthill (Dodd and Seenan, 2001). However, the Scottish Asylum Seekers Consortium, which was established in 1999, has announced that Fife, West Dumbartonshire and East Renfrewshire are among the other Scottish councils that have signed contracts with the National Asylum Support Service in 2001, with the expectation of housing many more thousands of asylum seekers in some of the most economically deprived and least multiracial areas of the UK.[9]

Case study 2: Caia Park Estate, Wrexham

> What we saw last night is not that different from when you see mobs of people hunting for paedophiles. It happens in hot weather: rumours fly around and people get angry . . . young people get involved because they get excited – it's the football hooligan mentality.
>
> (Shan Wilkinson, Leader of Wrexham Borough Council,
> in Press Association 2003a: 2)

On Sunday 23rd June 2003, the Caia Park Estate in Wrexham, North Wales was the scene of violent clashes involving Iraqi Kurd asylum seekers, local residents and police. On that Sunday night, the asylum seekers and local residents fought running battles armed with baseball bats and metal sticks (Al Yafai 2003). On the Monday night, violence returned to the estate when 200 or so youths gathered outside the Red Dragon public house armed with baseball bats, metal poles and petrol bombs. However, no Iraqi Kurd asylum seekers turned up to fight; they had already fled the estate after the disturbances the night before after being removed to secure accommodation (Al Yafai 2003). On Monday night, a battle was waged with hundreds of police in full riot gear brought in from neighbouring areas to deal with the White residents of the estate.

Caia Park is a tough and impoverished place; it is one of the largest and most troubled housing estates in the UK with high levels of unemployment and many acute social problems (Davies 2003). According to Shaun Wilkinson the Leader of Wrexham Borough Council, the number of asylum seekers dispersed to the Wrexham borough was relatively low compared with Sighthill; only 60–70 in the entire borough, with some of this number being housed on the Caia Park Estate (Press Association 2003a), most of whom were single men. This was, as was the 'rioting' in Bradford, a gendered affair. The women of the

Caia Park Estate marvelled at the comical stupidity of their men folk fighting with the police as they repeatedly retreated, regrouped and charged the police again.[10] According to one young woman: 'I shouldn't say it, but it was quite comical to watch them all going backwards and forwards'. Another woman, said of the young men involved in the disturbances: 'it is just something for them to do . . . they have two pints and it goes to their heads. They think they can take on the world' (Al Yafai 2003: 1, 2). However, the same woman pointed to a similar culture of resentment festering in the area, as found on the Sighthill Estate, in relation to the perception of preferential treatment and of asylum seekers appearing to be more affluent than the local residents: 'they are better off than our people. They come here with nothing but they soon have big cars and more money than us' (Al Yafai 2003: 1). As in Sighthill, it is the competition for scarce resources coupled with the protection of status and hierarchy (the assumption being that asylum seekers should remain less affluent and of lower status than local residents).

There are a lot of parallels with the Caia Park Estate disturbances and Bea Campbell's (1993) observations of the summer disturbances in housing estates in the early 1990s in her book *Goliath: Britain's Dangerous Places*. Not only are the time of year and the time of day (hot summer evenings) similar to the 'disturbances' explored by Campbell, there are also similarities in the type of environment the disturbances occurred in: the estates included in Campbell's study and the Caia Park Estate can all be described as 'miserable, anxious and angry' places (Trevor Phillips,[11] in Weaver 2003: 1). Another major similarity between the disturbances depicted by Campbell and the Caia Park disturbances, mentioned above, is the differential gendered experience of the disturbances. For example, in Campbell's account women were rarely directly involved in the disturbances and were relegated to trying to restore the community after violent clashes. The main difference between Campbell's depiction of housing estate disorder and the disturbances in the Caia Park Estate is that the latter erupted in the context of widespread anti-asylum seeker prejudice.

Local residents of Caia Park described themselves as defending their area from 'ruin' and destruction in June 2003: 'as the locals see it, they came down here and now they're trying to ruin the place. They destroyed our pub and the locals won't have it' (in Al Yafai 2003: 1). The war with Iraq as well as the media's depiction of asylum seeker affluence were also cited by local residents as adding to the culture of resentment in the area. Journalists noted that: '. . . residents' anger bubbled up during the Iraq war . . . the resentment increased by stories of refugees and asylum seekers driving Mercedes cars and throwing money around' (in Al Yafai 2003: 1). The war on terrorism and especially the war with Iraq was acknowledged in local residents' conversations with journalists. For example, some commented on the tragedy of the disturbances in which groups of people were being hounded from their neighbourhoods by angry mobs after seeking sanctuary from atrocities at the hands of Saddam Hussein. However, other journalists witnessed local residents on the estate demanding that the Iraqi asylum seekers should be deported because 'Saddam Hussain's gone now, they should go back to Iraq' (in Smith 2003: 1). Unlike in Sighthill, the residents of the Caia Park Estate contextualized their actions in relation to the conflict in Iraq. Although the racial elements of the disturbances in Wrexham have been played down, Lord Ousely suggested that racism exists in North Wales:

> It would be wrong for people to be in denial to suggest that race isn't a factor, that there isn't prejudice, that there weren't hostilities or indeed hatred. While it always takes a small incident it then brings to the surface the prejudices that exist, particularly as we have seen the way asylum seekers and refugees have been demonized.
>
> (Lord Ousely, in Smith 2003: 2)

Trevor Phillips, the Chairman of the Commission for Racial Equality, has welcomed the Home Office's plans to suspend asylum dispersal to some 'unsuitable' areas, but has also called for the Home Office to do some joined-up thinking that will result in a new approach to asylum dispersal that will place race relations at the heart of its vision, making 'community cohesion the main aim' (in Weaver 2003: 1). Phillips was damning in his criticism of the dispersal policy, accusing it of being 'the principal factor in destroying community cohesion in towns and cities in this country' because it 'dumps people in unsuitable places' (in Weaver 2003: 1).

The Far Right and neighbourhood nationalisms

In this chapter and in Chapter 2, British Far Right parties and groups, especially the BNP, National Front and Combat 18, have been a lurking malignant counter-modern force at the site of many of Britain's troubled areas, especially when these troubles are associated with relations between 'host' and migrant communities, whether established or temporarily dispersed communities and groups. The creeping influence of the Far Right has not gone unnoticed by government, especially in relation to immigration and asylum policy. For example, in an all-party House of Commons Home Affairs Select Committee report published in May 2003, fears were expressed over increasing applications by asylum seekers in Europe:

> If allowed to continue unchecked, it could overwhelm the capacity of receiving countries to cope, leading inevitably to social unrest. It could also, and there are signs this may already be happening, lead to

a growing political backlash, which will in turn lead to the election of extremist parties with extremist solutions.

(in Travis 2003: 1)

The Labour, Conservative and Liberal Democrat MPs on this Home Affairs Select Committee were concerned that the election of 16 British National Party councillors in local elections in 2003 was unprecedented and a sign of more Far Right election victories to come (Travis 2003). In June 2004, the BNP received more than 800,000 votes in the European elections and now has 21 councillors (Taylor 2004). The members of the Home Affairs Select Committee were unambiguous about where blame should be attributed, where the problem lies in relation to the UK's immigration and asylum policy: it is in the failure of the system to remove economic migrants – 'nothing is more likely to discredit the notion of asylum than the knowledge that most of the seekers are economic migrants, many of whom the system has failed to remove' (in Travis 2003: 1). It seems that the immigration and asylum debates under the Labour administration have come full circle, despite all of the many lessons to be learned from the introduction of the politics of deterrence in the provisions of the Immigration and Asylum Act 1999. It was the strategy of attempting to deter bogus asylum seekers in the first place that has in part made anti-asylum seeker prejudice socially acceptable in Britain. The solution once again is to get tough on 'the problem'.

Asylum is 'the issue' of the day, and this is an issue it seems 'ordinary' people, and even some established ethnic minority individuals in certain areas, are seeking a right-wing solution to. For example, the Shadow Home Secretary commenting on the Home Affairs Select Committee report stated: 'already we are seeing otherwise sensible people being enticed to vote for extremists because of their worries about the asylum system' (Letwin, in Travis 2003: 1). The BNP's exploitation of this situation can be observed in their manifesto (for council elections in 2003) under 'Asylum clampdown', which can be described as a direct attack on the alleged preferential treatment of asylum seekers by local councils, which in turn feeds into the emotional response to asylum seekers explored during this chapter. There are four main components in the BNP's policy summarized here:

1. Preventing asylum seekers being dumped in the area in the first place.
2. Prevent the upgrading of empty sub-standard council accommodation especially for asylum seekers when British people are homeless.
3. Push asylum seekers off the top of the housing lists and benefit queues.
4. Ensure that money spent on asylum seekers by local councils be

repaid by them through work programmes, for example, by cleaning up the streets and carrying out other tasks on behalf of the community.

(http://www.bnp.org.UK/elections/elections2003/manifesto/ manifesto20037.htm)

Immigration is the first on the list of BNP policies. With the subtitle 'time to say no', the focus of the BNP's policy is the exaggeration of the threat of gradual minoritization of 'British native people' who will be 'an ethnic minority in our own country within sixty years' (http://www.bnp.org.UK/policies.html). The emphasis of this policy is on defence – that is, defending the homeland (securing borders) and shoring up British identity. At the same time, the emotive issue of preferential treatment or positive discrimination, which is acting to disadvantage 'native Britons' and advantage migrant communities, is at the centre of BNP policy: 'we will abolish the "positive discrimination" schemes that have made White Britons second class citizens. We will clamp down on the flood of asylum seekers, all of which are either bogus or can find refuge much nearer to their home countries' (http://www.bnp.org.UK/policies.html). The BNP's strategy here is to offer disgruntled, misinformed and anxious 'host' communities the promise of a safe haven in a context of insecure borders. The BNP and other Far Right parties could end up being the only victors in the UK's current anti-asylum culture, as more and more desperate communities turn to them as an emotional solution to their increasing tabloid-fuelled ontological insecurity and resentment over being the alleged losers in the competition for scarce resources.

What these developments indicate is the creeping rise of a particular politics of 'Whiteness' that is of a White Britishness of 'the not very privileged' (Knowles 2003: 183). The BNP here are the defenders of 'White spaces' and 'White rights' linked with discourses of the tidal wave of immigration in which 'immigrants' are making 'indigenous' communities strangers or second-class citizens in their own land (Cohen 1996). Taking her inspiration from Philip Cohen's work in East London (Isle of Dogs), Knowles (2003) suggests that the 'blue collar' racism of the 'work habitus' has been transcended, in that, for example, in Sighthill and Caia Park, there is little evidence of the social anchorage of work in the form of industrial labour (Campbell 1993; McDowell 2003). As a result, the associations between the working class, masculinity and race require new forms of understanding. Knowles considers Cohen's suggestion that in places such as these, claims to 'the local', to 'the neighbourhood' are increasingly being expressed and lived as a form of nationalism: 'a nationalism of the neighbourhood'[12] where even slight privileges and entitlements are worth maintaining in a context where 'racism starts much closer to home' (Knowles 2003: 183).

Conclusion

There are a number of threats, risks and sources of anxiety depicted in this chapter, mostly associated with the fear that 'our' small island will be engulfed by 'strangers' who will bring their diseases, their crime, their neediness and even their sinister anti-Western malcontent into our midst. However, the counter-modern defences, depicted above in relation to Sighthill and Caia Park, associated with the heat of the narcissism of minor differences and neighbourhood nationalisms are clearly also associated with the dread of social unrest, as well as the fear that incidents such as these are in turn nourishing and strengthening the British Far Right day by day. As a result, the country is not only supposed to be terrified of being 'swamped' and over-burdened by asylum seekers, but as a direct consequence of this the country is also facing the risk of social unrest, which is directly related to the rise of the Far Right.[13] The result is an escalating and spreading sense of dread, of fear of potential catastrophe, which the government is attempting to ameliorate by getting tough on asylum, the alleged root of the problem. However, according to some, this strategy has backfired. For example, Mohammed Azam, a Labour councillor in Oldham, suggests that the government's legitimization of racism, through the politics of deterrence, brings the emotional spectrum of racism to the surface, and this is what the Far Right are exploiting:

> Throughout the past twelve months, there has been a legitimisation of the racism the BNP feeds off. The Government policy of curbing asylum seekers was supposedly designed to reverse BNP gains. It has failed to do so. Rather, it appears to have had the opposite effect.
>
> (Azam, in Renton 2003: 83)

It is increasingly clear that the government needs to operate in another, calmer emotional register when attempting to develop immigration and asylum policy. The discourses of 'getting tough on asylum seekers' and their attempt to legitimize the 'toughness' of their policies on the basis of the Gothic conventions of breached borders, insecurity and lurking menace has resulted in their dispersal policy, as observed in Sighthill, being doomed to failure before it started. The host communities in Sighthill and Caia Park were fully primed to give a negative reception to the asylum communities before they even arrived there. During 2004, another raft of 'tough' asylum legislation has been introduced associated with the controversial Asylum Bill 2003. One of the main provisions associated with this Bill was the reduction of the avenues of appeal available to failed asylum applicants. This was to be achieved through replacing the three-tier appeal system with a single appeal (Johnson and Womack 2003). The Bill also proposed the reduction in the amount of legal aid offered to asylum seekers; under these provisions, asylum seekers will be able to claim for only five hours worth of solicitor or accredited adviser time (Johnson and Womack 2003). The most controversial component of the Bill is the proposed policy of forcing failed asylum seeker applicants with families to return 'home', through threatening to take away their benefits and to put their children into care (Casciani 2003). The latter component of the Bill has been referred to as a 'BNP charter' by Karen Chouhan, the Chief Executive of the campaign group and think tank The 1990 Trust, in that the spiralling costs of councils looking after asylum seeker children taken into care would be ruthlessly exploited by the BNP, in that one of the main issues of contention, as observed above, is the financial cost of asylum seekers to local taxpayers (Black Information Link 2003).

In the next chapter, the rise of post-9/11 Islamophobia in the UK will be further explored, especially in relation to the Far Right's incitement of religious hatred. This will be achieved through examining the progress of the Religious Offences Bill 2002 through the two British Houses of Parliament.

The next three chapters, taken together, can be described as an investigation of the Labour Government's wider 'social inclusion' strategy in relation to ethnic, religious and sexual minority communities with regard to their protection from hatred. In these chapters, as observed in the Introduction and Chapter 1, the renegotiation of the boundaries of toleration will be explored in relation to discourses and initiatives dedicated to the protective inclusion of designated vulnerable communities, for example the Muslim community in Britain (in Chapter 4) and lesbian, gay, bisexual and transgender communities (in Chapter 5). I will show that the political strategy of attempting to outlaw specific forms of hatred, intolerance and prejudice that impact negatively on these communities is a component of a wider institutional and organizational reflexivity unfolding in Britain in relation to the place of minority communities in the nation (which will be further developed in Chapter 7), which is testament to the emergence of a more intolerant Britain – that is, a Britain which is becoming increasingly intolerant of intolerance.

4   Faith-hate in post-9/11 UK

> The attacks of September 11th underscored the most striking question
> of politics since the collapse of the Soviet Union: increased communal
> conflicts coming from religious, ethnic, and cultural identities.
>
> (Creppell 2003: ix)

Introduction

This chapter continues some of the themes developed in previous chapters in
relation to race, immigration and diversity. The focus here is on the incitement of religious hatred in contemporary multi-faith Britain. The emergence
of Islamophobia, and especially British Far Right organizations fanning the
flames of Islamophobia, is the particular social problem that is under scrutiny
here by policy makers (Parliamentarians and especially members of the
House of Lords and House of Commons Select Committees) and by members
of various pressure groups and organizations representing the Muslim
community.

   This chapter is therefore a detailed analysis of institutional reflexivity in
relation to the amelioration of a particular counter-modern 'social bad', that is,
hatred incited against a religious minority group. However, by also examining
the processes of reflexivity in determining the need for, and the extent of
problems associated with prohibiting in law undesirable behaviours and
practices that have a negative impact on certain minority religious communities, the chapter is also well placed to examine the governmental and
'social engineering' intentions of the 'hate crime' legislation (and related
legislation) from the perspective of policy makers.

   The specific focus of the chapter is less sociological (relative to the
previous two chapters) and more socio-legal in style, in that the analysis is of a
particular lack of legal protection endured by some religious groups, namely
multi-ethnic religious groups such as Muslims. The extent of provisions to

protect groups from the incitement to hatred will be explored in relation to race and religion through the examination of official documents: parliamentary debates (House of Lords and House of Commons) and select committee reports (House of Lords and House of Commons) on the issues surrounding the introduction of a proposed offence of incitement to religious hatred in the Religious Offences Bill 2002.

In many ways, this chapter is a continuation of some of the themes explored in Chapter 1 in relation to the definition of 'racist incidents' and the introduction of racial aggravation provisions in the Crime and Disorder Act 1998. In this chapter, the process of attempting to classify Islamophobia as one of the UK's 'officially designated prejudices' (Jacobs and Potter 1998: 29) is examined as part of a larger trend in which more and more forms of prejudice are being officially designated (Jenness and Broad 1997), and many more groups in society are coming forward to demand protection from hate. However, part of what the chapter does is to demonstrate that legislating against hate, especially incited hatred, is not a straightforward process. It requires a careful calibration of the reasonable and unreasonable, the lawful and the unlawful, to determine what actions or behaviour should, or should not, be legislated against.

The collection of official documents that will be examined in this chapter are particularly revealing of some of the recurring themes throughout the book. For example, as alluded to above, the institutional reflexivity of the Labour government and other public institutions (including organizations within the criminal justice system) as they attempt to come to terms with the changing cultural landscape of twenty-first-century Britain. Another major theme that will be examined here is the response to the 'shifting focus of bigotry' in the UK in recent years – that is, from race to religion in the post-9/11 context and how the government and the judiciary are (or are failing) to respond to this.

The main problem addressed in the documents examined below is that existent legislation, especially common law offences, including blasphemy, and criminal law provisions, including incitement to racial hatred, do not protect all social groups equally. In particular, the Muslim community, a multi-ethnic, minority faith group which in recent years has been the focus of an array of Far Right attention, remains unprotected from the incitement to religious hatred. In this chapter, some of the problems associated with attempting to adequately protect religious groups from the incitement of religious hatred will be explored in relation to: (i) international law (including European human rights law); (ii) the problems associated with balancing the legal protection of religious groups with the protection of the freedom of expression; and (iii) the relationship between provisions dedicated to the incitement to racial hatred, and the proposed provisions dedicated to the incitement to religious hatred.

The proposed offence of incitement of religious hatred in the Religious Offences Bill 2002 will also be placed within the socio-political context of the emergence of an observable (yet uneven) 'intolerance of intolerance' in New Labour public policy. The proposed Bill, it shall be argued, is a component of a wider political programme in which the government is attempting to send a 'clear message' to those individuals and groups who are intolerant of difference that the expression of this intolerance in certain activities will no longer be tolerated in Britain.

However, in the post-9/11 context, especially the war on terrorism and the introduction of the Anti-Terrorism, Crime and Security Act 2001, there have emerged some contradictions in UK legislation between recognizing the need to protect the Muslim communities in the UK from (Far Right incited) hatred, but at the same time the state of emergency legislation has been introduced partly to defend the UK against the potential 'Muslim threat' associated with terrorist activities.

Incitement to religious hatred in international law

In this section, international and national legislation and policy on the incitement of both racial and religious hatred will be examined. The section provides the legislative context in which both the introduction of emergency anti-terrorism legislation and the parliamentary and select committee debates on the need to protect the Muslim community in Britain from the incitement to hatred in the Religious Offences Bill will be explored.

Article 20.2 of the International Covenant on Civil and Political Rights (ICCPR) states that :

> Any advocacy of national, racial or religious hatred that constitutes incitement to discrimination, hostility or violence shall be prohibited by law.
>
> (HL Select Committee on Religious Offences 2003: para. 96)

According to the Muslim Council of Britain, the British government is in breach of this obligation in international law as the government currently does not protect religious minorities, especially the Muslim community, 'from being victims of violence, harassment and intimidation for their belief' (Memorandum from the Muslim Council of Britain, HL Select Committee on Religious Offences: 2003: para. 3.1). The UK ratified the ICCPR in 1976. However, in relation to article 20.2, the UK made a reservation saying that this provision must be taken to reflect no more than the law as it stood, which consisted of the common law offence of blasphemy and the provisions of the Race Relations Act 1976. However, in 2001 the United Nations

Human Rights Committee (which is charged with examining the record of states that have ratified the ICCPR as to their compliance with its terms) recommended that this reservation should be withdrawn and that criminal legislation be extended to cover offences motivated by religious hatred (UN Human Rights committee, 73rd session, CCPR/CO/73/UK, 6 December 2001).

The House of Lords Select Committee on Religious Offences (2003) noted that the European Commission against Racism and Intolerance (ECRI) had recommended that all Council of Europe member states should introduce criminal laws to penalize the following acts if committed intentionally: public incitement to violence; hatred or discrimination; public insults and defamation; or threats against a person or a grouping of persons on the grounds of their race, colour, language, religion, nationality or ethnic origin (HL Select Committee on Religious Offences 2003: para. 98). Almost all the proposed offences are already contained in the criminal law, but incitement to religious hatred is not. In the next section, the extent of the legislative protection in relation to race and religion will be examined.

UK religious offences and incitement legislation

Existing, related and recently proposed legislation is listed below in order to ascertain the extent of legislative protection afforded to faith groups in England and Wales:

- Criminal Libel Act 1819 – Blasphemy – the publication of contemptuous, reviling, scurrilous or ludicrous matter relating to God as defined by the Christian religion, Jesus, the Bible or the Book of Common Prayer, intending to wound the feelings of Christians or to excite contempt and hatred against the Church of England or promote immorality.
- Race Relations Act 1976[1] – prohibits discrimination on 'racial grounds' defined as 'colour, race, nationality, or ethnic or national origins'.
- Public Order Act 1986 (Part III) – Incitement[2] to Racial Hatred[3] – to behave in such a manner as to use or publish insulting or abusive words with the intent to stir up racial hatred or, in the circumstances, racial hatred is likely to be stirred up as a result of the action.
- Crime and Disorder Act 1998 (Part II) – Racially Aggravated Offences – harassment, violence and/or criminal damage to property motivated by racial hatred or where there is any aggravating evidence of racial hostility in connection with the offence.
- Anti-Terrorism, Crime and Security Act 2001 – Religiously Aggravated Offences[4] – harassment, violence and/or criminal damage to property

motivated by religious hatred or where there is any aggravating evidence of religious hostility in connection with the offence.

- Religious Offences Bill 2002 (Section II) – Incitement to Religious Hatred – to behave in such a manner or to use or publish insulting or abusive words with the intent to stir up religious hatred or, in the circumstances, religious hatred is likely to be stirred up as a result of the action.

Blasphemy provisions in the Criminal Libel Act 1819

The main problem with the common law 'blasphemy' provisions found in the Criminal Libel Act 1819 is that the Anglican Church, its adherents and Christian beliefs are protected but not those of all faith groups. The non-protection of Muslims living in Britain under the existing blasphemy legislation came to a head in 1988 with the publication of Salman Rushdie's purportedly 'anti-Muslim' book *The Satanic Verses* (Bonnett 2000: 126). The lack of legal redress during the Rushdie affair, according to Werbner, had the following impact on Muslims in Britain:

> as the affair continued, it became clear that Muslim religious feelings were not protected under the blasphemy laws. British Muslims discovered that their religion could be violated and mocked without the law affording them any protection . . . For Muslims in Britain, the Rushdie affair is experienced as a festering wound, an unpaid debt that demands redress . . .
>
> (Werbner 1997: 232–3)

Thus, existing blasphemy laws not only offer limited protection in law, the limited protection these laws afford has also had unintended consequences (during the Rushdie affair) of exacerbating the sense of exclusion, humiliation and discrimination in Muslim communities in Britain. At the same time, blasphemy laws offer no protection for any faith group (Anglican or Muslim) from the incitement of religious hatred or against harassment, violence and/or criminal damage to property resulting from such incitement (Forum Against Islamophobia and Racism 2002: 12).

Incitement to racial hatred and racially aggravated provisions in the Public Order Act 1986 and the Crime and Disorder Act 1998

Incitement to racial hatred was first made an offence under the Race Relations Act 1965. In both the 1986 and 1998 Acts, 'racial groups', following the Race Relations Act 1976, are defined by reference to colour, race, nationality or ethnic or national origin. The definition of 'racial group' is extended by case law to include mono-ethnic religious communities, such as Jews and Sikhs.[5] Although Jews and Sikhs enjoy protection from this offence, the protection is not extended to multi-ethnic religious communities. The *Mandla* decision does not recognize groups as being 'ethnic' solely on account of their religious identity. Thus, Christians, Hindus, Muslims and Rastafarians do not belong to a Christian, Hindu, Muslim or Rastafarian ethnic group. The crucial factor for Sikhs, and which distinguishes their position *qua* ethnicity from Muslims, is that their membership currently and historically has been drawn from just one cultural group (the Punjabis), whereas the world's Muslim population is drawn from many ethnically and culturally diverse groups[6] (Dobe 2000). As a result of this categorization, Christians, Muslims and most other faith communities in Britain remain unprotected from the incitement of religious hatred (Forum Against Islampohobia and Racism 2002). This has resulted in an iniquitous anomaly in the law producing a hierarchy of protected faith communities in the UK where multi-ethnic minority religious groups, like Muslims, do not on the whole benefit from such protection or provisions, unless it could be shown that the treatment, behaviour or circumstance was indirectly racial (Forum Against Islamophobia and Racism 2002).

Anti-Terrorism, Crime and Security Act 2001

Although this Act introduced nine new religiously aggravated offences, which like the racially aggravated offences introduced in the Crime and Disorder Act 1998 are sentence enhancement provisions that will expand the legislative protection of Muslim communities in Britain from hate crimes, this legislation is on the whole dedicated to protecting Britain from the threat of 'Islamic' terrorism.

The 9/11 attacks on the USA prompted swift anti-terrorism measures in both the USA and in the UK. The emergency measures in the USA (the Mobilization Against Terrorism Act and the Patriot Act of 2001) resulted in the rounding up of 800 immigrants immediately after the attacks on New York and Washington. This number increased to 1147 by November 2001. These laws allowed for the arbitrary detention without trial of suspected terrorists and greatly increased the powers of the FBI and government to gather intelligence and also to withhold information; all of these measures were justified by concerns about national security during the post-9/11 'state of emergency' (Fekete 2002).

It was not until 13 November 2001 that the former Home Secretary David Blunkett laid an order before Parliament declaring Britain to be in a state of public emergency due to the events of 11 September 2001. The legislation that was to be proposed in the UK during this state of emergency followed just 12 months after the passing into law of the Terrorism Act 2000, which was already cause for alarm due to the wide remit of the definition of 'terrorism' in this legislation, which could include other forms of protest, including anti-globalization protests (Hyland 2001). The 2000 Act was defended by the government on the grounds that, once in place, it would protect the lives and security of British people. However, after the 9/11 attacks the government claimed that the provisions in the Terrorism Act were not enough. The Anti-Terrorism, Crime and Security Act followed the example of the USA's emergency anti-terrorism legislation, especially provisions allowing the detention without trial of suspected terrorists. This was achieved through the derogation (opting out) of Article 5 of the European Convention on Human Rights,[7] which outlaws arbitrary detention and imprisonment.

The British state now has the power to arbitrarily arrest and hold anyone on suspicion of terrorist activity (irrespective of whether it has been carried out) and to deport them from the country, as well as powers to seize assets and personal materials which they believe may be related to terrorist activities (Hyland 2001). According to Fekete (2002), the result of the US and UK anti-terrorism emergency laws is that the governments of these two countries have been engaged in trawling for suspects in 'foreign', especially asylum seeker, communities. At the same time, the combination of xeno-racism with asylo-phobia, as identified in Chapter 3, is becoming increasingly combined with Islamophobia in the post-9/11 climate, which under the 2000 and 2001 Terrorism and Anti-Terrorism Acts has resulted in all asylum seekers being subjected to 'a special surveillance regime' (Fekete 2002: 105).

Under this legislation, 15 people have been detained in the UK; two of them have chosen to leave Britain rather than face detention, 13 have been interned without charge in British top security jails, including Woodhill Prison, Milton Keynes Prison and Belmarsh Prison in south east London. Most of the interned are asylum seekers who claim that they will be tortured if they are returned to their country of origin. Two have been named: a Palestinian refugee, Abu Rideh, who is now interned in Broadmoor High Security Mental Hospital (Travis 2003: 2); the other is the radical Islamic Cleric, Abu Qatada (also know as Sheikh Omar Abu Omar and Omar Uthman Abu Omar), of North London's Finsbury Park Mosque. The latter is a Palestinian with Jordanian nationality who came to Britain as an asylum seeker in 1993 after fleeing religious persecution in Jordan. Abu Qatada has been described by MI5 as the most significant extremist cleric in the UK. He has also been accused by police and judges on the continent of being al-Qaeda's spiritual leader in Europe (Johnson 2003). According to Fekete (2002), these anti-terrorism provisions will not stop another 9/11, as the conspirators and plotters will not be caught by this legislation. Instead, a few 'troublesome' Islamic fundamentalist refugees in London will be rounded up for being upfront and outspoken in their views, and destitute asylum seekers arriving in the UK will be targeted as 'suspected terrorists'.

In the post-9/11 climate, the links being made between Muslim terrorists, British Muslim suicide bombers, Muslim 'hate clerics' and the 'rioting' Muslim communities of Bradford, Oldham and Burnley are increasingly becoming 'seamless and almost incontrovertible' (Alexander 2003: 2). In this climate, Islamophobia in Britain, according to a report published by the Commission on British Muslims and Islamophobia (CBMI) (a think tank set up by the Runnymede Trust) in May 2004, is becoming increasingly institutionalized. This report suggests that if this institutional Islamophobia is not addressed, then more and more Muslims will feel excluded from British society and simmering tensions, especially in northern English towns, are in danger of boiling over (Doward and Hinsliff 2004). The Terrorism Act and Anti-Terrorism, Crime and Security Act were singled out in this report as creating a climate of fear among Muslims in Britain. Sadiq Khan (Chair of the Muslim Council of Britain's Legal Affairs Committee) told the CBMI that this legislation has 'led to the internment in the UK of Muslim men, respectable charities having their funds seized, and charities suffering because Muslims are reluctant to donate for fear of being accused of funding "terrorists" ' (in Doward and Hinsliff 2004: 2). Police stop and search practices were singled out as a key indication of institutionalized Islamophobia in the post-9/11 climate because more than 35,000 Muslims were stopped and searched in 2003, with fewer than 50 charged. Three years ago, only around 2000 Muslims were stopped and searched (Doward and Hinsliff 2004). Several sources cite a 300 per cent increase in police stop and search techniques against 'Asians' in Britain between July 2003 and July 2004 (Aaronovitch 2004, Tempest 2004a). Glen Smyth, a spokesperson for the Metropolitan Police Federation, suggested that this increase in stop and search figures was understandable in the context of the war on terrorism. That is, 'in terms of the numbers of people, it's a pretty small number bearing in mind the circumstances in which we are operating' (in Aaronovitch 2004: 5). The chair of the CBMI, Richard Stone, suggested that in this climate of institutionalized Islamophobia, 'if we don't take positive action to embrace the young Muslim men in this country, we are going to have an urgent problem . . . we are going to have real anger and riots with young Muslims pitched against the police' (in Doward and Hinsliff 2004: 2).

What reports such as these feed into in the current climate is the inevitability of Muslim violence that is embodied in young Muslim men. According to Alexander:

> The conceptual mapping of 'the Muslim menace' which links suicide bombers with extremist Muslim clerics and recent 'riots', articulates a very specific imagination of 'the Muslim community' in Britain – one which is marked by both gendered and generational difference.
>
> (Alexander 2003: 3)

The figures of the Bradfordian British-Muslim rioter, the potential young Muslim rioter in the CBMI report, the British-Muslim Tel Aviv suicide bombers[8] and of the increasing collection of 'asylum rioters', whether in Dover, North Wales or in Scotland, are being articulated in: 'a cascade of images which fuse violence, death, danger, anger and difference and which, in the wake of post 9/11 paranoia, increasingly define and engulf "the Muslim presence" ' (Alexander 2003: 3).

According to Alexander (2003), the emergent spectres of religious 'fundamentalism' and the threat of terrorism now mean that Muslim young men are becoming increasingly inseparable from the image of violence, which is evidenced in the explosion of the riots in 2001 and fermented in the extremist Islamic schoolrooms of the preachers of racial hatred. Young British men who volunteered to fight with the Taliban against Anglo-American forces in Afghanistan were singled out as being particularly problematic, and this prompted calls for these individuals to be charged with 'treasonable acts' by the former Home Office Minister Anne Widdecombe:

> Any British citizen who fights against British forces, in my view, has committed treason and, certainly, if they come back to this country, they shouldn't imagine that they can then just enjoy the democratic freedoms and rights of a free society, when they have fought against it.
>
> (Widdecombe, in Hyland 2001: 2)

The post-9/11 climate is both a culture of fear and a culture of indignation in which established and asylum seeker migrant communities are viewed with suspicion. In this context, the benevolence of the UK's immigration and asylum policies and championing of multiculturalism (especially in the British tabloids) is being thrown back in the taxpayers' faces. This is clearly fertile ground for Far Right political manipulation; however, as Widdecombe and especially Blunkett (below) demonstrate, the question of Muslim loyalty to Britain is not a Far Right preserve. For example, the former Home Secretary nailed his colours to the mast of the new common sense 'social' risk sensibility in relation to Muslims in Britain when he stated in the post-Bradford riots, post-9/11 but pre-Afghanistan war context of November 2001 that: 'We could live in a world which is airy-fairy, libertarian, where everyone does precisely what they like and we believe the best of everybody and then they destroy us' (Blunkett, in Hillyard 2002: 107).

According to Hillyard (2002), Blunkett's statement depicts the world of a frightened man where the enemy lies in dark places. Post-9/11 Blunkett is a man running scared and his statements are:

heavily partitioned and binary divisions of good and bad can be imagined everywhere: the terrorist versus the law-abiding citizen, the civilised versus the uncivilised world, or Christian against Muslim. It is a dangerous mindset 'them' and 'us', a mindset which has dominated the Home Office since its formation. Far from accepting difference and diversity and an all-inclusive society, it is a society where the enemy is everywhere.

(Hillyard 2002: 109–10)

The 'Home Office' mindset alluded to above by Hillyard is related to the 'clash of civilizations' discourses popularized by Huntington, in which religion is thought to be the most important differentiation (along with history, language, culture and tradition) between the meta-cultural entities of the world – for example, the Western, Confucian, Japanese, Islamic, Hindu, Slavic-Orthodox, Latin American and African civilizations (Huntington 1993). This gross simplification and reduction of the world into seven or eight 'major civilisations' has contributed to the anti-Islamic climate in the West, especially issues around loyalty[9] and the so-called treasonable activities of Muslims living in Britain. For example, the former Conservative Prime Minister Baroness Thatcher commented in an interview to *The Times* published on 4 October 2001 that she 'had not heard enough condemnation from Muslim priests' of the September 11 attacks. Baroness Thatcher was keen to present the attacks on the USA as an exclusive Muslim problem: 'the people who brought down those towers were Muslims and Muslims must stand up and say that it is not the way of Islam ... they must say it is disgraceful' (Thatcher, in European Monitoring Centre on Racism and Xenophobia 2002: 25). Here, moderate Muslims are being called to stand either with or against Britain, despite the serving Prime Minister's attempts to convince the country that there 'is no contradiction between being Muslim and being British' (Blair, in European Monitoring Centre on Racism and Xenophobia 2002: 24). Baroness Thatcher's understanding of Britain's relationship with religious minority groups is reminiscent of the former Conservative Minister, Norman Tebbitt's infamous 'cricket test' to judge migrant community loyalty in which he suggested African-Caribbean and Asian people residing in Britain should demonstrate their loyalty by supporting England in cricket tournaments rather than India, Pakistan or the West Indies (Malik 1996).

It was in this anti-Islamic climate, especially the fusion of Islam with the terrorist activities of al-Qaeda, that Muslim organizations in Britain, who condemned the attacks on 11 September 2001, also proposed that clause 39 (incitement of religious hatred) of the Anti-Terrorism, Crime and Security Bill be dropped. The main concern of Muslim groups was that by introducing this clause within emergency anti-terrorism legislation, Islam would be further associated with terrorism. At the same time, these organizations were also concerned that instead of protecting the Muslim community from the incitement to religious hatred, the proposed clause 39 'had the potential to be used as an instrument of targeting and oppressing Muslims rather than affording protection from others who stir hatred against them for being Muslims' (Memorandum from the Muslim Council of Britain, HL Select Committee on Religious Offences 2003: para. 3.3).

Clause 39 was eventually dropped at the eleventh hour from the Anti-Terrorism, Crime and Security Bill by the Home Secretary when the House of Lords voted down the measure by a large majority (240 to 141) as a result of fears over the impact of the clause on free speech (Wintour 2001). However, the result of this is that religious groups, especially Muslims, were left unprotected from the incitement of religious hatred during a particularly anti-Islamic period in British history.

The exploitation of legislative non-protection: Islamophobia unbounded

> Muslims in the United Kingdom feel particularly vulnerable, insecure, alienated, threatened, intimidated, marginalized, discriminated against and vilified since the 11 September tragedy.
>
> (Memorandum from the Muslim Council of Britain,
> HL Select Committee on Religious Offences 2003: para. 1.4)

Islamophobia is not exclusively connected to the 9/11 attacks on the USA and the subsequent war on Iraq, although, as will be demonstrated below, these events have certainly exacerbated it. Alexander suggested in 2000, a year before the 9/11 attacks, that during the 1990s some social scientists, academics and politicians in Europe were concerned with the emergence of 'problematic' religious identities in Europe, especially Muslim identities. This 'rush of concern' was described by Glavanis (1998) as a 'neo-Orientalism' (in Alexander 2000: 14). In the 1990s in the UK, Alexander (2000) rather prophetically suggested that concerns over 'religious fundamentalism have concurred in the positioning of Islam at the centre of political and academic discourse as Public Enemy Number One – Britain's most unwanted, as it were' (p. 14).

Since the events in September 2001, attacks on Muslim, Sikh and other Arab and Asian communities in the UK have increased four-fold in some areas, and an increase in attacks of more than 75 per cent on the Asian community has been reported in Tower Hamlets in London (Lord Ahmed, HL Hansard 30 January 2002: col. 318). Many of these attacks and much of the Far Right's activities in these and other areas have focused on the Muslim community.

The word Islamophobia has been introduced by the Muslim community to describe this new social reality:

> anti-Muslim prejudice has grown considerably and so rapidly in recent years that a new item in the vocabulary is needed so that it can be identified and acted against. In a similar way there was a time in European history when a new word, anti-Semitism, was needed and coined to highlight the growing dangers of anti-Jewish hostility.
>
> (Runnymede Trust 2002: 1)

Examples of some of the Islamophobic or anti-Muslim activities that have been reported since September 2001 include:

> Far right racist groups openly attacking Muslim communities in the media and in their websites . . . Muslim women wearing the hi'jab, Arab women in particular, have been subject to verbal abuse . . . Racist groups have openly displayed posters and distributed leaflets inciting religious hatred in the north of England.
>
> (Lord Ahmed, HL Hansard 30 January 2002: col. 319)

The reporting of the 9/11 attacks is crucial for understanding the context in which anti-Islamic feelings have been stirred up in non-Muslim countries. On the day of the attacks on New York and Washington, the culprits were very soon identified as being Muslims; thus, the connection between Islam and terrorism was fused as reporters and politicians across the world began to report and comment on the attacks as being Islamic in origin. In this context, it has been noted by, for example, the European Monitoring Centre on Racism and Xenophobia (2002) – in their report on Anti-Islamic Reactions in Britain – that verbal and physical attacks as well as attacks on (and threats to attack) Muslim property increased dramatically between 12 September and 31 December 2001. However, as well as the examples of attacks on Muslim individuals and their property in this context, various organizations noted the mobilization of British Far Right extremist groups, especially the BNP, the National Front and Combat 18, against Muslim communities in the UK in the months following the 9/11 attacks. The problem here is that within this context the incitement to anti-Islamic hatred is not prohibited in the criminal law, and that Far Right groups are actually aware of and exploiting this absence of legislation. For example:

> It is clear from the publications and activities of far right and Neo-Nazi organizations, like the BNP and the NF [National Front], that their campaigns against Islam and Muslims is deliberate and

premeditated; campaigns that have been devised to sit within existing laws.

(Forum Against Islamophobia and Racism 2002: 4)

The Forum Against Islamophobia and Racism listed in their memorandum to the House of Lords Select Committee on Religious Offences a number of publications, mostly pamphlets and posters distributed by the BNP in the aftermath of 9/11, which they say were designed to incite hatred against the British Muslim community within the law. The following are some of the titles of these BNP publications: 'Islam Out of Britain', 'Islam a Threat to Us All' and 'The Truth About Islam'. And on the BNP website: 'The Enemy Within', 'The Real Face of Islam', 'The Choice: Islam or the West?' and 'What if Islam Ruled Britain' (Forum Against Islamophobia and Racism 2002: 15–17). In one of these pamphlets, 'The Truth About Islam', the Forum suggest that the BNP set out a range of highly inflammatory reasons for hating Islam, for example: 'to find out what Islam really stands for, all you have to do is look at a copy of the Koran, and see for yourself . . . Islam really does stand for intolerance, slaughter, looting, arson, and the molestation of women' (BNP, in Forum Against Islamophobia and Racism 2002: 16). In the BNP pamphlet 'Islam Out of Britain', the threat to Britain depicted is more explicitly focused on the Islamic threat to Christian nations, stating that 'it won't be long before Christianity is dead and buried and Britain becomes an Islamic dictatorship' (Forum Against Islamophobia and Racism 2002: 17).

The memorandum from the Forum Against Islamophobia and Racism to the House of Lords Select Committee asserted that the issue is not just one of the inequitable protection of certain faith groups under the provisions of the 1986 and 1998 Acts, but that Far Right groups have been actively inciting hatred of the Muslim community within the limits of current legislation and that this has resulted in bigotry shifting from race, which is prohibited by legislation, to religion:

> It is our view that an offence of incitement to religious hatred is not only necessary to provide equality of protection from incitement across religious groups but critical to avoid 'the shifting focus of bigotry' we have witnessed in the UK from race to religion. In this shifting focus, the target remains the same, only the marker changes . . . unless the new offence of incitement to religious hatred is introduced, in our view, it leaves a loophole in the law that could potentially make a mockery of the current offence of incitement to racial hatred.
>
> (Forum Against Islamophobia and Racism 2002: 4)

Thus the unintended consequence of progressive provisions to outlaw the incitement to racial hatred has, from some Muslim organizations' perspectives, resulted in certain Far Right groups literally shifting their focus from race to religion, and this change of emphasis has been achieved within the parameters of the current law.

Incitement to religious hatred and the freedom of expression

This section of the chapter is dedicated to the two main problems that have been exposed in the official documents examined in relation to the Religious Offences Bill. These are: (a) negotiating the balance between incitement and freedom of expression and (b) the role the Attorney-General plays in consenting to the prosecution of offences of inciting racial hatred and will play in the proposed offence of inciting religious hatred.

The Attorney-General, police and Crown Prosecution Service (CPS) are bound to apply the principles of the European Convention for the Protection of Human Rights and Fundamental Freedoms (ECHR) in accordance with the Human Rights Act 1998. Articles 9 (freedom of thought, conscience and religion) and 10 (freedom of expression) are especially relevant to the proposed legislation in question. Articles 9 and 10 are qualified rights. In relation to Article 10 this means that the right provided for in Article 10.1 is not absolute, but may legitimately be subject to restrictions so long as they are prescribed by law and are necessary in a democratic society for the reasons listed in Article 10.2 (Memorandum from the Attorney-General, HL Select Committee on Religious Offences 2003: 1). The main concern here is that the gap between criminal incitement and permissible freedom of expression is narrow; and that it is difficult to define the point at which a particular expression takes on characteristics that can reasonably be proscribed in the spirit of Article 10.2 (HL Select Committee on Religious Offences 2003: para. 82). During parliamentary debates in the House of Lords, attempts were made to focus attention on the limited group of activities that could be prohibited in the proposed legislation in order to move away from some of the debates concerning the criminalization of 'fair comment' and 'religious humour' which emerged during the parliamentary debates on Clause 39 of the Anti-Terrorism, Crime and Security Bill of 2001:

> Much of the opposition to this proposal expressed fear for the curtailment of free speech. But what is at issue is not the right to free speech; no religion ought to have anything to fear from fair scrutiny and honest debate. No, what is at issue is the abuse of free speech to incite fear, prejudice, contempt and even violence.
> (Lord Bishop of Birmingham, HL Hansard 30 January 2002: col. 322)

What statements such as these reveal is the process whereby policy makers within the institutions of government and the criminal justice system attempt to map the coordinates between the desirable and the undesirable, the lawful and the unlawful, and the reasonable and the unreasonable within a wider and more general classification in society between tolerable and intolerable behaviours, especially in relation to 'hate crimes' and their impact on vulnerable or targeted minority groups. For example, as well as the difference between fair comment and incitement, there is also a distinction being made here between hateful acts that should be subject to law and other forms of hatred that are understandable in the form of 'a reasonable person's' 'reasonable' hatred of hateful acts. Lord Lucas provides some examples of what he thinks are 'reasonable' forms of hatred expressed in response to the hateful acts of particular religious groups which he suggests should not be 'caught' by the proposed provisions of Part II of the Religious Offences Bill. This demonstrates that, to a certain extent, the confluence of Islam, terrorism and the Taliban has become an accepted and acceptable articulation and at the same time it is only reasonable that we should hate such an enemy:

> it seems to me that one can reasonably get to the point of hating the Taliban – and it is a group which would define itself in relation to religion . . . Religion, sadly, often results in people – or groups within religion – doing hateful things.
>
> (Lord Lucas, HL Hansard 30 January 2002: cols. 328 and 329)

Therefore, the issue as to whether behaviour or a publication is an example of fair comment, reasonable hatred or an attempt to incite hatred is one of the major problems associated with this proposed legislation. An added dimension to this was uncovered at the House of Lords Select Committee in that the Attorney-General's refusal of consent to prosecute on the grounds of fair comment might result in the distinction between fair comment and incitement remaining unclear. At the same time, the Attorney-General's power to refuse prosecution on the grounds that the prosecution is not needed in the public interest, which will be examined in the next section, could also inhibit the clarification in law of the difference between fair comment or legitimate criticism of a religion or a religious group and incitement to religious hatred.

What is clear is that this proposed legislation is a practical attempt to criminalize the expression of hate. Under these provisions, it will be possible to tackle incitement resulting from: words or behaviour; the display, publishing or distribution of written material; public performances or plays; distributing, showing or playing a recording; broadcasting or the possession of racially inflammatory material (Lord Dholakia, HL Hansard 30 January 2002, col. 332).

However, as Lord Lucas has pointed out, there are concerns that instances in which 'reasonable haters' (of, for example, the Taliban) will be caught out here, especially if hatred is defined as 'hatred against a group of persons defined by reference to religious belief or lack of religious belief' that is expressed 'in public'.[10] A reasonable hater, such as the parent of a child who has allegedly been kidnapped by a religious 'sect', could plausibly find that they have incited others to hostility through communication, verbally (for example, in a TV or radio interview) or in published material (in an article in a newspaper, magazine or newsletter),[11] especially if they intended to incite others to hatred of this particular religious group.

The House of Lords Select Committee referred to the potential social implications of the proposed legislation, especially the 'chilling effect' such provisions could introduce in society in the form of the suppression of robust debate and opinion in relation to religious matters because of the fear that individuals could easily overstep an undefined boundary and become subject of prosecution (HL Select Committee on Religious Offences 2003: para. 82). However, as will be demonstrated below, the intention of these provisions is not to catch out: comedians performing *risqué* humour; fair comment in the form of 'legitimate' criticism; or parents railing against a religious 'cult' that has allegedly kidnapped their child. Rather, the target activities to be prohibited are the incitement to religious hatred expressed by extremist groups.

The role of the Attorney-General

Under Section 27(1) of the Public Order Act 1986, proceedings for a prosecution on the grounds of incitement to racial hatred can be instituted only with the consent of the Attorney-General. The proposed Bill on incitement to religious hatred carries the same requirement. The main problem with this requirement, according to certain lobbying groups, is that the Attorney-General's office is a political office which is part of the executive branch of government, and therefore in theory the Attorney-General could take decisions which are, in part at least, 'politically' influenced rather than purely legal and objective (Forum Against Islamophobia and Racism 2002). Therefore, it is conceivable that political pressure could be brought to bear on the Attorney-General's consideration of such cases:

> While we welcome new legislation against incitement of religious hatred we urge that sufficient safeguards[12] be put in place to avoid the misuse of such legislation ... the concern is that, following major international and/or national events, eg., September 11th or the northern cities disturbances, due to certain biases in political

and media discourses, where this influences and shapes a particular perception against a particular religious community, this could place specific pressures on the office of the Attorney General and thereby politicise his decision.

(Forum Against Islamophobia and Racism 2002: 25)

However, there are contradictory views as to whether the Attorney-General's role (and hence the political influence associated with incitement legislation) is a help or a hindrance in the documents under consideration. For example, the Muslim Council of Britain suggested that:

it is desirable to de-politicize acts that are potentially criminal. We recognize the need to regulate prosecutions in this area since such prosecutions have an element of public interest at stake but we cannot see why such decisions should not be left to the Director of Public Prosecutions, the normal prosecuting authority.

(Memorandum from the Muslim Council of Britain, HL Select Committee on Religious Offences 2003: para. 3.7)

A contradictory view is expressed by the Archbishop's Council of the Church of England, who note that:

by virtue of s. 27 (1) Public Order Act 1986 the consent of the Attorney General would be required for the bringing of any prosecution, a fact which also reassures us that the new offence would only be invoked in circumstances in which the nature of words or conduct in question was such as to lead to genuine concerns that religious hatred could be stirred up.

(Memorandum from the Archbishop's Council of the Church of England, HL Select Committee on Religious Offences 2003: para. 5)

A considerable component of the British-Muslim community's concern about the Attorney-General's political influence over incitement cases focuses on this office's power to consent or refuse the prosecution of such cases. In response to such concerns, the Attorney-General in his memorandum to the House of Lords Select Committee emphasized that as well as the considerations of the European Convention, the high threshold test of such cases must be that the prosecution would be in 'the public interest'. That is:

Where there is sufficient evidence that an individual has committed one of the relevant offences, the facts and circumstances of the individual case may give rise to European Convention considerations . . .

Equally, even where there is sufficient evidence to justify a prosecution he retains the discretion not to prosecute where he assesses that a prosecution is not needed in the public interest.

(Memorandum from the Attorney General, HL Select Committee on Religious Offences 2003: 2)

This is clearly a political decision rather than an exclusively legal decision based on proceeding to prosecution in the light of sufficient evidence that an offence has been committed. The House of Lords Select Committee suggested that the government needed to be clear about the proportionality principle that will inform the Attorney-General's reason for consenting to prosecution under the incitement to religious hatred provisions in terms of the necessity of restricting the freedom of expressions of individuals or groups; and that this decision is clearly related to the necessity of preventing disorder and crime arising from the deliberate provocation of hatred of particular religious groups, and the protection of the rights of those groups (HL Select Committee on Religious Offences 2003: para. 84). However, there is a sense from the documents under examination here, from a number of perspectives (as will be demonstrated below), that the proposed incitement to religious hatred legislation is, in itself, not perceived primarily as a mechanism of criminalization that will generate increased prosecutions. Rather, the proposed Bill (and also the provisions of the 1986 Act) can be better described as a governmental strategy intended to shape and guide, as well as deter and dissuade, specific forms of behaviour deemed 'undesirable' in contemporary British society.

The message is in the legislation: 'no hating here'

It came to light at Select Committee that incitement legislation, in the form of the incitement to racial hatred provisions in the Public Order Act 1986, has generated relatively few prosecutions; and it is predicted that religious incitement legislation will generate even fewer. However, this is not seen as a problem by the Select Committee because it is thought that: (i) racial incitement legislation has had a deterrent effect and this is the reason for low prosecutions; and (ii) that this type of offence has a declaratory purpose which cannot be measured by prosecution rates:

if this area of the criminal law were to be extended to encompass incitement to religious, as well as racial, hatred, and not many additional prosecutions ensued the effort would not have failed: a few convictions would be good enough to convey the clear message that such behaviour is no longer acceptable in the community but has been held by a court to be criminal. A condign sentence would have been imposed.

(HL Select Committee on Religious Offences 2003: para. 101)

While this is all very well, North American writers on hate crime, especially Jacobs and Potter (1998), have suggested that 'the message' hate crime legislation attempts to communicate is far from clear. These authors suggest that:

it would take some heroic assumptions to believe that bigoted and anti-social criminals, if they listened at all, will be any more responsive to this message than they have been to all the other threats and condemnations contained in the criminal laws that they regularly ignore.

(Jacobs and Potter 1998: 68)

However, in the case of the incitement to religious hatred legislation, 'the message' being sent appears to be more finely calibrated than Jacobs and Potter's critique of North American generic hate crime legislation. The proposed provisions have been designed to target a specific audience (Far Right groups) and a specific legislative problem (that is, the attempt to fill the gap in legal protection which is currently being exploited by Far Right groups). This is evident at Select Committee:

it might be said that it is important for Parliament and the Government to make clear that they did not expect a large number of additional cases to be prosecuted, but they did expect that publication of some of the most inflammatory material could be deterred by extremists' fear of the risk of prosecution.

(HL Select Committee on Religious Offences 2003: para. 84)

The Lord Bishop of Oxford, during the Anti-Terrorism, Crime and Security Bill of 2001 debates (on Clause 39), is very clear that this is indeed the intention of legislation 'of this type':

It may be that the smaller number of convictions [for incitement to racial hatred] itself highlighted the case for this kind of legislation. As we all know, the law has a declaratory purpose and a deterrent effect. It could be argued that the laws against incitement to racial hatred have in fact played a role making such hatred less frequent.

(Lord Bishop of Oxford, HL Hansard 21 November 2001: para. 1229)

There is clearly a self-conscious, governmental intention in the proposed Bill and in the 1986 Act to shape the conduct, especially the undesirable conduct, of others, which is akin to what Foucault refers to as 'the conduct of conduct' (Rose 1999: 3) in his lectures on governmentality. To govern in this Foucauldian sense, according to Rose, is to act upon action in that practices of government are deliberate attempts to shape conduct in certain ways in relation to certain objectives. In relation to curbing Far Right excesses with regard to the incitement to religious (and for that matter racial) hatred, the government, judiciary and organizations representing the Muslim community all seem to be concerned with the context rather than the causes of the poten-tial offence. This is an instrumental understanding of 'the problem' based on the assessment of how these groups have managed to incite religious hatred with legal impunity. Thus, closing the legal loophole in which these groups operate should have the desired effect of deterring further undesirable activ-ities. Beverly Hughes, in her former role as Parliamentary Under-Secretary of State for the Home Office, lends support to this governmental interpretation of the objectives of introducing (and expanding) legislation of this type (with specific reference to Clause 39 of the Anti-Terrorism, Crime and Security Bill of 2001):

> I do not think that the merit of the existing legislation is in terms only of the numbers of prosecutions. We do feel that the deterrent effect on the extent to which some of these racists groups would go otherwise without this legislation is a significant one in that, whilst they produce propaganda, they are mindful of the chances of prosecution and that does limit to some extent the excesses to which they would otherwise go . . . We are convinced that it is having a deterrent effect in relation to racial hatred and similarly we hope for the same effect in terms of religious groups.
>
> (Hughes, HC Select Committee on Home Affairs,
> Anti-Terrorism, Crime and Security Bill, Minutes of Evidence,
> 14 November 2001: cols. 230 and 231)

From the documents examined here, it becomes clear that incitement to hatred legislation (whether racial or religious) is an example of a particular type of legislation which is intended to promote self-censorship and self-policing in extremist individuals and groups. Much of the discussion above focuses on closing the legal gap in protection that is currently being exploited by Far Right groups. The emphasis here, therefore, is not on attempting to reform, understand or rehabilitate those engaged in the incitement to hatred. Much of the focus of the debates and discussion explored above coincides with what Young (1999a) describes as the process of *adiaphorization* within the 'actuarial attitude' (p. 67) associated with contemporary criminal justice systems in the Western world being increasingly concerned with risk mini-mization and the avoidance of 'trouble' and 'difficulty' rather than morally condemning undesirable behaviour. Adiaphorization is a concept developed by Zygmunt Bauman (1995) to depict the stripping of human relations of their moral significance, exempting them from moral evaluation, rendering them 'morally neutral'. This is not to say that the incitement to hatred is not being morally condemned by policy makers, as this certainly is the case. However, the suggested legislative solution to this problem in the form of closing the legal loophole in which incitement to religious hatred is conducted can be described as being motivated by the instrumental intention of attempting to minimize the risk of these activities disrupting the social order and infringing on the rights of others in the future rather than law as a technology of moral condemnation.

Yet there is also the issue that it is only the most severe and blatant incidents of Islamophobic propaganda that would be caught by this legislation (see Iganski's critique of 'incitement' and 'stirring up hatred' provisions in relation to the Public Order Act 1986 in endnotes 2 and 3) and that these groups will simply exploit the limitations of incitement of hatred legislation (whether racial or religious) by avoiding sending out obviously illegal material. This is clearly the case in relation to the BNP's response to the 1986 Act in its information sheet *Freedom of Speech in Britain – A Brief Legal Primer*:

> the fact of the matter is that the more politely one's case is expressed the more damning it is. Abusive language only gains support for the opposition. The Act, in substance, banned the use of wild language, not polite and reasoned argument. The legislation can work entirely to our advantage if only a tiny minority of people would just stop sending out abusive and illegal material anonymously.
>
> (BNP, in Iganski 1999a: 134)

However, extremism is not exclusive to the Far Right. Legislation of this type could easily by used to impact on the activities of extremists from the Muslim community. One has just to refer to the trial of Sheikh Abdullah el-Faisal in March 2003 to realize the potential impact of this proposed incitement to religious hatred legislation on Muslim extremists, especially the media-coined 'Muslim hate clerics'. For example, on 6 March 2003 at the Old Bailey, el-Faisal was found guilty on three counts of soliciting murder, two counts of using threatening or abusive words to stir up racial hatred (in the form of a combination of religious and racial hatred against Jews), and one count for distributing recordings of such speeches (Branigan 2003).[13] However, there is little detailed discussion of the consequence or 'use' of this proposed legislation for the purposes of deterring and/or prosecuting Muslim 'extremists' at Select Committee, where the overwhelming emphasis has been on curbing, through the introduction of criminal sanctions, Far Right Islamophobic activities and therefore engineering yet another obstacle to the expression of counter-modern difficulty.

The restrictions of the freedom of expression that the proposed incitement to religious hatred legislation could introduce (in the event that the Attorney-General grants consent to prosecute) can be described as being a strategy of consequentialist 'social engineering'. Stanley Fish explains what the consequentialist approach to freedom of expression means:

> What this means is that insofar as you have an answer to the question 'what is free speech for?' – you are already committed to finding in a particular situation that speech with certain undesirable effects should not be tolerated; and what that means in turn is that *there is no such thing as 'free speech'*, because from the very start your sense of just how free speech should be is shadowed by your identification of, and obligation to, the good in whose name acts of speech are to be justified. 'Free speech' always means for consequentialists 'free speech so long as it furthers rather than subverts our core values'.
>
> (Fish 1994: 14)

The core value that is being upheld in this proposed legislation is manifestly one of equal protection and non-discrimination before the law, which is emphasized in the following statement made by Lord Dohlakia in the House of Lords:

> one must feel concern about the security of all communities in Britain . . . Any law that discriminates in its application is a bad law and goes against the government's stance on equality legislation . . . the Bill . . . will introduce a common, universal definition that treats all religions equally.
>
> (Lord Dohlakia, HL Hansard 30 January 2002: cols. 331 and 332)

However, as well as the admirable attempt to ensure the equal protection of all communities, the complementary emergent value that is being promoted in this Bill is an intolerance of expressed hostility between social groups. As a result of the promotion of these associated values of equality before the law and the proscription of incitement to hatred, the Labour government's desire to create a new, superficial morality on the surface of social relations is also exposed. In this emergent social order, the inner enemy of extremism (whether Far Right or Muslim fundamentalism) will increasingly be prohibited from disrupting the image of Britain that the Labour government is attempting to promote. The problem with the proposed Bill is not its 'good' intentions, but rather its limitations. As well as the limitations listed above in relation to distinguishing between 'fair comment' and the incitement to hatred, and the politics of consent in relation to the Attorney-General's permission with regards to prosecution, another major source of concern about the proposed legislation is that it fails to protect many more vulnerable groups in society (not overtly defined by race or religion) from incitement to hatred. Patchy protection is not enough. It sets up hierarchies of victimization which devalue the impact of hatred and the incitement of hatred on other groups.

The need for the introduction of comprehensive legislation that would protect many more groups who are, or who are potentially, the victims of hatred or the incitement to hatred, other than groups targeted for race or religion, was suggested at Select Committee:

> The starting point for legislation may be the requirement on government to enact legislation to implement the draft Council Framework decision on Racism and Xenophobia,[14] which would not be confined to incitement to hatred in the two areas so far selected: race and religion. It is possible to forecast how this might be ripe to include incitement to hatred across the range of targets of hate crime, even beyond the list currently under the debate in connection with the decision, for example, the gay community, asylum seekers or whoever incurs the opprobrium of some branches of public opinion.
> (HL Select Committee on Religious Offences 2003: 135)

What this means is that this area of legislation could open up certain possibilities for the representatives of other minority groups (e.g. asylum seekers, lesbians, gays, bisexuals and transgender groups) to benefit from the development of a more comprehensive 'incitement to hatred' Bill. On several occasions, the House of Lords Select Committee Report referred to this need for comprehensive protection. For example:

> We repeat that there are now, and may arise in the future, more categories of victim in addition to racial and religious minorities who would welcome a more comprehensive approach to the identification of the vulnerable, and recognition that the courts have the power to punish offences against such persons with a more severe penalty. Such victims might then be encouraged more frequently to report incidents to the police.
> (HL Select Committee on Religious Offences 2003: para. 128)

The introduction of this more inclusive legislation could lead to a culture where legislation has a comprehensive rather than highly selective deterrent effect on all forms of incitement to hatred that impacts on the lives of all vulnerable groups targeted by hate in Britain, especially asylum seekers but also other groups in society, such as sexual minorities including the lesbian and gay communities in the UK.[15] This will be the focus of the next two chapters.

Conclusion

The progress of the Religious Offences Bill has not been a smooth one. This chapter has exposed the factors involved in attempting to protect one group from a form of harm (incitement to hatred) while simultaneously attempting to protect the rights of all (freedom of speech and expression) at the same time as recognizing the fact that non-protection (in the form of an exploited gap in protection) leads to inequity between groups (some which are protected and some which are not). At the same time, as suggested above, just filling a gap in protection for one community (for example, Muslims) will result in other groups who are also vulnerable to hatred and the incitement of hatred being left unprotected. This single issue, rather than a comprehensive approach to legislative protection, can lead to the creation of hierarchies of oppression that prioritize racist and religious intolerance but de-prioritize the impact of hatred on other vulnerable groups, including sexual minority communities and the members of disabled communities.

In June 2003, the Chairman of the House of Lords Select Committee on Religious Offences, Viscount Colville of Culross, released the following statements in relation to the findings of the Committee and the future of the Religious Offences Bill:

> After extensive public consultation we have analysed the merits of all the options, but feel it is up to Parliament as a whole to decide how it wants to proceed. Religion plays a vital role in our society and there should be a degree of protection equally available to all faiths, but there is no consensus among us on the precise form that protection might take. The introduction of a Bill to deal with any, or all of these issues is likely to run into profound controversy, despite the pressure to take action on incitement to religious hatred. The Committee also looked at the possibility of increasing maximum penalties for public order offences so that – through sentencing guidelines – aggravating factors could be taken into account when determining punishment of all convicted of offences motivated by hatred of vulnerable groups, not just racial or religious hatred. The Committee noted that an opportunity to consider amending legislation on religious offences could present itself if the proposed European Framework Decision on Combating Racism and Xenophobia is agreed.
>
> (Viscount Colville of Culross 2003: 1)

On 7 July 2004, the former Home Secretary David Blunkett announced that he would again press ahead with plans to criminalize incitement to religious hatred through Parliament (Tempest 2004b). Mr Blunkett stated on BBC Radio 4's *Today Programme* on the same day, that:

> The issue of incitement to religious hate is a tiny part of a much broader pattern that we are attempting, collectively, to put together, to create a society where cohesion, tolerance and understanding are natural, where people can settle their differences in ways that don't develop hate and where people feel free to be able to express sensible views and have sensible arguments.
>
> (Blunkett, in Tempest 2004b: 2)

That this controversial legislation could continue to face problems in Parliament is undoubted. The Conservative Party announced on 7 July that they would not back Mr Blunkett's proposal. At the same time, Labour peers in the House of Lords predicted that it would be 'very difficult' to get this new law through Parliament (Tempest 2004b).

The debates and statements examined in the documents referred to above offer insights into a number of wider themes that are being explored in this book. For example: (i) the shifting focus of bigotry in contemporary Britain from race to religion (which nevertheless contains subtle inscriptions of race through religion), and (ii) the gradual encroachment of common law provisions (incitement, hatred, etc.) into the criminal law in the context of successive governments' attempts to deter certain behaviours and activities with a view to promoting an image of Britain, which even if it is not totally comfortable with its diversity, will at least be seen to be discouraging extreme, incendiary and hateful views and behaviours which could disrupt the social order.

If the 'declaratory' role of incitement legislation is taken to its ultimate conclusion, then it could be assumed that those individuals and groups that have not acclimatized to the cultural diversity of twenty-first century Britain will, through legislative 'social engineering', be required to at least 'act' within the narrow confines that respects their freedom of expression at the same time as assesses the consequences of their actions in relation to the rights of others and for the well-being of society, especially in relation to the promotion of inter-community harmony (this theme will be developed further in Chapter 7).

In the official documents examined in Chapters 1–3, for example in relation to the killing of Stephen Lawrence and the resulting inquiry into his murder, in the documents dedicated to community cohesion in response to the disturbances in 2001 (in Oldham, Burnley and Bradford) and in the range of documents examined regarding recent UK immigration and asylum policy, all have, to different extents (and sometimes in contradictory fashions), been concerned with the government's reflexive project of attempting to understand and minimize social risks or social 'bads' associated with the migration, displacement and integration of the diverse communities that make up multi-ethnic, multi-faith and multicultural Britain. At the same time, I have demonstrated that much of this 'official' reflexivity is concerned with developing new ways of being British, with an emphasis on active participation and dialogue between different social groups in order to ameliorate specific social problems in the form of tensions, polarization and segregation between 'host' ('indigenous' White communities), established migrant communities and recent migrant or temporary migrant (asylum seeker) communities. This chapter had a slightly different emphasis, as it explored the ambiguous political location of the Muslim community in Britain. Yet the discussion above is also related to the issue of citizenship, especially equity before the law and the project of providing equal protection for vulnerable communities under the Labour government's strategy of protective inclusion. This strategy of including the excluded, especially 'minority' communities of various types, through offering them greater protection from hatred is a central theme that will also be developed in the next two chapters where attention will turn to how the government and police are increasingly taking homophobic hate crime seriously. In Chapters 5 and 6, what will be observed is the recalibration of the boundaries of toleration in relation to the discursive construction of sexual minority groups (especially gay men) in Britain from being a source of social danger (for example, as corruptors of youth, as emblematic of moral decline, as a threat to the hetero-familial sexual and gender order) to the construction of lesbian, gay, bisexual and transgender communities in recent years as communities who also deserve to be protected from hate.

5 Building trust – policing homophobia

A gay man who was kicked and beaten to death in an apparent homophobic attack in London had survived the Soho pub bombing five years ago, it emerged yesterday. David Morley, 37, died hours after being set upon by a gang of teenagers who carried out a spate of assaults near the Royal Festival Hall, on the South Bank in central London, in the early hours of Saturday morning. Police said some items were stolen but they were investigating all lines of inquiry. At least one of the other victims was a gay man and detectives could not rule out homophobia as a motive.

(Laville and Cowan 2004: 1)

Introduction

In this and the next chapter, attention moves away from race relations and immigration policy to look at other minority groups in society – namely, sexual minority communities in the UK. Like the religious and ethnic minority communities and asylum seeker communities examined in earlier chapters, the problems facing gay, lesbian, bisexual and transgendered (lgbt) communities have in recent years also been the subject of institutional (Home Office, Association of Chief Police Officers, etc.) reflexivity in relation to some of the social problems already raised in earlier chapters; for example, the crisis in confidence in policing, the harm of hate, and the civic and political detachment of minority communities.

Within this wider process of reflecting on the specific social problems associated with ethnic, migrant, religious and sexual minority communities, it is important to tease out some of the differences in relation to how these different communities are conceptualized. For example, religious, ethnic and asylum seeker communities in previous chapters have been classified in terms of length of stay – that is, as established, recent and temporary communities living in specific areas of the UK. The prefix 'British' has also been used to depict established ethnic and religious communities, especially the British-born second- and third-generation members of these minority communities. At the same time, the adjectives 'White', 'indigenous' and 'host' have been used to depict 'British' communities living in close proximity to these ethnic, religious and asylum seeker minority communities. However, lgbt communities are rather different, as they are not associated with the familial and biological characteristics of these other minority groups. In fact, lgbt individuals emerge from within all communities whether they are the communities of 'Middle England' or ethnic and religious minority communities. Rather than migrant status,[1] religious and cultural traditions, or physical 'racial' characteristics,[2] lgbt communities are communities whose minority status is marked out by sexual and gender practices. Despite these differences, what lgbt communities do share with religious, ethnic and migrant communities, apart from their minority status within mainstream society, is their vulnerability to hatred; and, as will be revealed in the next chapter, a shared history of oppressive policing. Homophobia[3] is the umbrella term used to describe the form of prejudice expressed by societies, institutions and individuals who hate (and fear) homosexuals. This classification of prejudice is also used to describe the hatred and fear of lesbians, bisexuals and members of the transgender community (although the term transphobia is increasingly being used to describe the fear and hatred of the members of transgender communities[4]).

This and the next chapter explore the place of the lgbt community within this emerging social and political landscape through a critical analysis of the strategies (usually local government and police 'multi-agency' strategies) by which lgbt communities in the UK are being transformed from being 'tolerated' communities on the margins of society into communities targeted by hatred that must be protected in the context of the post-Stephen Lawrence, community safety policing ethos implemented in the Crime and Disorder Act 1998. It will be shown that this transition in police–lgbt relationships in particular is to be achieved through the mechanism of a particular variety of British citizenship (already observed in earlier chapters), which, in this instance, takes the form of encouraging the civic engagement of marginal communities, through these communities becoming 'active' in the amelioration of the social problems that have a direct impact upon them.

In this chapter, the process of consulting with lgbt communities, auditing the extent of the homophobic violence they experience, and devising multi-agency strategies for dealing with homophobic violence and related issues will be examined in relation to initiatives developed in the city of Southampton[5] since 1998. The chapter will also consider the implications of such initiatives for the lgbt community. What will be the effect of these initiatives on these communities, especially lgbt communities being called to 'active' citizenship? Are there any hidden costs for lgbt communities that come with the benefits of greater protection and improved service provision? The chapter starts with an examination of the emergence of 'joined-up' government and community safety as the context for the emergence of 'active' citizenship, especially in the Labour government's wider law and order strategy.

Modernizing government: getting in touch with 'active communities'

Two areas of legislation are especially relevant to the exploration of the contemporary policing of lgbt communities in England and Wales: the Crime and Disorder Act 1998 and the Local Government Act 1999. Both Acts can be described as an attempt to re-imagine the way government (in programmes associated with 'joined-up government') and the police (in the ethos of 'community safety') interact with citizens and communities. A central aspiration of these Acts is the strategy of transforming citizens and communities into 'active' entities. I argue that with the passing of the Crime and Disorder Act in 1998 and the Local Government Act in 1999, Britain has entered into a political ethos in which 'community' in general, and 'local communities' in particular, are seen as the key instruments of government and policing. Community, in New Labour discourse, connotes a range of attachments and local relationships between people and places, for example 'geographical communities', 'neighbourhood communities' and 'communities of identity' (Clarke and Newman 1997)[6] that are to be utilized in strategic ways by local government and the police. In this section of the chapter, the focus is on the process of modernizing government, especially the emergent role of local governments in the Local Government Act, before moving on to explore policing and community safety.

According to the Department of the Environment, Transport and the Regions (DETR), local government is viewed as a problem because of the culture of apathy associated with local government elections (DETR 1998a,b; Brooks 1999; Chandler 2001); however, at the same time, local government is also viewed as an opportunity because it is the form of government most closely associated with citizens and their communities (DETR 1998a: para. 1.3). The problems and possibilities of local government are at the very centre of New Labour's most significant experiment in democracy to date, joined-up government. It is through the joined-up government programme that central government is attempting to become more closely connected to 'the individual' through modernizing local government. The involvement of local people is seen to be a crucial issue of democratic legitimacy (DETR 1998a: para. 2.1). Involvement, consultation and participation are pervasive notions that emerge in 'joined-up government' discourse, which indicates an emergent form of government that desires to govern through existing or potential 'indigenous' mechanisms (O'Malley 1996), whether these be of communities, cultural groups, neighbourhoods or some other entity (Dean 1999). Local government has a crucial intermediary role to play here as a point of connection between central government and local communities, through councils and local authorities being encouraged to take community leadership in the forging of partnerships with a broad range of local stakeholders.[7] Participation is central to this strategy and local government is being re-branded as the facilitator of participation and the enabler of engagement. This new role for local government is described in the following passage:

> It is in partnership with others – public agencies, private companies, community groups and voluntary organisations – that local government's future lies. Local authorities deliver important services but their distinctive leadership role will be to weave and knit together the contribution of the various local stakeholders.
>
> (DETR 1998a: para 1.9)

However, is does not mean that central government will become irrelevant and 'hands off'. In this model, stakeholder-orientated local government is subjected to even more central government control through the introduction of the culture of best value, in the form of centrally regulated monitoring regimes (Chandler 2001). As Giddens (2000) notes, in this Third Way strategy governments no longer row but steer, governments do not control but challenge, and the quality of public services is to be improved through performance monitoring.

Democratic legitimacy is to be achieved through shared responsibility and building consensus around policies. The joining-up of the citizen to government through the creation of participatory spaces of local government is in theory supposed to be a process of convergence in which information is shared by participants in an attempt to reach mutual understanding (Schedler and Glastra 2001). This convergence, this variety of participation, is synonymous with shared responsibility (Schedler and Glastra 2001), which has the added bonus of the government's role and the government's interventions becoming increasingly backgrounded (Fairclough 2000). This, according to Rose (1994), is governing 'at a distance' in both a constitutional and a spatial sense. This amounts to a process of 'de-governmentalizing government and de-statizing practices of government' through the detachment of the substantive authority of expertise from the apparatuses of political rule, in what Rhodes (1997) describes as 'the community government scenario' (p. 134).

Therefore, the whole point of the Third Way joined-up government programme can be described as a comprehensive programme of democratic renewal involving strategies of interactive and participatory democracy that are designed to win back government credibility and effectiveness through turning citizens from objects of policy intervention into sources of relevant knowledge (Schedler and Glastra 2001). However, this participatory ethos is not to be confused with the ideal of deliberative democracy. Deliberative democracy is a dialogic form of democracy characterized by a 'politics of presence' and the institutional framework that aims to facilitate a 'transformative discussion' among partners under the appropriate conditions of equality (Bohman 2000).[8] Rather than 'deliberative democracy', the Labour government's joined-up government programme should be viewed as a tendency towards extending participation in local democracy (Bucek and Smith 2000). Out of this context emerges what Rose (1996a) describes as the most fundamental and most generalizable characteristic of these new rationalities of government – the 'active citizen' in an 'active society'. Thus, in terms of citizenship, the movement from policy object to democratic resource (Young 1997) in this socio-political context involves the facilitation and promotion of a distinctive 'subjectivity' in the form of the 'active' and 'empowered citizen' (Thompson and Hoggett 2001).

This is all very well, but: (1) Is the citizen really becoming as 'enjoined' as all this 'on the ground'? (2) Are there any hidden costs incurred in signing-up to 'active citizenship'? And (3) who is and who is not being invited to become an 'active citizen'? These questions will shape the analysis of the response to homophobic incidents in the city of Southampton. Before that, however, the development of 'active citizens' in 'active communities' so central to New Labour's joined-up government strategy will be examined in relation to the policing of minority groups in the post-Crime and Disorder Act context.

Community safety

It was with the passing of the Local Government Act in 1999 that much of this joined-up thinking in relation to communities and local government came into being. However, a year earlier (in the first year of the Labour administration) a parallel development in relation to the mobilization of communities in the sphere of law and order was implemented in the Crime and Disorder Act 1998. Even though this legislation is better known for its shake-up of the youth justice system,[9] it was here that 'community safety partnerships', as first suggested in the Morgan Report (Home Office 1991), were introduced as a statutory requirement. The emergence of such partnerships and initiatives should be put in context. It was with the publication of the Morgan Report that 'police-driven' initiatives associated with crime prevention in general were seen as being limited in scope. It was suggested in this report that the term 'crime prevention' should be replaced with that of 'community safety', which is a wider interpretation that could encourage greater participation from all sections of the community in the fight against crime. The report suggested that the local authority was the 'natural focus for co-ordinating, in collaboration with the police, the broad range of activities directed at improving community safety' (Home Office 1991: 4). When these recommendations were eventually drafted in the Crime and Disorder Bill, they took the form of statutory partnerships (see Chapter 1), which required local authorities, the police and other bodies to come together to develop strategies for tackling crime and disorder (DETR 1998a: para. 1.15). This 'required community consultation process' in the implementation of community safety strategies and community representation in local partnerships has been described by Crawford (2001) as an attempt to implement a 'holistic, problem-oriented approach' to crime that offers:

> more plural understandings of and social responses to crime, drawing together a variety of organisations and stakeholders, in the public, voluntary and private sectors as well as from amongst relevant community groups in ways that are problem-focused.
>
> (Crawford 2001: 57)

The former Home Secretary, David Blunkett, was clearly attempting to build on the 'community safety' and 'community participation' ethos of the Morgan Report and the Crime and Disorder Act 1998. This is evident in the following passage from the White Paper *Policing a New Century*:

> the police alone cannot win the fight against crime and disorder. It requires a co-ordinated response by the community as a whole. Local authorities, schools, health services, the voluntary and private sectors, and individuals all have to work in partnerships with the police to develop and implement local crime and disorder reduction strategies.
>
> (Blunket, in Home Office 2001b).

What both the Crime and Disorder Act and the Local Government Act, together with the programmes and reports that have followed in their wake, signal is the attempt by the government to enjoin local authorities and local police forces to the local communities that they serve in the name of ensuring democratic legitimacy and increasing community safety and community confidence in the police (and government). In this context, all citizens are to be active citizens who are attached to, live in or identify with 'active' participating communities. This, however, poses particular problems for some minority groups (e.g. ethnic and religious minority groups, sexual minority groups), which might have good reason not to trust the police and other service providers.[10]

The social harm of hate

According to Chandler (2001), the emphasis on community safety in the provisions of the Crime and Disorder Act should be placed within the broader context of central government's attempts to address 'problems of social cohesion'. Social cohesion, social exclusion and especially community cohesion have already been explored in earlier chapters with reference to some of the problems experienced in relation to asylum seeker dispersal, and more overtly in relation to programmes devised for post-riot Bradford, where the specific problems of White and Pakistani-Muslim community polarization was to be addressed through strategies aimed at de-antagonizing these communities. However, there is another momentum behind these initiatives that is strongly associated with crime and disorder, and this has an important bearing on the issues associated with hate crimes that will be discussed below: New Labour's commitment to improving 'social well-being'. The promotion of social (alongside economic and environmental) well-being was a duty to be placed on councils in the Labour Party's manifesto. That is:

> the government has given careful thought to how councils should meet this new duty. Making this a duty rather than a power would mean that this is something local authorities must do – it would be a mandatory function. Such a responsibility would require local councils to take a holistic view of their local communities and take steps to promote its well-being.
>
> (DETR 1998a: para. 6.11)

'Social well-being', as well as the facilitation of active communities and the empowerment of citizens, is crucial to understanding much of the Labour government's 'crackdown' or criminalization of 'incivility' and 'anti-social behaviour' in an attempt to foster social and community cohesion. It shall be argued below that what is emerging in the local government and police discourses and practices (in an attempt to foster and promote social well-being and social cohesion) is a distinctive appreciation of the mechanisms that promote social 'detachment', especially among minority groups such as ethnic and religious minorities as well as asylum seeker communities. This appreciation has resulted in the government's 'social exclusion' discourses undergoing a process of expansion, as noted in Chapter 2, in the face of segregation, hatred and polarization between communities in society. This 'expanded' concern over the mechanisms that can detach individuals and groups from the social mainstream does, as will be suggested below, also have a bearing on lgbt communities. However, much of the emphasis of this 'concern' in recent years has been associated with racial disharmony. One could say in relation to the policing 'of' and the policing 'with' the multi-ethnic and multi-faith communities that make up twenty-first-century Britain that the development of 'holistic problem-orientated' approaches to community policing has a well-documented relationship with racism, racial tension and high-profile racially aggravated disturbances and incidents since the 1980s. From Lord Scarman's Report in 1981 on the Brixton disturbances, to the murder of Stephen Lawrence and the MacPherson Inquiry Report (1999), to the publication of the White Paper *Policing a New Century* in December 2001, what can be observed is the gradual movement and pressure on police forces (to paraphrase from the Scarman Inquiry Report) to develop 'styles of policing' that are designed to secure public approval and respect in order for policing to be more effective in multi-ethnic, multi-faith and multicultural Britain.

The Association of Chief Police Officers (ACPO) was one of the first organizations in the UK to focus on the problems facing minority groups in society that are targeted by hatred. Significantly, the ACPO's *Guide to Identifying and Combating Hate Crime*, published in 2000, listed homophobic hate crime and racist hate crime as the two most high-profile hate crimes perpetrated in the UK. Both of these forms of hate crime, according to the ACPO, are associated with high-profile media events, for example the Stephen Lawrence Inquiry and the nail-bombing of the Admiral Duncan (gay) public house in Soho in London in 1999 (ACPO 2000).

Hate crime in the ACPO's guide is taken to mean any crime where the perpetrator's prejudice against an identifiable group of people is a factor in determining who is victimized (ACPO 2000). The centrality of victimization in relation to racist and homophobic hate crime is evident in the ACPO's definitions. For example, a racist incident (as observed in Chapter 1) is defined as 'any incident which is perceived to be racist by the victim or any other person'. Homophobic incidents are similarly defined as 'any incident which is perceived to be homophobic by the victim or any other person. In effect, any incident intended to have an impact on those perceived to be lesbian, gay men, bisexual or transgender' (ACPO 2000: 13). According to the ACPO, hate crimes are special crimes that require special police attention because:

> Hate crimes can have a devastating effect on the quality of life of its victims and those who fear becoming victims. That is why we must give it priority. Hate crime victims feel the added trauma of knowing that the perpetrator's motivation is an impersonal, group hatred, relating to some feature such as skin colour, physical disability, or visible features relating to core personal values such as religion or being lesbian, gay, bisexual or transgendered. A crime that might normally have a minor impact becomes, with the hate element, a very intimate and hurtful attack that can undermine the victim's quality

> of life . . . hate crime is a powerful poison to society . . . it breeds suspicion, mistrust, alienation and fear. It promotes isolation and exclusion and sets up barriers to communication.
>
> (ACPO 2000: 20–1)

According to Moran (2000), the ACPO's definitions of racist and homophobic hate crimes are significant as they focus on the 'special circumstances' and the 'unique effects' of these 'value-added' crimes, which, although impersonal, are experienced as being very personal and thus are the source of greater harm. For example, homophobic hate crimes have been described as having a particularly spatial impact on victims and victim communities in that these incidents have been described as a mechanism for 'policing the closet', or the boundaries of 'privacy' that work to keep lesbians and gays marginalized in the secret fringes of society. Thus, homophobic violence can be viewed as 'a punishment for stepping outside culturally accepted norms and a warning to all gay and lesbian people to stay in "their place", the invisibility and self hatred of the closet' (Herek and Berrill 1992: 3). According to McManus and Rivers (2001), in the context of crime and disorder, homophobia is not just a fear; it is also a hatred of, or prejudice towards, people who are lesbian, gay or bisexual, or who are perceived to be. It can be subtle or overt and can take many forms, including:

- verbal abuse and harassment
- physical assault and emotional violence
- property damage
- other crimes (e.g. extortion).

(McManus and Rivers 2001: 3)

For McManus and Rivers, the victims of homophobia and homophobic incidents can experience a number of long-term mental health problems as a result of the victimization or discrimination they face. For example, it has been suggested that adolescent victims of homophobia are more prone to self-harm and suicide[11] than their heterosexual counterparts. Also, exposure to violence and harassment increases the prevalence of depression, anxiety and relationship problems among lesbians, gay men and bisexual men and women.[12] There is also the suggestion that the victims of homophobic incidents may also suffer from post-traumatic stress disorder (McManus and Rivers 2001). However, the ACPO stresses that it is not just individuals who are affected by hate crimes, but also the families and friends of victims (their wider 'community'). According to the ACPO, it is 'society' that is the ultimate victim of hate crime. In answer to the question 'why is it important to identify an incident as a hate incident?', the ACPO stresses the following:

- It does not just affect the victim;
- It can impact upon entire communities;
- There can be hundreds of 'victims';
- Society as a whole is a victim;
- There is a very high risk of repeat victimization.

(ACPO 2000: 76)

Thus hate crimes, whether racist or homophobic, are perceived by organizations such as the ACPO as a serious threat to individuals, neighbourhoods and communities. The policy solutions to hate crime, other than introducing higher tariff offences, such as for racially aggravated offences in the Crime and Disorder Act 1998, are also associated with attempting to encourage the communities affected by hate crime to work with police to fight it. The Crime and Disorder Act requires that both the police and local authorities in partnership with other agencies should become involved in both mapping and thereafter reducing crime in local areas (Blackbourn and Loveday 2004). This translates into the requirement that crime reduction partnerships should actively seek out and record offences identified as 'hidden crime' (Blackbourn and Loveday 2004). The following is a five-step plan devised by McManus and Rivers for the development of a generic police–lgbt community crime reduction partnership:

- prepare the ground of partnerships
- prepare a common policy statement
- consult and involve lesbian, gay and bisexual communities
- audit homophobic crime
- develop and implement a strategy for dealing with homophobic crime.

(McManus and Rivers 2001: 4)

It is suggested below that much of the focus of police–lgbt crime reduction partnerships is on the third and fourth steps of this five-step plan – that is, consultation with certain individuals who 'represent' the lgbt community and the auditing of homophobic hate crime. But what is being audited in homophobic victimization surveys? According to Moran and Skeggs (2004), homophobic victimization surveys represent violence in two main ways: (i) as hidden violence and (ii) as unreported violence. Moran and Skeggs suggest that victimization surveys are mechanisms for recognizing 'what is not recognized' in official criminal statistics. Moreover, the conducting of a homophobic victimization survey is often perceived as a reflexive act by institutions within the criminal justice system that have previously failed to take these instances of violence seriously to begin the process of doing so. According to Moran and Skeggs, the lack of data on homophobic victimization is reflected in the limited number of police investigations into the perpetration of such crimes, as well as the dearth of prosecutions and convictions for such offences.

However, homophobic victimization surveys do not exclusively focus on homophobic violence and the experience of homophobic victimization in local lgbt communities. Homophobic violence and victimization is only one side of the problem to be audited:

> Research shows that lesbian, gay, bisexual and transgender popula-
> tions are at a greater risk of being victims of crime. They are also
> disadvantaged when they experience crime and find it more difficult
> to access the range of services available to many other victims of
> crime.
>
> (McManus and Rivers 2001: 2)

Service provision – or, more accurately, the obstacles obstructing victimized communities accessing the range of services that should be open to them – is therefore another important aspect of homophobic victimization surveys or audits of homophobic crime. The presence or absence of adequate services and policies to deal with specific crimes is a significant part of the ACPO's classification of victims of homophobic and racist crime as hate crime victims. The controversial exclusion of domestic violence from the ACPO's guide on hate crime, according to Moran, is particularly revealing of this classification process:

> this violence is not 'hate crime' [in the ACPO guide], in part because
> of the existence of well-established services and policies relating to
> violence against women. We must assume that the argument here is
> that there is no need to add value to women as victims, as their needs
> are already well met.
>
> (Moran 2000: 12)

The presence of an institutionalized prejudice in service provider organ-
izations is also one of the prerequisites for the ACPO's classification of hate crime. Lack of trust in service providers results in a further layer of value-added 'harm', which can impact on individuals and whole communities because hate crime offenders 'can often keep the same victim or group of victims locked in isolation and fear by keeping the physical extent of each attack at a level where it is unlikely to be reported' (ACPO 2000: 21). Thus, just as with racist incidents examined in Chapter 1, homophobic crime is only one aspect of the problem, as the reporting behaviour and access to services in relation to the victims of homophobic crime is seen as another layer of 'added-value' in relation to these 'special victims'. Part of the problem in establishing

police–lgbt crime reduction partnerships, according to McManus and Rivers, is the perception among members of lgbt communities that the police as an organization is homophobic. McManus and Rivers have produced a definition of institutional homophobia modified from the definition of institutional racism[13] found in the Stephen Lawrence Inquiry Report:

> The collective failure of an organisation to provide an appropriate and professional service to people because of their actual or perceived sexual orientation. It can be seen or detected in processes, attitudes and behaviour that amount to discrimination, through unwitting prejudice, ignorance, thoughtlessness and homophobic stereotyping, all of which disadvantages lgbt people.
>
> (McManus and Rivers 2001: 3)

The ACPO suggests that the perception of police institutional prejudice towards lgbt communities results in victims of homophobic violence assuming:

- that the incident/crime will not be taken seriously by the police
- that there may be a homophobic reaction from an officer
- that others may find out about your sexuality as a result of reporting
- that information about your sexuality may be recorded/stored; and
- that you will have to disclose/talk about your sexuality to an officer.

(ACPO 2000: 81)

Many of the problems and issues surrounding the policing of the lgbt community raised above, including issues of trust, overcoming the perception of institutionalized prejudice, as well as the combination of victimization surveys with audits of service provision, will be explored in the case study below.

Hidden targets: experiences of homophobic crime and harassment in Southampton

Here, attention turns to the roles played by various agencies and organizations in the Gay and Lesbian Community Multi-Agency Group (Hampshire and Isle of Wight),[14] with particular emphasis on organizations or agencies based in Southampton. The significant agencies and stakeholders in this multi-agency group are listed below together with a description of their roles in relation to police–lgbt anti-hate crime initiatives.

1. *Hampshire Police Authority*. The Authority is the governing body of the Hampshire Constabulary. According to the Chairman of the Hampshire Police Authority, 'public safety and crime prevention and detection is best achieved through partnership' (Hampshire Police Authority 2001: 3). The Police Authority's stated objectives in its annual policing plan are 'to consult as widely as possible on policing issues with the people of Hampshire and the Isle of Wight' (Hampshire Police Authority 2001: 13). Since the passing of the Crime and Disorder Act 1998, the Police Authority has been actively involved in forging partnerships and consulting widely on the social problems associated with police discrimination towards the members of the lgbt community and the policing of homophobic incidents.

2. *Hampshire Constabulary*. The Constabulary's team of lesbian and gay liaison officers (LAGLOs) predates the Crime and Disorder Act 1998. This service was established in 1996. These volunteer officers are trained by the Constabulary's Community Support Team (similar to the Community Safety Units in the Metropolitan Police Service, see Chapter 1), in collaboration with the Southampton Gay Community Health Service, to deal with crimes motivated by homophobia. Hampshire Constabulary is a partner in the Hampshire Anonymous Reporting Scheme and the Community Support Team also holds regular 'police surgeries' in local lgbt venues.

3. *Southampton Gay Community Health Service (GCHS)*. The GCHS is primarily dedicated to services relating to HIV-AIDS in Southampton and South West Hampshire Health Authority. The GCHS has been working with the police since 1994. This partnership emerged in response to: (1) the high number of suicides in the early 1990s among men who were waiting prosecution for gross indecency offences; and (2) a survey undertaken in 1994 which indicated that, among gay and bisexual men in Southampton, the police were the least highly rated service (Mallett 2001). In 1997, the then Gay Men's Health Project (GMHP), in conjunction with Hampshire Constabulary, was awarded both regional and national Health Alliance awards in the category of mental health as a result of their work to reduce suicide rates among men awaiting prosecution for gross indecency offences.[15] The GCHS is a partner in the Hampshire Anonymous Reporting Scheme. It provides training for LAGLOs and beat officers in Southampton, and is a member of the National Advisory Group on the policing of the lgbt community.

Within the remit of the Local Government Act 1999, it is the local authority that is supposed to take the lead on multi-agency crime and disorder partnerships, which is admittedly difficult in a group such as this which encompasses all of Hampshire and the Isle of Wight. This multi-agency group can be more accurately described as being a police and lgbt community liaison group, as it was only Hampshire Constabulary, Hampshire Police Authority and various lgbt agencies that were represented at these meetings. This was to change, especially in Southampton, in the second quarter of 2001 with the publication of the report 'Hidden targets: lesbian women and gay men's experiences of homophobic crime and harassment in Southampton' (Mallett 2001).[16] The research upon which this report is based was commissioned by the Southampton City Council's Social Cohesion Team and was conducted and written by the GCHS. The Social Cohesion Team launched this report in July 2001 with a structured programme of presentations from various representatives of the GCHS, the Hampshire Constabulary Community Support Team, Southampton Gay Community Network and the city council's Crime and Disorder Steering Group, in Southampton Civic Centre in July 2001 to an audience of invited stakeholders. The purpose of this launch was to promote a wider understanding of: (1) the extent of homophobic incidents in the city, (2) the existing initiatives that have been set up to deal with the problem, and (3) the ways the various agencies might work more closely together.[17]

In response to the Hidden Targets Report, the Hidden Targets Multi-Agency Group was established in Southampton in October 2001. The membership of this group includes representatives from 17 statutory and voluntary organizations and agencies across Southampton and wider Hampshire. Southampton City Council's Community Safety Team and not Hampshire Constabulary (as in the Gay and Lesbian Community Multi-Agency Group, Hampshire and Isle of Wight) is the lead organization in this multi-agency group. It is the city council that is responsible for: establishing the multi-agency group in the first place; arranging and facilitating the quarterly meetings; and leading a sub-group to develop monitoring and reporting mechanisms (Mallett 2001).

In relation to the Gay and Lesbian Community Multi-Agency Group (Hampshire and the Isle of Wight) and the Hidden Targets Multi-Agency Group (Southampton), it is important to critically examine what is on offer in response to hate crime and the policing of the lgbt community. I have examined the various documents and used Nikolas Rose's suggested 'analytics of government'[18] to clarify what these multi-agency groups are trying to achieve.

1. *What is it that these multi-agency groups want to happen?*
   - Increase confidence in the police.
   - Increase the reporting of homophobic incidents.
   - Create a better referral system for the victims of homophobic incidents.
   - Ensure a coordinated multi-agency response.
   - Increase communities' awareness of the services available.
2. *What is the problem, how is it defined?*
   - Social disengagement, homophobia as an exclusionary mechanism.
   - Lack of confidence in police resulting in a lack of reporting.

3. *What are the objectives?*
   - Increase confidence in the police so as to increase reporting.
   - Improve community relations.
   - Reduce the fear of homophobic crime in the city.
   - In the long term, reduce the amount of homophobic offences.
4. *What are the strategies and techniques being employed?*
   - Steps taken to uncover the extent of homophobic incidents in the area through anonymous reporting schemes and victimization surveys.
   - Police 'out reach' programmes set up; for example, police surgeries in local gay venues.
   - Improve police training (carried out by Community Safety Team and Gay Community Health Service).
   - Increase police liaison with the lgbt community.

What becomes obvious from the above is that the multi-agency response to homophobic incidents at city level in Southampton and at county level in Hampshire gives the reduction of homophobic incidents a relatively low priority in relation to increasing liaison and improving communication between the police, partner agencies and the lgbt community (although, obviously, these are not unrelated factors). Thus, within the context and climate of these 'community safety' and multi-agency interventions, we do see the welcome creation of what Mathews and Pitts (2001) describe as new alliances and new lines of responsibility between police and the communities they serve. However, it is important to note that in this context the roles of key regulatory agencies, such as the police, are changing significantly and this has important implications in that 'the police have been "let off the hook" and can now legitimately claim that neither crime control nor community safety is their sole responsibility' (Mathews and Pitts 2001: 5). This is an emergent policing culture that requires the police to participate in an increasingly wide range of interventions, which shifts the balance of 'policing' away from crime control towards interventions that are described by Mathews and Pitts as being increasingly related to public order maintenance and akin to 'social work' functions.

Not only is 'homophobic incident reduction' relegated to the category of a long-term objective here, so too is the direct participation of 'lay' (non-agency-affiliated) lgbt 'citizens'. What can be observed from the 'confidence -boosting' and self-esteem building initiatives (and aspirations) listed above can be more accurately described as a developmental stage before the emergence of the active citizen in active communities so central to the Labour government's joined-up government programme. That is, the central objectives of the multi-agency partnerships in Hampshire and in Southampton can be more accurately described as being 'therapeutic' (see Chandler 2001) rather than 'participatory' in orientation. The Crown Prosecution Service (CPS), in their guidance on homophobic crime, suggests that there is little that can be done at the initial stage of a police–lgbt anti-hate crime initiatives other than building bridges and increasing community confidence in the various criminal justice agencies:

> many homophobic incidents go unreported because the victim makes an immediate decision not to involve the police. There is little that we can do to prevent this from happening, although by building links with the lgbt communities and by using those links to help the communities have confidence in us, more victims from the lgbt communities may be willing to come forward and report crimes to the police.
>
> (CPS 2002a: 10)

Trust and confidence are at the heart of the police–lgbt liaison culture, which, in turn, is connected with wider concerns about governance, especially the governance of detached, marginalized communities. This theme will be further developed in subsequent chapters; however, it is important at this stage to explore some of the assumptions behind this strategy of 'increasing' trust. According to Misztal (1996) (talking about the trusting relationship between subjects and governments), it is assumed that people who believe that political power is appropriately exercised have good grounds for compliance. At the same time, if they feel that their government will deal with their demands fairly and equally, they are more likely to press those demands on government. Therefore, for Misztal, there is a connection between trust and the expectation of being treated fairly and equally by a public institution, which, in turn, is related to political and civic participation. The social necessity of trust is therefore a two-way process that sustains social relationships; trust is thus well placed as a potential basis for social solidarity, cooperation and consensus in late modern societies associated with the erosion or decline of many institutions (family, work, discipline, the welfare state and national sovereignty) and the rise of others such as culturally specific (ethnic, sexual orientation and territorial) identities (Misztal 1996). However, trust, like those other centre left (and centre-right) staples – community, civil society and citizenship – is an ambiguous concept. Trust, as Misztal elaborates, is employed as the new basis of democratic civil society in rather circular ways:

> first trust – as one of the important sources of cooperation – is seen as a socially desirable aim. Secondly, it is argued that, in order to achieve it, we must proceed in a trustworthy way. It is this double and ambiguous meaning that makes the concept of trust difficult to examine yet simultaneously attractive to use.
>
> (Misztal 1996: 8)

Trust, according to Misztal, is therefore a process; trust is to be achieved, increased, development, earned. However, confidence should be distinguished from trust (which Misztal describes as a matter of individual determination and involves choosing between alternatives). Confidence is the end point of building trust in that confidence is a more 'habitual expectation' (Misztal 1996). One could say that the police–lgbt liaison culture that is unfolding in Southampton and all over the country is an attempt to turn the habitual mistrust between police and lgbt communities into trust in an attempt to eventually facilitate 'habitual confidence' in lgbt communities in the form of the expectation that they will be treated fairly.

It could be suggested that lgbt trust (never mind habitual confidence) in police is still far off in relation to the lgbt community in Southampton and in Hampshire. This conclusion is supported by the following passage from the 2001 Hidden Targets Report:

> This research shows that lesbians and gay men are subject to homo-phobic incidents. Over half the sample[19] have experienced one or more incidents and over a third have experienced an incident in the last year. Only a quarter of these incidents were reported to the police. The data show that it is not just 'minor' incidents that are not reported. Respondents often did not report incidents such as rape and blackmail. This study identifies a number of possible reasons for the under-reporting of homophobic incidents. These reasons include a distrust or fear of the police; concerns around disclosure of sexuality; belief that the incident will not be taken seriously; or feeling that the incident is not serious enough to warrant reporting.
>
> (Mallett 2001: 71)

What this indicates is that the problems associated with the reporting of homophobic incidents to the police are multi-causal yet are all strongly associated with trust. The vast majority of the multi-agency group (Hampshire and Isle of Wight and Southampton) initiatives and many of the recommendations taken up by the assembled stakeholders at the launch of the Hidden Targets Report in Southampton in the summer of 2001 is a project of trust and esteem building where the promise of inclusion, participation, protection and justice are all bound up with the project of encouraging homophobic incident 'reporting behaviour'. The problem that lgbt communities have in Southampton is not merely 'voter apathy' and political indifference with regard to local government (which is one of the things the joined-up government programme has been set up to address). This is a historical deep-seated mistrust of official organizations and institutions, directly related to the perception, widespread in lgbt communities, of police institutional homophobia.

The ACPO recognizes that institutional prejudice, whether racist or homophobic, can become an obstacle to the goal of creating an equitable police force that 'must be – and be seen to be – entirely fair to every individual and to all sections of the community' (ACPO 2000: 18). The way to address lgbt communities' lack of trust in policing, according to Hampshire Constabulary, is to create a more informed and sympathetic police force by: (1) encouraging police officers to volunteer for LAGLO service, with its specialist training in conjunction with local lgbt organizations and agencies; (2) providing special outreach surgeries in local lgbt venues; and (3) expanding and improving access to anonymous 'homophobic incident' reporting facilities.

The multi-agency responses to homophobic incidents in Southampton are extremely important developments that do begin to point to a positive change of culture in relation to the interaction between the lgbt community, local authorities and the police. However, what can be seen emerging here is not the trinity of joined-up government in New Labour discourse – that is, central government, local government and active citizens attached to an active community. This trinity is disrupted 'in practice' by the mediating presence of various agencies and services in local authority areas that can be described in Durkheimian terms as 'intermediate groups' in the form of 'third-sector' organizations, for example voluntary organizations, not-for-profit concerns, cooperatives, self-help associations, neighbourhood groups, community associations and other social organizations (Bucek and Smith 2000). What can be observed in relation to the democratic processes that are unfolding in response to homophobic incidents is multi-agency collaboration that conceptualizes the lgbt community in Southampton as a 'targeted community'.[20] That is, a local sub-population in need of empowerment through a programme of confidence and trust building. What New Labour's joined-up government discourses do not tend to prioritize, especially in relation to engaging disengaged 'targeted populations' such as lgbt communities, is that these sub-populations are already 'serviced' by a range of fragmented and disjointed agencies. These are the intermediate groups in the form of agencies and services that designated target populations have been, or are expected to think of themselves as being, enjoined to. It is these agencies and services that are being increasingly joined up with local authorities and local police to respond uniformly and efficiently to homophobic incidents in Southampton, and not lay lgbt citizens *per se*. The following is stated in the conclusions of the Hidden Targets Progress Report in relation to the work that had been carried out by the Southampton multi-agency group during its first year:

> The Hidden Targets Multi-Agency Group is working towards building greater confidence in the reporting process and the court service. This is being achieved by both training for staff working in these services and making them more accessible to the lgbt community through outreach and publicity . . . the work completed in the past year has

enabled services to respond more effectively to people experiencing homophobic and transphobic harassment. The next step for the Hidden Targets Multi-Agency Group will be to ensure services are well publicised and promoted, and that the lgbt community are aware of the improvements.

(Mallett 2001: 18)

These are all very welcome developments; however, one could suggest that too much priority is given here to improving the efficiency (and awareness) of the agencies and organizations that come into contact with the lgbt community (even though this is undeniably important work). This is a problem associated with all community safety multi-agency approaches. Ballintyne and Fraser (2000) suggest that 'public services and multi-agency partnerships do not have a strong track record in consulting and engaging local communities' (p. 164). The emphasis in the Hidden Targets Progress Report appears not to be on participation, engagement and consultation with the wider lgbt community, but improving the agencies and organizations that might service the lgbt community and publicizing these improvements to the lgbt community. Rather than producing active citizens embedded in active communities as was envisaged in the Local Government Act and in the Crime and Disorder Act, what can be observed on the ground in relation to anti-homophobic hate crime initiatives in Southampton is a programme dedicated to creating a more active sector of service providers to deal with the victims of homophobic violence.

This focus on the 'third sector' presents, just as local government does, both problems and opportunities for the government's modernization programme and for 'community policing'. The major opportunity here, as recognized by the Southampton Hidden Targets Multi-Agency Group, is that improved and well-publicized service provision in relation to dealing with homophobic violence and the problems facing lgbt communities in general will ameliorate some of the problems associated with lack of trust, the perception of institutional homophobia and the impact of homophobic violence at the individual and community level. However, there is also a need to acknowledge one of the major problems in relation to the role of the 'third-sector' agencies in this context – that is, the issue of representation, which is well rehearsed in studies of participatory democracy and deliberative democracy (see Schedler and Glastra 2001). The main problem that arises here is: who is representing which communities in these consultation processes, with whose authority, and to what ends?

In Southampton, there are few lesbian and transgendered 'community representatives' in multi-agency fora. In this city, the lgbt 'community' is overwhelmingly represented by what can be described as a group of highly motivated and extremely well-organized gay men from the local health promotion agencies and HIV services in the city. In more metropolitan settings, one is increasingly finding that 'political professionals' in the form of 'freelance consultants' on community discrimination issues dominate lgbt advisory groups in certain London boroughs. All of this raises the questions: Who is being empowered here? Is this really about creating 'active lgbt citizens'? Or is this a matter of consulting with the usual suspects, the same faces, the same self-selecting 'community representatives'? And what can be done to make the lgbt multi-agency groups more representative of the wider communities they are aiming to serve? These problems associated with consultation and representative 'representatives' is not isolated to lgbt–police anti-hate crime initiatives but can be found in, for example, ethnic minority community–police anti-hate crime initiatives as well.

What this critique demonstrates, therefore, is that there is more to joined-up government than the trinity of central government, local government and 'active citizens'. Active citizens have to be made, especially when these potential 'active citizens' are to be made from 'detached' and designated high-risk and 'hard-to-reach' sub-populations. The first step to achieving this type of citizenship is to recognize and understand the work of the agencies and services that are attempting to offer services to these groups already. These agencies and organizations must be recognized, in these processes of democratic renewal and the promotion of community safety as a crucial stratum that creates bridges between communities, such as the lgbt community and the police. However, these agencies are often service providers to specific communities (e.g gay men). It does not always follow that these agencies can be consulted on behalf of all the communities the police and local authorities assume they represent (e.g. lesbian and transgender communities).

Anti-hate crime and emergent subjectivities – towards conclusions

The questions that will be explored in this section are concerned with empowerment, subjectivity and self-government in advanced liberal democracies. I argue here that these issues are particularly relevant to the themes of 'active citizenship' and 'community safety' explored above in relation to the policing of lgbt communities. Despite the existence of detailed critiques (e.g. Stenson 1998), I am still convinced, to a certain extent, by the work of specialists in governmentality such as Rose and Cruickshank, who have consistently encouraged a culture of suspicion in relation to the promises of liberation and the promise of 'inclusion'. I cannot but be concerned that the invitation extended to lgbt communities to take up and take part in their right to fair, sympathetic and equitable policing (despite the obvious benefits) comes with certain familiar trade-off responsibilities that will be borne by these communities.

Sexual minorities, especially gay men, in England and Wales have certainly come a long way from the Wolfenden Committee's recommendations for the partial decriminalization of 'homosexual offences' through the encouragement in the criminal law of the discrete, self-policing homosexual subject of privacy (Moran 1996a; McGhee 2001); this is developed further in the next chapter. The strategy of decriminalizing homosexuality, in the Sexual Offences Act 1967, is an example of an act of toleration, in that homosexuals and the practice of homosexuality were disapproved of (morally justified in the 1950s and 1960s through discourses of homosexual abnormality). Yet through advocating decriminalization for homosexual offences, the Wolfenden Committee (1957), and later Parliament, demonstrated restraint (by decriminalizing that which they found abhorrent). This act of toleration was associated with a strategy of attempting to marginalize homosexual acts, through attempting to distance them from the social mainstream by banishing homosexuals and homosexual practices to decriminalized 'privacy' (Wilson 1993).

This toleration of homosexuals and homosexual acts has been replaced in recent years with concerns focusing on the social harm homophobic incidents can cause members of the lgbt community and wider society. These developments can be described as a reversal of the Wolfenden Committee's recommendations for driving homosexuality underground, in that the police and local authorities in cities, towns and counties across the UK are currently appealing for the members of lgbt communities to come forward and let their experiences of victimization and discrimination be fully documented. What this amounts to is a project where the alienated lgbt victim of hate crime is to be (eventually) transformed into an empowered citizen who can be confident that their report to police, local council or any other agency will be taken seriously and dealt with sympathetically. This, on the surface at least, can be described as an invitation to an element of 'fuller' citizenship, not previously enjoyed by many members of the lgbt community.

However, there is a need to unpack this to explore some of the potential problems arising from this alleged de-abjection of 'homosexuality' from the closeted margins of society. The questions we might ask include: Are all lgbt community members welcome? And will all lgbt community members want to become 'active' and responsible citizens in the first place? Alongside these questions must be the consideration of the relationship between power, subjectivity and the price lgbt community members might have to pay to become active, responsible and empowered citizens.

Several key studies that deal with empowerment, 'self-esteem' and subjectivity can contribute to this analysis, especially those of Rose (1990) and Cruikshank (1994, 1996). According to Cruikshank, the line between subjectivity and subjection is crossed when I subject myself, when I align my personal goals with those set out by reformers – both expert and activist – according to some notion of the social good. The norm of self-esteem links subjectivity to power.

(Cruikshank 1996: 235)

This is clearly a critical perspective on the project of building self-esteem, especially in relation to 'technologies of citizenship'.[21] However, there are obvious connections to be made between the Labour government's attempts to govern at a distance and to govern through consensus in the context of 'interactive policy making', including policing policy and what Foucauldians such as Rose and Cruikshank have to say about power and subjectivity. Governance, according to Rose, is something we do to ourselves in advanced liberal democracies and not something done to us by powerful others; governance is therefore in keeping with the 'hands-off approach to governing' or the governing at a distance component of the Labour government's modernization programme: that is:

government of subjectivity has taken shape through the proliferation of a complex and heterogeneous assemblage of technologies. These have acted as relays, bringing the varied ambitions of political, scientific, philanthropic, and professional authorities into alignment with the ideas and aspirations of individuals, with the selves each of us want to be.

(Rose 1990: 213)

The major assumption in the Labour government's modernization programmes and in the emergent practices for the effective policing of the lgbt community in Southampton is that 'we', to use one of New Labour's favourite pronouns, all want to be 'active' and responsible citizens. The norm of self-esteem and the generation of politically able selves which is at the heart of the programmes discussed above links subjectivity to power. According to Rose (1990), power 'binds subjects to a subjection that is more profound because it appears to emanate from our autonomous quest for ourselves, it appears as a matter of our freedom' (p. 256). Power is embedded here; government interventions are 'backgrounded' yet extended 'through opening lines of force across a territory spanning space and time' (Rose 1994: 364–5) through the reflexive discourses, policies and practices of modernization, democratization and community safety. In this instance, the lgbt community's liberation from the bondage of mistrust, social detachment and marginalization is promised through the nurturing of 'self-esteem', increasing trust and through building tentative bridges and avenues of communication with the agencies and organizations that 'serve' these communities.

However, as the Labour government repeatedly informs us, there are no rights without responsibilities. The invitation extended to the lgbt community to take up and take part in their right to fair sympathetic and equitable policing comes with certain familiar trade-off responsibilities that will be borne by this community. This could be interpreted as a return to familiar dividing practices and categories, for example of the responsible and the irresponsible, the good and the dangerous in relation to specifically male homosexuals that emerged in the deliberations of the Wolfenden Committee in the 1950s and the continuing debates over Section 28 in the 1980s and late 1990s (this will also be explored in greater detail in the next chapter). Recent Crime and Disorder Act community safety initiatives targeting lgbt communities in the form of encouraging their participation in the policing of their community could prove to be a further episode in the continuing pressure for the lgbt community to normalize.

From this perspective, it is important to consider the price of citizenship before lgbt communities buy into it wholesale. But what are the alternatives for emergent sexual minority citizens? Paying the dues and taking up the responsibilities of the active citizen, or remaining 'hidden targets' existing on the secret fringes of society? In the next chapter, the focus will be on the wider implications of anti-hate crime initiatives for lgbt communities, in conjunction with calls to reform sex offences legislation, to explore what all this might mean for sexual minority citizenship in the UK.

6 Beyond toleration: privacy, citizenship and sexual minorities in England and Wales

Introduction

In this chapter, sexual minority citizenship in England and Wales will be explored in relation to two significant moments of review and reform in which the 'place' of sexual minority groups in British society was subject to renegotiation. The first of these occurred in the 1950s and 1960s in relation to the reform of sex offences, especially the partial decriminalization of homosexual acts. The primary artefact associated with this moment is the Report of the Committee on Homosexual Offences and Prostitution (1957), know as the Wolfenden Report after the committee's chairman Sir John Wolfenden. The second is one we are currently experiencing in England and Wales, when sex offences legislation is again being subjected to review. However, at the same time, as introduced in Chapter 5, the service that the police provide to sexual minority communities is also being reviewed, alongside that of other minority groups (especially ethnic minority groups). In Chapter 5, the analysis focused on police–lgbt community initiatives, especially multi-agency crime reduction partnerships in the context of New Labour's associated programmes of democratization, modernization and community safety. In this chapter, observations regarding the implications of anti-hate crime policy for the lgbt community made in Chapter 5 will be expanded, especially with regard to the designation of lgbt communities as a 'hard to reach group' by the Home Office in relation to their strategy of improving police–community consultation. However, at the same time, the place of lgbt communities and the anti-hate crime initiatives targeted at them will be contextualized within a wider analysis of shifting boundaries of tolerance and intolerance in Britain. The primary argument that will be made here is that these two moments (the Wolfenden-decriminalization moment and the anti-hate crime moment) within the set of 'civil and legal rights' in the Marshallian model of citizenship (alongside social and political rights) (Marshall 1977; Richardson 2000) demonstrate two very different mobilizations and spatializations of minority sexual citizenship in relation to 'mainstream society': the first was based on toleration whereas the second is based on inclusive protectionism. At the same time, this chapter also maps the transitions in the technology of subjectivities in these two moments. The first moment is associated with the production of the 'private' homosexual subject in an explicitly heteronormative society, whereas the second moment is associated with the 'mainstreaming' or normalization of certain sexual minority subjectivities in a more subtle, yet enduring, heteronormative culture in which family life, marriage and stable and loving relationships (Department for Education and Employment 2000) are, it seems, being promoted for both heterosexual and lgbt communities alike.

In the first moment of review and reform of sexual minority citizenship, the objective was to tolerate yet restrict sexual minority communities (especially 'homosexual' men) to a private existence in order to protect 'ordinary' citizens and 'normal' society, especially the most vulnerable members of this society, including impressionable young people from the social threat of homosexuality (McGhee 2000, 2001). However, in the current moment, as will be revealed below, this impulse of social defence, through legal restrictions, especially the privacy provisions associated with 'homosexual acts' introduced in the Sex Offences Act 1967, is currently the subject of reform in which the object is one of attempting to eradicate discriminatory elements in the criminal law which impact negatively on sexual minorities (especially lesbians and gays). At the same time, as the privacy provisions are being dismantled in the criminal law, the police in England and Wales are also reviewing and improving their service delivery to the lgbt community, partly in response to the high-profile accusations of institutional prejudice (especially in relation to ethnic minority groups, but increasingly, as was revealed in Chapter 5, in relation to institutionalized homophobia too) and more significantly in their response to the statutory requirements of the Crime and Disorder Act 1998. The result of the latter, as revealed in Chapter 5 and as will be further developed below, is that the police, and the wider criminal justice system, are attempting to turn themselves into a progressive force in society and a significant mobilizer of a variety of 'active' sexual minority citizenship in which lgbt communities[1] are being encouraged to move out of the shadows to be embraced by mainstream society. As in Chapter 5, this invitation to a 'fuller' citizenship embodied in the second (anti-hate crime) moment of sexual minority citizenship will not be taken at face value. The chapter ends with a consideration of what the proposed reforms of sexual offences might mean for sexual minority citizens (and also heterosexual citizens) with a view to examining the transition between these two moments as being not only a shift from Wolfendenesque tolerance to the 'acceptance' of lgbt communities in the Labour government's ethos of inclusive protectionism, but as being also the advent of a shift from private to pubic spheres of control for all 'sexual' citizens.

Wolfenden and the spatialization of decriminalization

The Wolfenden Committee was appointed in 1954 to consider the law and practice relating to homosexuality and prostitution. The final report was published 3 years later in 1957. In many ways, the appointment of the Wolfenden Committee was a response to the liberal backlash against the 'controversial' policing of homosexual offences in the early 1950s in which all 'homosexual acts' between men, whether in public or in private, were an offence (West 1977). In the 1950s, the policing of homosexuality was carried out with considerable zeal and the pursuit of convictions of homosexuals at that time led to some sordid prosecutions involving in some cases:

> gross violations of privacy, the use of compromising letters unearthed in the searches of doubtful legality, and dependence upon guilty persons prepared to give evidence against their friends in return for immunity from prosecution that began to alienate public opinion.
>
> (West 1977: 282)[2]

The Wolfenden Committee's recommendations (on 'homosexual offences') can be described as offering two interdependent recommendations for the reforming of the criminal law. First, the decriminalization of homosexual activities in specific circumstances, resulting in the creation of a 'realm of privacy' in which two men over the age of consent could engage in homosexual acts. Secondly, the promotion of a specific homosexual subject who, regardless of the criminalization or decriminalization of homosexuals, would be well-adapted to society and be discreet in his 'private' practices. The means of achieving this was to create a realm of circumstantial legal indifference for homosexuals based on a particular definition of 'privacy':

> there must remain a realm of private morality not the law's business. To say this is not to condone or encourage private immorality. On the contrary, it is to emphasize the personal and private responsibility of the individual for his own actions, and that is a responsibility which a mature agent can properly be expected to carry for himself without the threat of punishment from the law.
>
> (Wolfenden 1957: para. 61)

The Wolfenden Committee's description of this 'private' realm became a spatial and ocular arrangement between homosexual bodies and the eyes of members of the public – that is, between observers, viewed as the embodiment of heteronorms – that is, the watchers – and the self-policing homosexual 'watched':

> It is our intention that the law should continue to regard as criminal any indecent act committed in a place where members of the public may be likely to see and be offended by it, but where there is no possibility of public offence of this nature it becomes a matter of the private responsibility of the persons concerned and as such, in our opinion, is outside the proper purview of the criminal law.
>
> (Wolfenden 1957: para. 64)

Thus, a 'homosexual act', according to this definition, would be determined as being 'in private' if it was conducted in a place where it was unlikely to be witnessed by, and thus cause offence to, a member of the general public. Here, the Wolfenden Committee incorporated a definition of homosexual privacy that was intended to decriminalize homosexual acts yet also protect society from 'offensive' homosexuality at the same time. According to Rose (1990), what the Wolfenden privacy-visual offence criterion amounted to was the self-policing of 'the external manifestations of morality in "visible" conduct' (p. 225). The result of this was that this conceptualization of 'in private' evoked 'the public' and 'the private' as a 'lived distinction' in and around 'bodily behaviour' (Young 1990: 140). This Wolfendenesque privacy thus produced two subject positions: (1) 'private homosexuals' whose membership was provisional on their circumspection; but it also produced (2) 'the ordinary citizen' as the easily offended 'innocent' who must be protected from witnessing homosexual acts. The outcome of the Wolfenden Committee's recommendations was that in the Sex Offences Act 1967, homosexual activities participated in by two adult males (over the age of consent, at that time 21) 'in private' was no longer to be a criminal offence. On the passing of these Wolfenden Committee recommendations into law in the Sex Offences Act 1967, public homosexual activities and indiscreet homosexual acts were subject to even more rigorous policing. This project was described by Weeks (1989) as initiating a contradictory series of effects – that is, 'that privatisation did not necessarily involve a diminution of control'; the Wolfenden reforms were 'restrictive in one direction, liberal in the other' (p. 243). That is, following decriminalization in the form of the Sex Offences Act 1967, arrests for homosexual offences 'in public' actually increased.

Decriminalization and the promotion of 'private homosexuality'

The privacy provisions introduced in the Sex Offences Act 1967 can be described as attempting to manipulate the space in between what Gayle Rubin (1992), in her essay 'Thinking sex', has described as the two poles of 'good' and 'bad' sex in order to create the specifically packaged homosexual subject's place in society. According to Rubin, heterosexual, married, reproductive, monogamous relations are the best example of 'good' or 'normal', 'natural' sex. By contrast, under the heading 'bad' or 'abnormal', unnatural, sick, sinful, 'way out' sex, Rubin catalogues the ensuing group of deviants: transvestites, transsexuals, fetishists, sadomasochists, those engaging in cross-generational sex, as well as those involved in prostitution. However, between these poles of good and bad, according to Bristow's reading of Rubin:

> she designates the 'major area of contest' where one finds sexual behaviours and lifestyles that signal how attitudes are shifting across the moral terrain. In this liminal in-between zone, we find the following: unmarried heterosexual couples; promiscuous heterosexuals; masturbation; and long-term, stable same-sex relationships. Located somewhere closer to 'bad' sex are lesbians in the bar and promiscuous gay men in public places.
>
> (Bristow 1997: 201)

It was in this major area of contest, between the poles of 'good' and 'bad' sex, that the Wolfenden Committee attempted to shift the moral terrain (with special reference to male homosexuals) in favour of the decriminalization of homosexuality. Anna Marie Smith (1990) refers to this strategy as the promotion of good homosexuality. Smith suggests that the promotion of the good homosexual subject was simultaneous with the demonization of his antithesis: the flaunting, unassimilable 'bad gay'[3] in most of the high-profile legislation (for example, Sexual Offences Act 1967, Section 28 of the Local Government Act 1988) that has emerged since the 1960s.

This distinction between 'good' and 'bad' homosexualities is achieved through a particular spatialization. That is, according to Smith (1994), legal indifference to homosexual activities was possible when homosexuals knew their 'proper place' on the secret and discrete fringes of mainstream society. Knowing one's proper place amounted to discreet and controlled homosexuals existing non-offensively in the narrowly defined realm of privacy created for them in the Wolfenden Report, which was subsequently written into law in the form of the Sex Offences Act 1967.

One could argue, and this will be demonstrated below, that this Wolfendenesque 'realm of privacy' has had a profound effect on the place of sexual minorities, especially the lesbian and gay community in England and Wales, for almost 50 years. Evans suggests that:

> The progressive movement of gay men and lesbians into partial and specific civil, political and social rights has been facilitated in the post-Wolfenden era by the Law's retreat from homosexual liaisons between consenting adults in private, liaisons which, however, have

remained stigmatized as deeply immoral. As a consequence both status groups have become structurally and ideologically contained within the semi-public space which lies between the boundaries of legality and morality which surround the 'moral community'. In this cultural space is sited specifically gay and lesbian associations, friendship networks, institutions and political associations, but it is a space increasingly dominated by consumerism and the pursuit of leisure and lifestyle commodities.

(Evans 1995: 117)

Ken Plummer (2001) updated Evans's observations when he suggested that within the multiplicity of late modern public spheres, lesbians and gay men have created, among other things, a visible culture that has led to increasing recognition (coming out, finding a voice, making space, creating texts), increasing equality (in law, equal opportunities, anti-discrimination, 'gay rights'), and the emergence of more 'gay institutions' (political organizations, commercial 'pink pound' organizations and welfare-support organizations).

However, despite all of this, arguably some of the most high-profile sociological work to emerge in recent years in relation to sexual minority citizenship has not focused on the rapid expansion and innovation of lesbian and gay publics or semi-publics. There has been a discernible inward turn in that same-sex families and relationships are at the centre of these studies. For example, Weeks (1986) agrees with Evans and Plummer that 'new social-sexual movements have created, in effect, an alternative public sphere of personal interaction, debate, publications and intellectual concourse' (p. 105). However, Weeks's later work also places special emphasis on the home, same-sex relationships and intimacy; all conducted in the post-Wolfenden spaces of privacy as the particular site of the emergence of these alternative public spheres, and the new political movements and political claims that emerge from them:

> The sexual citizen . . . makes a claim to transcend the limits of the personal sphere by going public, but the going public is, in a necessary but nevertheless paradoxical move, about protecting the possibilities of private life and private choice in a more inclusive society.
>
> (Weeks 1999: 37)

In recent years, Plummer has also turned to the intimate, domestic sphere to explore the spaces of sexual minority citizenship. Plummer's focus has been on the new politics, life politics or the emancipatory politics described by Giddens as 'a generic outlook concerned above all with liberating individuals and groups from constraints which adversely affect their life chances' (Giddens, in Plummer 1995: 166). According to Plummer (1995), the emergence of 'life politics' – or, as he refers to it, the politics of 'intimate citizenship'[4] – has resulted, and will result, in new sets of claims emerging 'around the body, the relationship and sexuality' (p. 149); that is, 'all those matters linked with our most intimate desires, pleasures and ways of being in the world' (p. 151). Plummer (2003) describes his intimate citizenship as emerging out of feminist and sexual citizenships movements. His particular focus is on emerging 'intimacy groups' (e.g. surrogate mothers, 'lost' fathers, test tube citizens, post-divorce citizens, elderly citizens, transgender citizens) and their need for recognition 'in emerging zones of conflict, which suggests new kinds of citizens in the making' (p. 66). It is within the context of works like these that a particular sub-genre in lesbian and gay studies has emerged – namely, sexual citizenship studies – in which the experience of, and the politics emerging from, private same-sex relationships in the domestic sphere are central.

Space it can be argued is central to sexual citizenship literatures. 'The private' and 'the domestic' are presented as creative spaces in these literatures. They are also presented as spaces from whence to make claims, address injuries and seek recognition in the public 'political' realm. It is, therefore, from privacy that 'the sexual citizen' (as Weeks refers to them) makes his or her political and legal claims, and it is to the private realm of same-sex familial or relationships that any political gains are brought. Bell and Binnie (2000) suggest that the scenario depicted by Weeks and others is a thoroughly domesticated one in that the desired outcome of the sexual citizen's rights claims is to secure the private space of the home. At the same time, these examples of life and/or emancipatory politics, intimate and/or sexual citizenship are highly circumscribed in relation to what type of sexual minority citizen is most likely to make a successful rights claim. Here we return to Smith's observation that in the post-Wolfenden context the citizenship that is promoted with regard to sexual minority communities is one where they know their good and proper (private) place in society, as noted by Bell and Binnie in the following passage:

> in our reading of sexual politics, rights claims articulated through appeals to citizenship carry the burden of compromise in particular ways; this demands the circumscription of 'acceptable' modes of being a sexual citizen. This is, of course, an age-old compromise that sexual dissidents have long had to negotiate, the current problem is its cementing into rights-based political strategies, which forecloses or denies aspects of sexuality written off as 'unacceptable'. In particular . . . this tends to demand a modality of sexual citizenship that is privatized, de-radicalized, de-eroticized and *confined* in all senses of the word: kept in place, policed, limited.
>
> (Bell and Binnie 2000: 3; emphasis in original)

The problem that is being recognized here is that the tactic of attempting to increase, for example, lesbian and gay rights through the vehicle of citizenship creates problematic divisions in the lesbian and gay community (between good and bad, assimilable and unassimilable, mainstream and subaltern, gay and queer[5]). Richardson also observes the high price of sexual citizenship:

> sexual citizenship is heavily circumscribed and simultaneously privatized, its limits set by the coupling of tolerance with assimilation; thus, lesbians and gay men are granted the right to be tolerated as long as they stay within the boundaries of that tolerance, whose borders are maintained through the heterosexist public/private divide.[6]
>
> (Richardson 2000: 77)

Sexual citizenship studies have thus contributed the following insights in recent years: sexual minorities in the post-Wolfenden context have increased their spaces of association, contestation, recognition, celebration and consumption (as described by Evans and Plummer); and there is much to celebrate in terms of transformations in the sphere of same-sex relationships, households, families, etc. (especially Weeks), and that these transformations in the intimate sphere are emblematic of the emergence of new politics and new public spheres (Plummer 1995, 2001). These are all extremely valuable observations, which, without doubt, have enriched sociology. However, there is a problem here. All of the latter are constrained by the post-Wolfenden restrictions on gay men that have come to dominate the wider lesbian and gay community for almost 50 years. What is suggested below is that sexual citizenship studies will need to develop among and beyond these parameters in order to appreciate the changes, especially in relation to sexual minorities, with regard to space, toleration and citizenship, that are currently unfolding, especially in relation to violence. Plummer (2003) describes the oxymoron intimate citizenship as suggesting a potential bridge between the personal and the political. However, his focus seems to be all one way; that is, on 'doing intimacies' associated with the relational, experimental, corporeal and sexual inventiveness of individuals and groups moving from the private to recognition in ever emerging public spheres.

Plummer rarely mentions violence and protection from violence[7] in emergent sexual and other citizenships. As was observed in Chapter 5 in passages from the Association of Chief Police Officers' (ACPO) guide on hate crime, a homophobic incident is not merely an attack on one person. The impact was presented as causing a ripple effect, with potentially devastating effects on community relationships, neighbourhoods, areas and wider societies. Thus, in certain situations (for example, involving vulnerable social groups), intimate or individual violence has a wider public and societal-wide impact, which can fuel social detachment and feelings of exclusion. Violence and how violence is dealt with in society, especially what the ACPO (see Chapter 5) refer to as 'value-added' incidents, is thus also a bridge from the personal to the public that is currently being reflected on (as will be further developed below) by key agencies within the criminal justice system, but ignored on the whole in British sexual citizenship studies.

British society has changed much in the past 50 years. Britain, it seems, is a multicultural society, which is being encouraged to embrace and celebrate its diversity. With the recognition and celebration of British diversity, there have also been numerous calls to reconsider what citizenship could or should mean in a country that should or could be more at ease with its own diversity. Race, ethnicity, immigration and religion are clearly at the epicentre of these developments as examined in previous chapters. However, sexuality in the form of minority sexual communities such as the lesbian and gay community is also being drawn into this 'national' renegotiation of British identity and British citizenship. Ellison (1997) describes this process as evidence of the emergence of reflexive citizenship. Reflexivity for Ellison means:

> the general process, driven by social, political and economic change, by which social actors, confronted with the erosion, or transform- ation, of established patterns of belonging, re-adjust notions of rights and membership to new conceptions of identity, solidarity and the institutional foci of redress.
>
> (Ellison 1997: 711)

Ellison's observations are useful for contextualizing emergent forms of citizenships in the late modern world. However, they are, like the vast majority of sexual citizenship literatures reviewed above, 'actor-centred'. I would suggest that an actor-centred or an activist-centred perspective is too limited an approach for appreciating the mobilizations of citizenship associated with the second moment of sexual minority citizenship that will be examined below. What is evident in the second moment of sexual citizenship is not defensive reflexive citizenship, as described by Ellison;[8] rather, national policing organizations such as the ACPO and Her Majesty's Inspectorate of Constabularies, (HMIC), as well as all police forces under the requirements of the Crime and Disorder Act, suggest reflexivity at an institutional level, an institutional reflexivity (Giddens 1994a) that is motivated by the amelioration of the mechanisms of exclusion that inhibit the lesbian and gay communities (as well as wider lgbt communities) from a fuller experience of citizenship, as these institutions reflect on wider patterns of social change, increasing diversity and the de-traditionalization associated with reflexive modernization.

I argue below that the criminal justice system is a particularly revealing sphere in which the spatialization of sexual minority rights claims (from the private to the public in order to secure the private) and the spatialization of citizenship (especially in relation to the promotion of 'good', private lesbian and gay citizens) might need to be reconsidered. The reason for this is that privacy, especially the particular 'Wolfendenesque privacy' that lends (or has lent) 'partial citizenship' to lesbians and especially gay men since the 1960s (Richardson 1998), is currently the subject of parliamentary scrutiny and legislative reform.

Policing sexual minority communities since the Crime and Disorder Act 1998

Here, the impact of certain provisions within the Crime and Disorder Act are examined with specific reference to the requirements within this legislation for involving local communities, especially hard to reach communities with a history of being detached from the social mainstream.

In the foreword of the guidance issued by the Home Office on the Crime and Disorder Act 1998, Jack Straw (a former Home Secretary) described the rationale of the Act as the provision of a framework for the 'radical new empowerment' of local people in the fight against crime and disorder (Straw, in Home Office 1998b). Thus, one of the key intentions of this Act was the involvement of local communities at every stage of the process:

> It is self-evident that we cannot make communities safer if we do not find out the extent to which local people currently perceive them as unsafe: and it is clearly right that these people should be invited to participate actively in the process of tackling local problems, not just passively consulted about them.
>
> (Straw, in Home Office 1998b)

The involvement of local communities in this Act was initiated through the imposition of responsibilities on local authorities and the police to:

- Conduct and publish an audit of local crime and disorder problems;
- Consult locally on the basis of the audit;
- Produce and publish a strategy for tackling issues identified in the audit;
- Monitor progress; and
- Repeat the process every three years.

(Home Office 1998b)

Statutory crime and disorder partnerships are at the heart of these provisions. That is, in Section 5(1) the Act identifies that 'responsible authorities' (police and local authorities) are to lead the statutory crime and disorder part-nerships, which will also involve, under Section 5(2), other 'co-operating bodies' (such as the police authority, probation service, health authorities) (Newburn and Jones 2002). However, provisions under Section 5(3) stipulate that various other groups must be invited to participate in partnerships, including a wide range of community groups and statutory voluntary bodies. For example, some of the following were included in the Home Secretary's guidance: parish and/or county councils, NHS trusts, social landlords, drugs action teams, Training Enterprise Council, Crown Prosecution Service, Court Managers, Chambers of Commerce, Race Equality Council, Neighbourhood Watch, Victim Support, Rape Crisis Centres, Tenants' and Residents' Associ-ations, local MPs and MEPs. Included in this list were gay and lesbian groups (Newburn and Jones 2002). One of the intentions of these statutory partner-ships, according to Newburn and Jones (2002), was to make sure that the process was made as 'inclusive' as possible, through the concerted effort 'to incorporate the views of disadvantaged or marginalized groups within the population' (p. 4). The Crime and Disorder Act guidance provided to partnerships listed the following social groups in this regard: young men, the homeless, drug users, the gay community, members of ethnic minority com-munities, children, those who suffer domestic abuse, and older people (New-burn and Jones 2002). According to Jones and Newburn, this list of 'potentially disaffected and vulnerable social groups' has become designated (by the Home Office) as 'hard to reach' groups, whose views were essential to the 'inclusive' ambitions of the Crime and Disorder audits and strategies. According to the Home Office's guidance, referring specifically to gay and lesbian groups:

> It is absolutely central to the success of the partnerships that they should be seen as credible and inclusive by *all* sections of the com-munity. It is likely that the Home Secretary will use his powers under Section 5(3) of the Crime and Disorder Act to require the police and local authorities to invite the full participation of gay and lesbian groups in the work of the new partnerships. This should do much to ensure that issues of concern to these groups are not overlooked when the audit is conducted and the strategy developed.
>
> (Home Office 1998b: 2.44; emphasis in original)

Jones and Newburn (2001) suggest that the label 'hard to reach' to depict social groups, such as the lesbian and gay community, should be changed to reflect the context of the type of disengagement associated with communities so described:

> It is clear that there exists a range of different groups that have trad-itionally had difficult relationships with the police, as targets of law

enforcement activity or as victims of hate crime (or in combination).
However, few of these groups are hard to reach in any fundamental
physical sense. It seems fair to say that there are a number of groups
who have at least some elements in common in terms of their difficulties with the police. But in many cases 'hard to reach' actually means
'hard to engage with on a positive level'.

(Jones and Newburn 2001: 13)

This change of label from 'hard to reach' to 'hard to engage with on a positive
level' is rather useful for the purposes of this chapter, which is concerned with
the two different moments of sexual citizenship with special reference to the
lesbian and gay community in England and Wales in the last 50 years. The
reason for this is that the partial citizenship afforded to the gay community in
the privacy provisions of the sex offences legislation in the 1950s and 1960s,
and the subsequent policing of this community in line with this legislation,
are fundamental components in the designation of the lesbian and gay community as being hard to reach. Jones and Newburn (2001) suggest that 'the
term "hard to reach" implies that it is some characteristic of the community or
group that makes it difficult to "reach", rather than a characteristic of the
police or a characteristic of policing' (p. 14).

By replacing 'hard to reach' with 'hard to engage with on a positive level',
as well as attempting to appreciate the context of the police–community relationship, especially those of sexual and ethnic minority communities feeling
that they have been over-policed and under-protected, then it becomes clearer
to police and other statutory partners why some groups, including the lesbian
and gay community, do not trust them. The 'historical reasons' for the lesbian
and gay community's lack of trust in police and this community's detachment
from the social mainstream are appreciated by the Home Office:

seeking the involvement of the gay and lesbian community must be
an active process not a passive one. This community is not always
visible,[9] and may for historical reasons not find it easy to engage in a
dialogue with some of the groups involved in the partnerships;[10] it
will *not* be enough just to write to the local pressure group inviting it
to send a representative to a meeting and then thinking that your
obligation to this sector of the community is discharged. You must
develop creative and flexible ways to break down any barriers which
may exist locally, and to encourage full and active engagement in the
work by local gay and lesbian people.

(Home Office 1998b: 2.44)

The main ways in which police forces have been attempting to break
down the barriers between themselves and the lesbian and gay community

(and the wider lgbt community) is through primarily taking homophobic (and transphobic) hate crime seriously. Evidence of lgbt 'trust-building' and homophobic hate crime initiatives are appearing all over the country as observed in Chapter 5. These initiatives testify to a new mobilization of sexual citizenship that introduces a significant modification of the private, detached homosexual subject promoted by the sex offences legislation in the 1960s. These initiatives can be described as attempting to de-marginalize lesbian and gay (as well as the wider lgbt) community through inviting them to enjoy an expanded form of citizenship hitherto unavailable to them.

What all of this adds up to, despite the reservations expressed in Chapter 5, is a centripetal 'inclusive' strategy which invites, in an unprecedented way, lesbian and gay communities (and wider lgbt communities) to become increasingly involved in the provision of public services such as policing. These developments are in marked contrast to the centrifugal 'exclusive' strategy that promoted the attempted evacuation of sexual minorities (especially gay men) from the sphere of public visibility in the Wolfenden recommendations and in the post-decriminalization context. However, it also has a great deal to do with the police and other agencies taking hate crimes, such as racially motivated and homophobic hate crimes, seriously. In relation to the latter, the ACPO, HMIC and CPS are attempting to send out a clear message:

> By working together against hate crime we can turn the tables; we can include the excluded and liberate the fearful. Joint action across society can change attitudes and push racism, homophobia and other group hatreds outside the limits of acceptability. The police service is committed to making a significant contribution by taking positive action against racist and other hate behaviours.
>
> (ACPO 2000: 17)

In a similar vein, HMIC have the following to say about policing in a multicultural society, with special reference to lgbt communities:

> The policing of a diverse community has one certainty, diversity will increase, and society itself will become more tolerant of what was previously and suspiciously referred to as difference. HM Inspector encourages forces to recognize this fact as a challenge for the future and to adopt an appropriate professional and ethical stance towards the lesbian, gay, bisexual and transgender communities whilst remaining cognizant within a society that is becoming refreshingly more tolerant and less judgmental.
>
> (HMIC 2000: 47)

The CPS in their policy statement, exclusively on homophobic crimes, also encourage police and other criminal justice agencies to send out a clear anti-hate crime message:

> Prejudice, discrimination or hate of members of any part of our community based on their sexual orientation or gender identity has no place in a civilised society; any such prejudice, discrimination or hate that shows itself in the commission of crime must be thoroughly and properly investigated and firmly and rigorously prosecuted in the courts.[11] A clear message must be sent so that those who commit such crimes realise that they will be dealt with firmly under the criminal law: the CPS has a vital role to play delivering this aim, not only in terms of its own role but also in terms of advising its partners in the criminal justice system – the police, the courts, magistrates, judges and those in the voluntary sector – that this sort of crime must no longer be tolerated.
>
> (CPS 2002a: 1)

Since the murder of Stephen Lawrence and the ensuing inquiry in which the institutional prejudices of British police forces (in particular the Metropolitan Police Service) were exposed, organizations such as the ACPO, CPS and HMIC have been attempting to expand the provision of fair and equitable policing to many more communities in England and Wales. It is here that the homophobic climate of the 1950s and 1960s, evident in the discussion above concerning the promotion of a tolerated (only if private) sexual citizens with regard to gay men is in marked contrast to the explicitly anti-homophobic sentiments that have emerged from police forces and from national policing and criminal justice organizations in which groups targeted by hatred are to be welcomed into the protective ambit of 'mainstream society'.

Homophobia, especially in the form of institutionalized homophobia, within criminal justice agencies and homophobic incidents perpetrated against the members of lgbt communities are in this emerging culture no longer to be tolerated. Rather than reflect the values of a homophobic, yet tolerant society, as in the Wolfenden Committee's deliberations in the 1950s, the ACPO, HMIC and the CPS can be described as acting reflexively in that they are: (1) attempting to purge their own organizations of institutionalized homophobia, while also, through policy commitments, (2) making efforts to send out a clear message to society that homophobic incidents (in appropriate evidence situations) will be subjected to the full force of the law. These powerful institutions within the criminal justice system can be described as attempting to create a moral economy, akin to strategies observed in earlier chapters (especially Chapters 2 and 3) where diversity and difference are to be presented and experienced as a social good and intolerance and hatred are presented as a social bad. The ACPO, HMIC and CPS in the process of releasing statements such as those above, are exhibiting a declaratory intention akin to that examined with regard to incitement of racial and religious hatred legislation (and proposed legislation) described in Chapter 4. All of these anti-hate crime initiatives, whether they be in the form of legislation (associated with racial and religious aggravated offences; incitement to racial hatred) or the commitment to prosecuting (in appropriate evidence situations) crimes aggravated by homophobic prejudice, can be described as a social project which has a particular image of Britain in mind, especially in relation to the place of minority communities (in particular racial, religious and sexual minority communities) in this emergent Britain. This inclusive strategy of inviting isolated community groups to join 'mainstream' society is a significant moment in the re-spatialization of minority groups, including lgbt communities, in their trajectory from the isolation of tolerated privacy and the marginalization in gay spaces and semi-publics in between 'legality and morality' to the membership of 'the public', the 'mainstream'.

The North American sociologist Steven Seidman (2002) notes that in relation to the lesbian and gay community in the USA, the recognition that homophobic hate crime is a social bad with adverse individual, community and national implications seems to amount to a politics of equality through the vehicle of protection which threatens the continuity of toleration as an organizing principle of mainstream society's relationship with lgbt communities:

> To date, tolerance has been the dominant type of social accommodation. Tolerance entails decriminalization and the de-legitimation of blatant homophobic behaviour. Gays are to be acknowledged as part of America, but not necessarily accepted or valued as equals. It is hard, however, to draw the line at tolerance. Once homophobic practices are criticized as hateful and hurtful, there is an implicit acknowledgement that gays are ordinary folk deserving of respect and equal treatment.
>
> (Seidman 2002: 195)

Thus, the acknowledgement of the need to protect lgbt communities and to punish homophobic incidents is for Seidman (talking about the USA) a watershed moment in sexual politics and sexual citizenship. It opens up an area of contest, which is less concerned with good homosexuals and bad gays and more concerned with 'social bads', such as homophobic hate crime, that harm minority groups in culturally diverse societies.

In the next section, which is dedicated to the contemporary review of sex offences legislation, a similar process is unfolding in which the boundaries of protection and toleration are, for some sexual minority groups, being recalibrated. Here, the emphasis is on proposals for the introduction of equitable and fair sex offences legislation with a particular emphasis on de-homosexualizing certain aspects of the criminal law.

The de-homosexualization of sex offences

The review of sex offences was announced on 25 January 1999. The first stage of the review process was reported in the form of a consultation paper, *Setting the Boundaries: Reforming the Law on Sex Offences* (Home Office 2000). The White Paper, *Protecting the Public: Strengthening Protection Against Sex Offenders and Reforming the Law on Sex Offences*, was subsequently published by the Home Office (2002a). I demonstrate below that these documents, alongside the statements, concerns and strategies examined above in relation to the policing of lgbt communities since 1998, represent what can be described as parallel and interdependent developments that signal the advent of an anti-homophobic culture in the sphere of criminal justice in England and Wales.

There are two discernible strategies informing the current attempts to reform sex offences in England and Wales: an inclusive strategy that is anti-discriminatory in intention, which is dedicated to respecting and supporting the personal, private relationships of consenting adults; at the same time, these legislative reforms can be described as an attempt to increase protection to those members of society who are thought to really need it. These reforms and the provisions they introduce are in a similar vein to the Wolfenden Committee's recommendations in that they are liberal in one direction (dedicated to the protection of individual privacy, in certain circumstances) yet also coercive (introducing tighter social controls to police the boundaries of legality) in another. The Home Office describes this two-pronged approach in the current review of sex offences as being organized around the following reference points:

- To provide coherent and clear offences which protect individuals, especially children and the more vulnerable, from abuse and exploitation;
- To enable abusers to be properly punished; and
- To be fair and non-discriminatory.

(Home Office 2002a: 34)

In the rest of this section, the third reference point will be the focus of attention. According to the Home Office (2002a), the role of the criminal law in society is 'to establish what is and what is not acceptable behaviour' (p. 10). This passage could have easily appeared in the pages of the Wolfenden Report.

However, the Home Office completes the sentence above with the following qualification: 'yet it must also treat everyone in society the same' (p. 10). The latter passage would be a rarer occurrence on the pages of the Wolfenden Report. In many ways, the latter statement is a reflection of the Europeanization of UK law that has led to the review of sex offences.[12] According to Bhattacharyya (2002), it was through the incorporation of the European Convention on Human Rights into UK law that sexual minorities (especially lesbians and gays) have been transformed from a minority to be tolerated to a minority whose rights also have to be protected.

With regard to the anti-discrimination agenda of the White Paper, the main obstacle to fair and equitable sex offences law is that: 'certain existing offences criminalise consensual sexual activity in private between men, which would not be illegal between heterosexuals or between women' (Home Office 2002a: 10).[13] It was suggested in the White Paper that to remedy this inequity in sexual offences legislation, a non-discriminatory 'generic' offence that would treat everyone equally and thus protect everyone (including 'homosexuals') equally should be introduced:

> In order to provide common sense and make policing the law fair and practicable, these offences will be replaced with generic offences. This will ensure that the criminal law protects everyone equally from non-consensual sexual activity, but does not criminalise sexual activity that takes place between consenting adults in private.
>
> (Home Office 2002a: 10)

The attempt to introduce generic offences is an example of the suggested dehomosexualization of sex offences in this review. The review noted that the laws used in relation to sexual activity in public tended to be:

- Sections 12 and 13 of the Sex Offences Act 1956 (Gross Indecency[14] and buggery).
- Section 32 of the Sex Offences Act 1956 (Soliciting by a man).
- Common Law Offences: outraging public decency;[15] and public nuisance.

> (Home Office 2000: 124)

The review recommended that Sections 12, 13 and 32 be abolished (these were all repelled eventually in the Sex Offences Act 2003). The recommended abolition of these offences was justified by consideration of the effect of these laws on the gay and lesbian community:

> There is a strong perception, particularly in the gay and lesbian community, that law can be used in an unfair and discriminatory way,

and there is clear evidence that it has been so used in the past. The present law derives from a time when male homosexuality was illegal and to be openly homosexual was extremely difficult. Meeting places tended to operate around public facilities like lavatories. These meeting places could become nuisances, and prosecutions would be undertaken on the basis of observations by police or by *agents provocateurs*.

(Home Office 2000: 124)

As well as recognizing the negative impact of such provisions on the lesbian and gay community, the de-homosexualization of sex offences was demanded by the responses to the consultation exercise on the theme of the extent and nature of discrimination, where the review committee reported:

a consistent message that the law discriminates against certain sections of our society, most notably homosexual men. This message was supported by the research commissioned by the review, the views expressed at conferences and seminars, views of legal professionals, academics, social commentators and the personal experience of members of the review groups themselves.

(Home Office 2000: 97)

In the public consultation exercise, one-third of all submissions to the review directly expressed concern over the discrimination in law against homosexuals (Home Office 2000: 98). However, it is here that the de-homosexualizing strategy in the consultation paper gives way to a rather more explicit process of eradicating homophobic discrimination from the criminal law. In fact, the White Paper reported that submissions to the review:

argued that this differential treatment was not only wrong in principle, it implied that those taking part in such behaviour [homosexual acts] were inferior and abnormal. This was counter to the Government's avowed principles of equality, and hindered the establishment of a safe, just and tolerant society. Differentiation in law can be seen as justifying discrimination and homophobia in society; neither of which is acceptable in a civilised country.

(Home Office 2000: 98)

What statements such as these, as well as those above made by the ACPO, CPS and HMIC, suggest is that homophobia and discrimination based on sexual orientation are increasingly being presented as 'undesirable', 'abnormal', 'inferior' and 'uncivilized' in the institutions of criminal justice in England and Wales. That being said, in terms of the distinction between good homosexuals and bad gays examined above in relation to the post-Wolfenden culture, there is some continuity with the present review of sex offences. There is a consistent promotion of the right to private, consenting sexual relationships between adults throughout the consultation and White Paper, as would be expected. In many ways, these documents are at pains to present homosexual and heterosexual relationships of this kind as the norm in society. However, the language of 'homosexual' toleration is difficult to detect in the recent review reports. In relation to the promotion of private, consenting same-sex relationships between adults, there is the recognition in these reports that society has changed, and the 'necessity' for many of the laws, if there ever was such a necessity, is now absent in contemporary society.

At the same time, anti-hate crime initiatives and the de-homosexualization of sex offences presents an aperture through which to observe the convergence of at least two discourses of British citizenship: the 'active citizen' and the 'familial citizen' (Probyn 1998). Perhaps it is time that the lgbt active citizen (especially associated with anti-hate crime initiatives) and the familial citizen should be viewed not as contradictory elements of centre-left politics – that is, as being inclusive of lgbt communities one minute within the ethos of protective inclusionism and exclusive the next, for example when 'family values' are being promoted as the key values in society. The recent review of sex offences suggests that the members of lgbt communities are also expected to be 'familial' in the sense that they too are expected in this climate to be engaging in private, monogamous, stable, loving relationships with other adults. This is all well and good if lgbt people fall into the category of assimilable, 'good' private citizens; but what about those members of these communities who don't, whose 'tastes', predilections, practices and ways of life do not fit into the convergent discourses associated with, for example, 'the normal gay'? As observed above (and see Note 5, p. 200), many lgbt activists and theorists see little compatibility between 'queers' and good citizenship; they see little value in trying to persuade 'straight society' that lgbt people are 'as good as' straights, through becoming, for example, good parents, good soldiers, good priests (Bersani 1995). Perhaps 'the gay outlaw' (Bersani 1995), 'the sexual dissident' (Dollimore 1992) and various other romanticized sexual and gender 'outsider' positions will be further erased in the current culture of protective inclusionism through the compulsion to ' "acceptable" modes of being a sexual citizen' (Bell and Binnie 2000: 3). At the same time in this climate, even same-sex sexual acts in public seem to be less a matter of policing the boundaries of tolerated 'homosexuality' (as in Wolfenden discourse) than 'managing a problem'. For example, 'the policing of public facilities has also changed with much greater attention being paid to managing a problem to tackle the nuisance . . . such an approach is already part of the current problem-centred policing approach' (Home Office 2000: 124).[16] However, the Home Office was concerned (as was the Wolfenden Committee) to allay fears that the anti-discrimination flavour of the recommendations would lead to unregulated homosexual acts:

> Concerns have been raised, encouraged by some media misrepresentation, that the replacement of these offences will result in the legalisation of cottaging and gay sex in public. This is not the case. There is a clear difference between private and public sexual activity. No-one wishes to be an unwilling witness to the sexual behaviour of others and everyone is entitled to the protection from it by the law. Sexual activity in public that offends, irrespective of whether the people engaging in the activity are heterosexual or homosexual, will remain criminal and will be dealt with by a new public order offence dealing with sexual behaviour in a public place.
>
> (Home Office 2002a: 10)

The CPS also attempts to tackle the problem of the public interpreting the new policing of public sexual acts as allowing people to commit these crimes with impunity. However, the CPS commits itself to an anti-homophobic agenda rather than an anti-homosexual public sex agenda when it comes to encouraging homophobic incident reporting, when it suggests police and court discretion in overlooking minor offences. For instance, if a gay man, while engaging in an act of gross indecency becomes the victim of a more serious offence while engaging in that activity, it is the more serious offence, rather than the minor offence related to gross indecency, that should be the focus of police attention (CPS 2002a: 7).

Seidman (2002) is on the right track when he suggests that in the USA the bringing of gays into the fold of the good citizen may not bring about expanded choice for all citizens. The process of de-homosexualizing sex offences might have the effect, as Seidman suggests, of shifting the focus of the social control from the boundaries of toleration in relation to homosexuality to the sexual activities of a wider proportion of the population (gay, straight and bisexual), as well as to the obvious targets of this legislation, the serious sex offenders (especially those who sexually abuse children). These individuals and groups in society, especially those who engage in public sex, might find that they are the unintended focus of this particular anti-discrimination strategy. As Seidman (2002) suggests, perhaps 'the bad citizen today is someone who violates romantic, intimate, familial norms, regardless of his or her sexual identity. The bad sexual citizen, not the homosexual, at least not "the normal gay", is becoming a chief focus of social control' (p. 161).

Conclusion: beyond toleration?

Much of the policy initiatives and legislative developments (and proposed developments) examined in this chapter in relation to the second moment of sexual citizenship amounts to a systematic dismantlement of the sex offences laws and policing practices established in the first moment associated with the Wolfenden Committee in the 1950s and eventually with the decriminalization of homosexual acts in the 1960s. As a result of the de-homosexualization of discriminatory and homophobic sex offences provisions, eventually introduced in the Sex Offences Act 2003, and of the police attempting to win the trust and confidence of sexual minority communities, one could assume that non-heterosexuality, especially homosexuality, no longer poses the threat to society it was once believed to.

Does this mean that homosexuals and other sexual minority groups (lgbt communities) associated with consenting sexual activities involving adults are now beyond toleration and privacy? Richardson reminds us of how things were:

> the private/public distinction is then, a sexualised notion: it has a different meaning depending on whether one is applying it to a heterosexual or homosexual context. For lesbians and gays the private has been institutionalized as the border of tolerance, as the place where you are 'allowed' to live relatively safely as long as one does not attempt to occupy the public.
>
> (Richardson 1996: 15)

In the anti-discrimination and inclusive policing strategies examined above, I would suggest that sexual minorities (especially lesbians and gays) are being invited to participate in social life beyond the post-Wolfenden boundaries of privatized toleration described by Richardson. Bhattacharyya (2002) supports this conclusion by suggesting that 'recent attempts to refashion the boundaries of public and private life, to re-imagine the terms of propriety and to agree the proper place of sex, could all be regarded as responses to larger social changes' (p. 154). The social changes alluded to here by Bhattacharyya, especially the proposed introduction of generic de-homosexualized sex offences in relation to sex in public, can be described as establishing the proper place of sex (all sex) as being non-public. This would certainly tie in with Seidman's (2002) concern in relation to the USA that the normalization of lesbians and gays is an extension of the dominant sexual culture that encourages private, tender, caring, genitally centred relationships linked to love, marriage and monogamy. What we might see emerging in England and Wales in the first decade of the new century is an unfolding proprietorial sexual culture that works in parallel with dominant heteronormativity, in which 'normal' lesbians and gays are becoming more like their heterosexual counterparts in order to put society's (including the institutions of the criminal justice system) energies into seeking to control those sexual minority groups and individuals who do pose (or allegedly pose) a threat to society, especially to vulnerable groups in society, in particular children.

What is interesting about this current process of reviewing sex offences is that it does not set out to be the search for a new morality (Weeks *et al.* 2001). Here the search for a form of morality that would be acceptable to everyone is avoided in favour of learning to negotiate the hazards of social complexity, moral pluralism and sexual diversity and to learn to live with the challenge of uncertainty (Weeks 1995). Instead of attempting (and failing) to find a new morality as the guiding principle of the consultation, the review committee chose instead guiding principles congruent with the European Convention on Human Rights based on the interdependent rights which both protect individuals from harm while simultaneously respecting their privacy:

> our key guiding principle was that the Criminal Law should not intrude unnecessarily into the private lives of adults. Applying the principle of harm means that most consensual activity between adults in private should be their own affair, and not that of the Criminal Law.
>
> (Home Office 2000: iv)

The result is that, even though privacy is central to these provisions, it is a de-homosexualized privacy, which protects and encourages both homosexual and heterosexual propriety. However, the extent of the process of de-homosexualizing sex offences in relation to the social control of all inappropriate (public) sexual liaisons is yet to be fully realized.

In the next chapter, I proceed to explore and develop some of the wider themes and issues encountered throughout the book. In this 'concluding' chapter, the future of British national identity and of British citizenship will be explored in relation to observations, insights and problems identified in the present chapter and in previous chapters in relation to the renegotiation of the boundaries of tolerance, the acceptance of the irreducible diversity of the British population, and especially in relation to the current problematization of multicultural politics in favour of a project of radical cosmopolitanization.

7 Cosmopolitan citizenship: New Labour, 'new Britain'

> Let's build a new and young country that can lay aside the old preju-
> dices that dominated our land for a generation. A nation for all the
> people, built by the people, where old divisions are cast out. A new
> spirit in the nation based on working together, unity, solidarity,
> partnership. One Britain. That is the patriotism of the future.
>
> (Blair 1995)

Introduction

Despite some problems identified in Chapters 1, 2 and 3 which suggest contradictions or inconsistencies,[1] it will be argued in this chapter that the government and many other institutions and organizations in England and Wales
are in the process of promoting a new Britain through promoting new forms of
British citizenship and British national identity within the wider context of
the Labour government's 'big tent' politics (Driver and Martell 2002). This
strategy is to be achieved through instituting 'differentiated universalism' in
relation to twenty-first-century British citizenship. Differentiated universalism
was first introduced by Ruth Lister (1997) as a mechanism for introducing a
woman-friendly citizenship rooted in the differences between men and
women.[2] The differentiated universalism that is increasingly present in political and academic discourses on citizenship that I will be addressing here has
expanded the scope of Lister's feminist analysis to differentiation based on
ethnic, religious, migrant and sexual others under the banner of protective
inclusionism. In this context, differentiated universalism has been modified to
a generalized other-friendly citizenship grounded in difference, through a process described below as 'cosmopolitanization'. Differentiated universalism
depends on boundaries remaining present, but requires that they must be
flexible and, importantly, open to change. Trust, reciprocity and, above all,
'tolerance through dialogue' (Creppell 2003: 4) are central to this evolving

model of other-friendly cosmopolitan citizenship. The main enemy of this emergent model of citizenship is loyalty and commitment to communities, cultures, traditions and identities which are not open, not flexible, and that are detached and hostile to others. These cultures, traditions and identities inhibit the interdependent political strategies that are at work in contemporary Britain: the cosmopolitanization of British citizenship within an ethos of participatory democracy.

Whereas a multicultural and anti-discrimination strategy would attempt to promote respect for diverse cultural and other minority groups at the same time as attempting to devise anti-discrimination policies in the institutions that serve these communities, a cosmopolitan strategy attempts to interrupt the recourse to defensive: communities, identities and traditions associated with counter-modern social problems such as racism, Islamophobia, asylophobia and homophobia exhibited by, for example, 'host' or indigenous White groups. At the same time, a cosmopolitan strategy also exposes and attempts to dismantle the defence of, or retreat to, community, culture, tradition and identity by, for example, minority groups as their primary defence against these hostilities. Thus, the disgust, fear and hostility of the British racist, Islamophobe, asylophobe and homophobe are a counter-modern symptom associated with the perception by individuals and groups that the British 'culture', traditions and identity they privilege are somehow threatened by the presence of ethnic, religious, asylum seeker or sexual others. In turn, the response of ethnic, religious, asylum seeker and sexual minority groups to racism, religious intolerance, asylophobia and homophobia are to affirm and find support in their own communities, cultural traditions and social identities in the face of these and other hostilities. What will be observed below is that in a cosmopolitan strategy it is not the effect of prejudice, discrimination and intolerance that is the target of cosmopolitan citizenship alone, rather it is the recourse to defensive monolithic cultures, traditions, identities and community formations that are the target of this model of citizenship, which is dedicated to the promotion of dialogue between groups and across boundaries within the general principles of participatory democracy. The problem here is that the processes of cosmopolitanization are too focused on transforming minority groups (especially ethnic minority, migrant and established migrant groups) and not focused enough on transforming the hostile defence of monolithic White, 'indigenous', 'host' identities and communities.

In the first part of the chapter, 'party' political and academic discourses that attempt to imagine a future or 'new Britain' will be examined. Some of the themes encountered in previous chapters, especially in relation to loyalty and commitment, reappear here in the context of debates concerning what Tony Blair (2000) referred to as 'a revitalised conception of citizenship' suitable for an emerging 'new Britain'.[3] In the second part of the chapter, attention turns to what is presented as getting in the way of the new Britain and this revitalized British citizenship, namely the multiculturalist emphasis on community, culture, tradition and identity. I demonstrate below that commitment to community, culture, tradition and identity are increasingly being seen as pernicious stumbling blocks to the image of the new Britain being promoted by the Labour government. These forms of social attachment and being are viewed as past-oriented rather than future-orientated phenomena, which inhibit the emergence of a new Britain populated with citizens committed to the shared values of the wider political community. In the third part of the chapter, the mechanisms for achieving this new Britain are explored through themes already examined in previous chapters – for example, active citizenship, active communities and dialogic mechanisms of participation. In this section, theories of cosmopolitanization (Beck 2002) are examined in the context of the Labour government's strategies of protective inclusionism. The final section of the chapter critically examines what these discourses (and the policies and practices they have engendered and might still engender) will mean for certain sections of British society who could find themselves increasingly subjected to compulsory cosmopolitanization. This section looks at the potential dark side of this process of revitalizing British citizenship and the dream of a future-oriented, convivial Britain (Gilroy 2004) which might in practice (especially in areas such as Sighthill, Wrexham, Bradford, Oldham and Burnley, to name just a few, recently notorious areas in Britain) be experienced more as imposed social engineering than 'right on' progressive policy interventions.

The 'new' Britain

According to Lash (1999), the programmes of social engineering associated with modernity have brought with them their own side-effects, unintended consequences that set the stage for reflexive modernity. Here, I examine both sociological and government reflexivity in relation to the problematic 'unintended consequences' of multiculturalism, especially in relation to the integration of 'migrant' community groups, beginning with the former Home Secretary's thoughts on the disturbances in Oldham, Burnley and Bradford in 2001. The problem, according to David Blunkett, is that:

> The UK has had a relatively weak sense of what political citizenship should entail. Our values of individual freedom, the protection of liberty and respect for difference, have not been accompanied by a strong, shared understanding of the civic realm. This has to change.
>
> (Blunkett 2001b: 2)

The solution to this imbalance between respect for freedom and liberty and the development of shared understanding in the 'civic realm', according to Mr Blunkett, is through developing 'a stronger understanding of what our collective citizenship means, and how we can build that shared commitment into our social and political institutions' (Blunkett 2001b: 2). What Mr Blunkett is proposing is the development of an emergent British unity – that is, unity as 'outcome' achieved through the negotiation and conciliation of 'naturally different' interests (Bauman 2000). According to the former Home Secretary, this is a matter of encouraging flexible or complex meta-loyalties above and beyond competing micro-loyalties:

> There is no contradiction between retaining a distinct cultural identity and identifying with Britain. But our democracy must uphold fundamental rights and obligations to which all citizens and public authorities adhere. Citizenship means finding a common place for diverse cultures and beliefs, consistent with the core values we uphold.
>
> (Blunkett 2001b: 2)

It is time, according to the government, for Britain to face up to its inherent multiplicity, but this will not be achieved by merely respecting and embracing the value of the multicultural. This new Britain is to be achieved through a specific programme of extracting 'the common' from what Maffesoli (1991) describes as the 'swarming multiplicity of heterogeneous values' in complex societies (p. 12). In many ways, the government is intent on presenting the overarching goal of inclusion through advocating commonality in societies characterized by diversity through developing a common framework of citizenship (Young 2003). There are a number of academic sources (on both the right and left of the political spectrum) informing the government's conception of a renewed and revitalized British citizenship. For example, Yasmin Alibhai-Brown (2000) attacks multiculturalism for 'getting in the way of our doing what we need to together' (p. 11) because it focuses not on our shared future but rather on our past. In the new Britain, according to Alibhai-Brown:

> we need to re-imagine our collective culture with ties that bind, when the old multiculturalism debate is still looking inwards, erecting new barriers between groups in our own society, instead of enabling us to collectively benefit from our diversity.
>
> (Alibhai-Brown 2000: 3)

This emphasis on finding shared commitments, strengthening the ties that bind 'our' common culture in societies characterized by diversity, have a lot in common with Etzioni's (1997) thesis in *The New Golden Rule* concerning the re-moralization of society through the strengthening of a single core set of moral values (Rose 1999). In this text, Etzioni (1997) refers to the need to develop 'commonality in difference' that will become the 'frame and glue' (of basic agreement) which holds the mosaic of diverse communities in place (p. 193). The problem with models such as these, which emphasize the need to find the common ground of shared values, is that they are based on the assumption that the apparently different values of all communities actually operate around a shared common core of decency and that this can be based within a common constitutional framework (Rose 1999). This model for creating unity in diversity at the level of 'the nation', and the assumption that this commonality of values is in fact an achievable outcome for the nation is problematic. For example, Parekh highlights some of the practical problems associated with finding a baseline of 'core' or 'shared' values and principles from whence all this can unfold in multi-ethnic, multi-faith, multicultural and multilingual Britain in the following passage:

> what values and loyalties must be shared by communities and individuals in One Nation?[4] How should disputes and incompatible values between different communities be handled? How is balance to be struck between the need to treat people equally, the need to treat people differently, and the need to maintain shared values and social cohesion?
>
> (Parekh 2000a: xv)

From the outset, the attempt to create unity out of diversity through the isolation of core principles and establishing core values shared by all is a highly problematic political project. However, there are signs (in academic and New Labour discourse) that the dream of creating a common culture of core values is not to be achieved through the problematic process of trying to please all social groups. Rather, for New Labour, shared values are to be found in the process of all social groups undergoing transformation. In this dream of a new Britain, no one (or no group) is allowed to remain in place, the multicultural rainbow is to be shaken up, the multicultural mosaic is to be disturbed, and no group will be allowed to demand anything from their fixed position. What this represents is a renegotiation of 'the non-interference pact' under what Alibhai-Brown (2000) describes as 'distorted multiculturalism', wherein increasingly differentiated groups each pursue their own case for attention and resources, while jealously protecting their rights not to be criticized by others. In the new Britain, separate and competitive group interests and loyalties are to become secondary to emergent forms of citizenship and patriotism. This is evident in Young's (2003) call for a new sort of multiculturalism – a multiculturalism of genuine diversity. In this Britain, according to Young, the stress will be on the ongoing creation of culture rather than the inheritance of a weighty tradition. He elaborates:

A diverse society is not Oldham or Bradford or Burnley, where fixed and monolithic cultures confront one another, nor is it the neo-tribalism of Northern Ireland where tradition is glorified and the problems of identity are seemingly solved by consulting the fixed geographical contours of an atlas. In contrast genuine cultural diversity is about creating new lifestyles and values, it is about bricollaging bits from here and there, it is the hybridization of culture rather than the pursuit of a fake authenticity. It is, in fact, the actual lived culture that young people in schools which recruit from a wide range of ethnic and class backgrounds create every day of the week. The enemy of diversity is segregated housing policies, single faith schools, backward looking community leaders and, above all, the glib allocation of people to fixed ethnic categories.

(Young 2003: 459–60)

This fluid-future orientated multiculturalism (of genuine diversity) is therefore contrasted against what social commentators and academics such as Alibhai-Brown and Young, and politicians such as David Blunkett, describe as the problematic monolithic past-orientated multiculturalism in which community, culture, tradition and identity are privileged and respected above all else. In Young's (2003) dream of a new sort of multiculturalism, the sacred cows of community, culture, tradition and identity are to be disrespected – 'everbody changes', no group remains the same. Beck (2002) has described processes such as this as taking the form of a re-traditionalization in which a collective future consciousness takes over from tradition and memory in the past-oriented national imagination. In this process, 'tradition' becomes the tradition of the future. Therefore, rather than trying to please all communities in their difference, this process is to be achieved through commitment to action in the form of participation and dialogue between groups to find the common ground of shared values.

In multicultural societies, community, culture, tradition and identity were assumed to define one's politics; they gave minority groups their position from which to act politically,[5] to stake their claim, demand recognition, resources, equality of opportunities, for example as a Black person, as a Muslim person, as a gay person against the power of 'the centre'. In the new Britain, community, culture and identity will no longer be seen as key political resources, and sites of action, as they were in the competition for resources in a multicultural society (Solomos 2001). In part, the re-traditionalization process 'beyond multiculturalism' is also influenced by the post-structuralist understandings of identity, especially in the form of the shift in 'minority politics' from a politics of identity to a politics of representation. For example, in relation to race and ethnicity, Solomos is keen to point out that the politics of representation (a politics which focuses not on who I am/we are but rather on how my/our difference is represented and undermined in society) makes a mockery of 'identity-based' minority politics. According to Solomos (2001), in societies that acknowledge difference rather than diversity the capacity for using difference as a resource will emerge, and this will supersede difference as being portrayed as a threat. What Solomos is alluding to, when it is transposed into thinking about the creation of a revitalized form of British citizenship, is the fusion of the politics of difference, with what Stevenson (2003) refers to as a cultural understanding of citizenship. These will be examined in turn, below.

Cosmopolitan citizenship

The politics of difference refers to 'the who', 'the what' and 'the why' of cultural exclusion, detachment and marginalization (Stevenson 2003). The main problem with identity politics from the perspective of a politics of difference is that by affirming minority identities, dominant identities (for example, heterosexual, White, male identities) are also affirmed in and through the attempt to preserve, value and mobilize the subordinate term. The politics of difference can be described as a change of tactic, in which the relatively powerless 'minority' or subordinate groups in society mobilize not by affirming their own identities, but rather through attacking dominant representations and codes in society that reproduce and maintain their subordination. For example, lesbian and gay politics became queer politics and instead of exclusively affirming lesbian and gay identities, queer activists began to also attack the dominant sexual and gender codes in society in the form of a new enemy: heteronormativity (Warner 1993; Berlant 1997; Berlant and Warner 1998; McGhee 2001). Thus queer politics attacked the very structures, discourses and assumptions that supported the minoritization, othering and ultimately the exclusion of lesbians and gays as quasi-citizens.[6] This was influenced by developments in race and ethnicity studies where, according to Stuart Hall, the politics of difference recognizes that 'black' is a politically and culturally constructed category which cannot be grounded in a set of fixed transcultural or transcendental racial categories. In this political context, Hall (1998b) called for the end of the 'innocent black subject', as the new cultural politics of difference and race needed to respond to and acknowledge the shift in dominant regimes of representation. Like the objective of exposing and deconstructing heteronormativity in a queer politics of representation, in relation to race and ethnicity, the politics of difference was to be employed in deconstructing, in historical and relational terms, not only the central categories of 'otherness' but also the dominant discourses and representations that secure 'Whiteness' as a universalizing norm (Giroux 1994).[7]

At the same time, cultural understandings of citizenship are a component of this wider politics of difference, which involves the deconstruction of 'the normal citizen', through emphasizing the exclusion and marginalization of women (Lister 1997; see also Yeatman 2001), lesbians and gays (Evans 1993; Plummer 1995, 2003; Weeks 1999; Richardson 2000), ethnic and religious minorities and migrant communities (Hall and Held 1990; Parekh 2000a; Solomos 2001; Schuster and Solomos 2001, 2002; Hussain and Bagguley 2003), and the disabled (Marks 2001). According to Stevenson:

> Cultural understandings of citizenship are concerned not only with 'formal' processes, such as who is entitled to vote and the mainten-ance of active civil society, but crucially with whose cultural practices are disrespected, marginalised, stereotyped and rendered invisible.
>
> (Stevenson 2003: 23)

Thus, like the politics of difference, cultural understandings of citizenship are sites of struggle concerned with the marginalization of certain social practices and the privileging of others (Stevenson 2003). Cultural citizenship is con-cerned with differentiating rather than universalizing citizenship (Lister 1997), in order to encourage more inclusive forms of citizenship.

Whereas multiculturalism attempts to make permanent that miracle in which dog, cat and mouse eat from the same plate (Mario Vargas Llosa, in Beck 2002: 36), cultural citizenship infused with the politics of difference has larger ambitions. In the dream of the new Britain, cats, dogs and mice will be trans-formed into a common 'political' animal in order to eat off the same plate. This is a project beyond the limitations of a politics of assimilation and the later multicultural project, in that this is a political strategy in which the col-lective image of humanity is fostered beyond the individual's (multicultural-ist) dependency on his or her cultural sphere (Beck 2002). For Stevenson, a cosmopolitan view of culture:

> Would emphasize that no community is self-sustaining and that individuals do not live their lives in cultural enclaves . . . we need to dispense with the idea that cultures act as pre-constituted billiard balls that strike up against each other.
>
> (Stevenson 2002: 9)

But how is this to be achieved? Beck (2002) suggest that a cosmopolitan perspective, which he describes as an 'alternative imagination, an imagination of alternative ways of life and rationalities, which includes the otherness of the other' (p. 18), is one way of breaking out of the essentializing fixity of culture and identity under multiculturalism. This perspective has much in common with the Arendtian perspective that was employed in Chapter 2 to make sense of the mechanisms for promoting community cohesion in Bradford. Arendt's model for developing an enlarged mentality or thinking informed by the internalized voices of the other has many similarities with Beck's theories of cosmopolitanization, which he refers to as a 'globalization from within', an internalization of many of the social processes associated with late modernity or the second modernity, especially what he refers to as the dialogic imagination (Beck 2002). According to Beck (2002), the dialogism of cosmopolitanization corresponds to the co-existence of rival ways of life in the individual experience, 'which makes it a matter of fate to compare, reflect, criticize, understand and combine contradictory certainties' (p. 18). Thus, where the multicultural project consists of an (often contradictory) array of measures dedicated to: (a) promoting respect in society for diverse cultures; at the same time as (b) attempting to de-essentialize encoded and racialized identities; while rising to the challenge of (c) questioning the ways in which national cultures privilege certain identities over others, thus beginning the process whereby dominant groups 'unlearn their own privilege' (Stevenson 2003: 53). The cultural understandings of citizenship informed by the politics of difference can be described as viewing culture and identity as minor differences (to further modify Ignatieff's reading for Freud, discussed in Chapter 3), which have been inappropriately championed under multicultural policies at the expense of the major similarities all groups in contemporary Britain should share (according to the Government) in the form of common core values which would privilege loyalty to the political community above all other communal identifications (Laxer 2003). Chantal Mouffe's problematization (and solution) to the crisis in political allegiance in contemporary societies has much in common with David Blunkett's pronouncement above. Like Blunkett, Mouffe asserts that the allegiance to the political community must take precedence over other forms of association:

> While it is important to defend the widest possible pluralism in many areas – culture, religion, morality – we must also accept that our participation as citizens in the political association cannot be located on the same level as our other insertions in social relations. To recover citizenship as a strong form of political identification presupposes our allegiance to the principles of modern democracy and the commitment to defend our key institutions. Antagonistic principles of legitimacy cannot coexist within our single political association; to accept pluralism at that level automatically entails the [disappearance] of the state as a political reality.
>
> (Mouffe 1992: 11–12)

Many diverse theories of transformative democracies (deliberative, participatory, dialogic), as well as the other bodies of work referred to above on cultural citizenship and the politics of difference, seem to be converging around the issue of how individuals and groups in complex, diverse societies have, and might in the future, 'act' politically. Forms of associations and attachments associated with community, culture, tradition and identity are seen as relatively limited political resources in that they foster a culture of diversity rather than a culture of difference. A culture of diversity, from this perspective, is viewed as a centrifugal system where group allegiance moves away from a desired place of commonality; whereas what is being advocated in the form of cosmopolitan citizenship is a variety of centripetal citizenship beyond allegiance to minor differences, which embraces the similarities of shared principles and common, core values. Thus, following Mouffe, the battle that is being waged over citizenship in the new Britain is between citizenship (in the form of active citizenship) and identity. This reflects the well-rehearsed conflict between citizenship and identity, when they are conceptualized as a status expressed in juridical norms that define the rights of the members of a polity (citizenship) and a relational entity which begins outside of the purview of legal rules and regulations but is quickly drawn into the legal field (identity) (Isin and Wood 1999). Identity, culture and tradition (and community, see below) in this discursive formation, which includes academic discourse on the left and the Labour government's confection of centre-left and centre-right discourses, are seen as unpredictable, recalcitrant and emotionally 'hot' patterns of solidarity (Turner 2002; see also Furedi 2004) in that they are the source of strong emotions, defensive impulses and 'thick' patterns of solidarity. As a result, identity, culture and tradition are seen as conducive to prejudice, antagonism, polarization, mistrust, hatred and overt (fanatical) loyalty associated with preservationist or past-orientated orientations. According to Turner (2002), given the complexity and hybridization of modern society, there is no convenient place for 'real' or 'hot' emotions – these are to be replaced with a 'calmer' cosmopolitan mentality which is characterized by flexibility, 'cool' loyalties and thin patterns of solidarity. The process of creating cosmopolitan citizens is thus to be achieved through the creation of cosmopolitan patriots (Stevenson 2002), wherein a balance is struck between loyalty and commitment to particular cultures, traditions and identities, which are, in turn, conducive to the fostering of wider civic and political allegiances. This is an attempt to introduce on the ground what Yuval-Davis (1994) described as a 'transversal' or dialogic politics, which is a process involving 'rooting' and 'shifting' in which participants remain 'rooted' in their cultures, traditions, identities and values, as long as they are cooled down, and as long as they demonstrate their willingness to have their views shifted and challenged through dialogue with those who have different cultures, traditions, identities and values. In relation to the case studies contained in previous chapters, this can be seen in operation most clearly in post-riot Bradford (see Chapter 2), where complex varieties of social capital are being encouraged (more bridging, less bonding) to facilitate less rooting and more shifting so that the hold of thick solidarities can be decreased in the strategy of promoting an increasingly networked sociality across the cultural divide between Muslim and White communities. Following Appiah (1998), this can be described as an attempt to overcome the contradictions that emerge in complex identities, for example in the second-generation British-born Pakistanis where commitment to culture and tradition is to be fostered simultaneously with the process of cultivating openness towards difference and otherness.

Participation and cosmopolitanization

It is important to reflect on what is driving the debate between the principles of cosmopolitanism versus those of multiculturalism. According to Giddens (2001), the state and government do not represent the public domain when they become detached from their roots in civic association. 'Civil society' rather than the state, according to Giddens, supplies the grounding of citizenship and is hence crucial to sustaining an open public sphere. In both the academic and political discourses explored above, there is a shared emphasis on participatory models of democracy which takes the form of a republican emphasis on 'popular participation', especially in the form of dialogue. When this is understood, it is possible to see that the cosmopolitanism versus multiculturalism debate is less about identity, culture and tradition *per se*, and more about how identity, culture and tradition might obstruct the emergence of a society of actively engaged citizens. Cosmopolitan citizenship clearly moves the goal-posts of a Marshallian rights-based citizenship model as well as the model of communicative citizenship developed by Raymond Williams. According to Stevenson (2003), the model of cosmopolitan citizenship is one that recognizes that merely providing abstract rights (Marshall) and fostering administrative transparency for an increasingly educated electorate (Williams) is not enough in complex and culturally diverse societies. Instead of focusing on privileging rights, transparency and education, it is dialogue between diverse cultural groups that is at the very heart of cosmopolitan citizenship. Dialogue in this model is the path to greater understanding and greater participation and hence the means to the ends of the republican ideal of an actively engaged citizenry. According to Benhabib, there is no end to the Russian doll of participation as a social good of and in itself:

> participatory models of democracy see participation as a good in itself, to be extended as widely as possible. In these theories, both the domains in which the public is entitled to exercise political

> judgement and their institutional possibilities for doing so become
> political issues.
>
> (Benhabib 1992: 125)

For this ideal of participation to be achieved, the barriers to it have to be identified. In previous chapters, ethnic, religious, asylum seeker and sexual minority groups were conceived, to different extents, as forging intra-community loyalty and commitment and thus privileging culture, tradition and identities over other allegiances. In the case of ethnic, religious and sexual minority groups, intra-community loyalty was conceived in terms of a symptomatic culture of mistrust and often segregation forged through episodes of discrimination, prejudice, violence and injustice in the interaction between these communities and the dominant culture's institutions. What is emerging in the new Britain is a particular project of social engineering that is concerned with 'managing' the source of non-participation rather than the effects. In this climate, community is central. However, there is a dividing practice between good and bad communities (Alexander, in press) inherent in this project. In, for example, community cohesion discourses (explored in Chapter 2), the overly bonded, self-segregating Pakistani community in Bradford was seen as an undesirable form of social association (in terms of its potential inhibition of participation with mainstream society and neighbouring 'cultural groups'). At the same time, the self-segregating local lgbt community in Southampton (explored in Chapter 5) was also seen as an undesirable community formation cut off from the mainstream (and thus wider civic and political participation) by the spatialization of 'privacy' laws (see Chapter 6), fear of exposure, hate crime and a lack of trust in the police and other service providers (see Chapter 5). In both of these cases, it is defensive minoritization that is the challenge of the process of cosmopolitanization. What this amounts to is a politics in which recourse to, or justification of action through, the defensive affirmation of community, culture, tradition and identity is viewed as a bad habit to be broken in order to encourage dialogue, facilitate participation and thus achieve the dream of a cosmopolitanized society of active citizens in active communities, which is a component of the Labour government's strategy of increasing their 'democratic legitimacy'.

What is distinctive about exploring cosmoplitanization in relation to the 'social problems' included in this book – and this will be explored in more detail in the next section – is that here theories of cosmopolitanism are not limited to elite groups in society who live urban, middle-class if not 'international lives'. That is, people who trade internationally, work internationally, love internationally, marry internationally, do research internationally, and whose children are growing up and are being educated internationally (Beck 2002).[8] Instead of cosmopolitanization being a process which occurs through the requirements, functions and 'everyday' patterns of those living an international life, what will increasingly emerge in Britain, and is evident already in places, is that cosmopolitanization will become a process of social engineering which, as will be explored below, has both progressive and draconian elements. Whatever the residents of the Manningham area of Bradford, the Caia Park Estate in Wrexham, the Sighthill Estate in Glasgow and the Newton-Nicholson (SO14) area of Southampton have in common it is not the challenges of living an international lifestyle.[9] Rather, it is the problems of dealing with diversity in local, emotionally charged contexts, where resources are scarce and the presence of cultural differences is perceived as a social threat rather than a social benefit.

Compulsory cosmopolitanization?

The transition from modernity to late modernity, according to Young, involves a remarkable change, a reversal of structures of tolerance in societies. Young describes this transition as follows:

> The modern world is intolerant of *diversity* which it attempts to absorb and assimilate and is relatively tolerant of *difficulty*, of obdurate people and recalcitrant rebels which it sees as more of a challenge to rehabilitate and reform. The late-modern world celebrates *diversity* and *difference* which it readily absorbs and sanitizes; what it cannot abide is *difficult* people and *dangerous* classes which it seeks to build the most elaborate defenses against, not just in terms of insiders and outsiders, but throughout the population.
>
> (Young, 1999b: 390; emphasis in original)

Young (1999b) suggests that in the late-modern world, the marginalization of 'the difficult' is experienced in three main forms: economic exclusion from labour markets; social exclusion between people in civil society; and the ever-expanding exclusionary activities of the criminal justice system and private security. All too often it is the economic forms of exclusion from labour markets (Levitas 1998) and consumption (Rose 1996b, 1999), alongside the exclusionary practices evident in 'the new penologies' of risk management and prudentialism (Feeley and Simon 1992, 1994,[10] Rose 1999; Young 1999b), that are the focus of contemporary sociology and criminology. However, I would suggest that the social problems encountered in this book in the form of hatred, antagonized segregation, violence and incitement to hatred tick all three of Young's 'marginalization boxes' above in that most of the social problems examined in the previous chapters resulted from the competition for scarce resources in contexts associated with economic marginalization. At the same time, they were also related to inter-community tensions, especially the relationships between diverse cultural groups in local areas or neighbourhoods in civil society. A certain actuarialist tendency is also discernible in the mobilization of the criminal justice system in relation to the 'legal remedies' designed to curb the expression and incitement of hatred, which were described as declaratory mechanisms that were more governmental than moral in orientation (see Chapter 4). However, I would also suggest, as explored above, that the affirmation of defensive identities is increasingly being viewed as a central marginalizing 'difficulty' getting in the way of the Labour government's dream of the new Britain.

In very simple terms, the dream of cosmopolitan citizenship in a democratic culture characterized by participation is inhibited by (a) the fear and hatred of difference which is interdependent with (b) the defensive recourse and excessive loyalty to one's cultural traditions and/or identity. This 'negative' orientation to diversity and otherness (for example, in the form of racism, Islamophobia, homophobia, fundamentalism, excessive inter-cultural bonding and community defensiveness) is collectively described by Bauman (1995) as mixophobia. Bauman contrasts this negative relationship to difference and diversity, with the ideal of individuals and groups who are comfortable with, and celebrate difference, which he describes as the relational orientation of mixophilia. Mixophobia is akin to Putnam's (2000) description (see Chapter 2) of social capital directed towards malevolent, anti-social purposes, or to excessive in-group loyalty and associated out-group antagonism, and to the mobilization of counter-modern community formations against encroaching otherness (Beck 1997). All too often mixophobic social problems are associated with how 'poor', 'under-educated', 'blue-collar' and/or 'low-income' groups, whether White, African-Caribbean, Pakistani, English, Scottish or Welsh, sometimes respond to living in culturally and ethnically diverse areas that are blighted by economic deprivation. In this particular take on counter-modernization, the mixophobic 'poor' are pathologized as intolerant anti-integrationists. However, the problem with this is that it leaves the prejudice and intolerance (towards ethnic, religious, migrant and sexual minority groups) at the heart of middle-class 'Middle England' untouched.

Mixophilia, on the other hand, equates closely to Putnam's description of outward-looking social capital, with its associated broadened horizons and broadened identities flushed with a wealth of diverse networks, which are the building blocks of the ideal of dialogic cosmopolitanism. This dividing practice between the mixophobic and mixophiliac has implications for the process of examining how the ideal of a transformative politics of difference is to be implemented in contemporary Britain. With regard to the social problems explored in earlier chapters, and in the discourses examined above, one can begin to see the emergence of a two-tier conceptualization of British citizenship, in terms of those who are sufficiently mixophiliac (or sufficiently cosmopolitan) and those who remain mixophobic, whether through hatred of other social groups or through self-segregation in the form of being too loyal, too committed and thus too rooted to their cultural traditions and identity. The mixophiliacs are increasingly being conceived as belonging to the 'inclusive we' (Fairclough 2000)[11] of right-minded cosmopolitanized citizens who, according to the Prime Minister, are people who want to live in a country free from prejudice, but not free from rules (Blair 1999). At the same time, the mixophobics are increasingly seen as products of their milieu, as 'works in progress', as communities of potential cosmopolitanized-mixophiliacs awaiting a change in local or neighbourhood social capital or, more accurately, the disruption of the identification processes ingrained in the habitus of their communities.

There are concerns being voiced that underneath the progressive utopianism of tolerant, cosmopolitan societies characterized by their 'intolerance of intolerance' lies a darker underbelly. For example, political theorists such as Robert Weissberg suggest that in US society:

> the rush toward the imposition of tolerance through educational indoctrination seems to be everywhere. The eradication of racism, sexism, homophobia, and similar aversions is so 'hot'. Hundreds of thousands of students and workers find themselves involuntarily enrolled in sensitivity workshops and similar campaigns.
>
> (Weissberg 1998: ix)

Weissberg (1998) describes this, rather too strongly, as 'the easy first step in the march towards totalitarianism' in the name of an unproved, unchallenged utopian panorama (p. ix). Similarly, Jacobs and Potter (1998) are concerned that in the USA low-level hate crime offenders (individuals involved in aberrant, *ad-hoc* hate crimes perpetrated during heated disputes rather than high-level organized ideological hate crime offenders) are being subjected to 'sanctions designed to correct wrongful prejudices . . . to correct their thinking' (p. 150). Jacobs and Potter see serious dangers lurking in these types of sanctions: 'the line between education and indoctrination may be fuzzy, but it is important that we be alert to staying on the right side of the line' (p. 150). In the UK, there is evidence of what Furedi (2004) describes as the emergence of regimes of therapeutic education, which are wedded to forms of behaviour modification that not only target conduct, but also attempt to alter feelings and emotions.

In the UK, the best example of these types of interventions can be found among the various community and educational initiatives that have sprung up in Oldham to tackle 'segregation'. One of these initiatives is the Inter-Community Peer Support (ICPS) Project, associated with the Peacemaker Project based in Oldham,[12] which has been set up to encourage positive cross-cultural experiences. The ICPS Project has been described as 'a hard-hitting approach to tackling racism and race-related crimes' (James 2003: 1), which is dedicated to 'changing the mindset' of racist (Asian and White) young people. These programmes focus primarily on young boys aged 12–14 who are deemed to be 'at risk' of crime, especially racially aggravated incidents. These boys come to the project through referrals from other agencies, in particular the Oldham Youth Offending Team (Peacemaker 2001a). Young people referred to the project undergo 'personal development' workshops to challenge their prejudices and racial stereotypes; these young people, if successful, have the opportunity of becoming 'accredited peer educators' who will assist the organizers running anti-racist workshops for 'race crime offenders' who will also be referred by Oldham's Youth Offending Team (James 2003). It was suggested on their website that these teenage peer educators 'will become race harmony ambassadors on their own council estates after making friends with young Asian men' (Peacemaker 2001b: 1). For both the White and Asian young people from Oldham involved in this project, this cross-cultural contact will be 'the first close contact they have had with each other in their entire lives' (Peacemaker 2001b: 1). This project is an attempt to educate young people out of a racist future through personal development and inter-community contact. This is an attempt to nip the counter-modern tendencies of defensive hatred in the bud to demystify and destabilize the 'abstract, conceptual, ideological' basis of collective and often inherited group prejudices (Ignatieff 1996), of stereotypes as fixated forms of representation that deny the play of difference (Sibley 1995) through what Bhabha (1995) describes as anxious repetition. Here the emphasis is on changing mind-sets and habitual prejudices through personal development and exposure to the other, thus interfering with the two central mechanisms of the power of stereotypes: (1) that they are based on fear and ignorance and (2) that they often remain unchallenged as a result of little or no interaction with others (Sibley 1995). In relation to similar programmes for adults, probation services are leading the way. There is evidence of schemes for dealing with adults convicted of racially aggravated offences in Leeds, Liverpool and Birmingham (Dean 2002). However, probation services in the London Borough of Greenwich (which is part of a Home Office targeted policing initiative) has the most extensive programme for working with racist offenders (Court 2003). David Court, who leads the programme, describes the autobiographical components – that is, the keeping of 'race diaries', wherein participants note and consider their interaction with Black and Asian people, and discuss these encounters with their probation officers on a weekly basis as 'a powerful tool in prompting behavioral change' (Court 2003: 56).[13]

Programmes such as these will become a common feature in probation services across the country in the next few years. The momentum for probation mechanisms dedicated to hate crime offenders is rising. For example, the Diversity Directorate of London Probation, led by Liz Dixon, held a conference in May 2004 entitled 'Addressing hate crime – a multi-agency approach', in which probation professionals from all over the country met to share expertise on how to effectively 'rehabilitate' these types of offenders, which will no doubt spill out into programmes dealing with Islamophobes, homophobes and other hate crime offenders in the future.

With regard to the above, these are all clearly necessary and much-needed projects undertaking valuable work. It is difficult to take up an oppositional-critical position here. How do you dismiss initiatives that attempt to work with offenders to prevent further racist, homophobic and Islamophobic hate crimes if you yourself are committed to anti-racism, anti-homophobia, anti-asylophobia and anti-Islamophobia? However, one potential criticism (and this was pointed out in Chapter 2 in relation to the centrality of 'cultural integration' and 'cultural dialogue' in the community cohesion discourses and programmes in Bradford, Oldham and Burnley; but is also relevant to other areas around the country) is that the current problematization of so-called negative emotions and prejudices distracts attention from the fact that perhaps it is the conditions (the social and economic context) that give rise to them that also needs to be addressed (Furedi 2004). Thus, the emphasis in all of these programmes, whether they be in Oldham or in Greenwich, is on cleansing or sanitizing 'polluting persons',[14] of breaking the habit of hating, which could result in the decontextualization of these counter-modern mobilizations from their location in multiple forms of deprivation in which groups are competing for scarce resources. Once again the cultural takes precedence over the material in the solutions to counter-modern social risks such as group hatred and antagonism between communities. In these programmes, transgression becomes a matter of the inappropriate emotions, allegiances and attitudes that are prevalent in a group's or individual's evident lack of commitment to allegedly commonly held norms and values and practices (e.g. anti-racism), which individuals or groups are expected to go along with (Driver and Martell 1997). The reorientation of 'hot' or 'defensive' allegiances (to community, culture, identity, tradition) and inappropriate hateful attitudes here is an attempt to move British society beyond half-hearted multiculturalism towards compulsory mixophilia through the process of cosmopolitanization.

An important question to ask here is, is this for everyone? Will all areas and neighbourhoods in Britain become implicated in such programmes? My suspicion is that this process, like many other 'programmes' before it, is an other-directed moral enterprise dedicated to:

> reforming human capacities, focusing its activities on a particular grouping of persons which it then seeks to reform, regulate, punish or reintegrate in various ways. Moral expertise, we might say, is

> other-directed in that the object is to work on and reform a constitu-
> ency deemed to be outside of the normal run of things.
>
> (Osborne 1998: 75)

The intention here of focusing on the potential dark side of the ideal of cosmopolitanization is to suggest that the progressive aspects of attempting to de-marginalize certain community groups through offering protection, inclusion and greater participation has hidden costs for these communities, in that the culture of cosmopolitanization will introduce a pernicious politics of assimilation where sexual minorities are vanillized, migrants are Anglicized and mixophobics are re-orientated to mixophilia through the mobilization of pedagogies of 'allegiance' and 'attitude' re-orientation and modification in 'problematic communities' deemed to be outside 'the normal run of things'. This process of cosmopolitanization is far from the elitist privileges of wealthy, international, 'jet-set' lifestyles; this darker side of cosmopolitanism is concerned with the thinning out of solidarity, the cooling down of loyalties and commitments, the un-bonding of social capital, as well as an attempt to foster trust and confidence. Following Foucault and de Certeau, these are governmental strategies for ensuring that the difficulties that can arise in relation to culture, tradition and identity do not undermine the political necessity under New Labour of building 'inclusive and democratic communities' (Stevenson 2003). Yet again, it is difficult to take up a knee-jerk oppositional position here. As an anti-racist, anti-homophobic, anti-asylophobic and anti-Islamophobic liberal, it is difficult to side with 'the victims' of this political strategy – the alleged mixophobes who are to be cosmopolitanized. It is dishonest to hide behind an oppositional posture here, rallying against the blurred boundaries of behaviour modification, indoctrination and the activities of criminal justice in the name of exposing the way society is (or hopes to) deal with racists, homophobes, Islamophobes and asylophobes, when in my heart of hearts I am committed to these types of attitudes and behaviours ceasing. However, this is not tantamount to a resignation of engaged criticism, it is an attempt to negotiate and explore the progressive as well as the problematic aspects of the emerging world around us. For example, in relation to the problematic aspects of many of the discourses, policies and initiatives examined in the chapters contained in this book, potential problems can be emphasized in which the right to be different, the right to enjoy, express and practise one's cultural traditions and identity in the future will be increasingly subject to the following provisos:

- As long as you are a competent English speaker.
- As long as you respect and embrace 'British culture'.
- As long as you are sufficiently integrated with communities other than your own.

- As long as you conduct yourself (sexually) with propriety.
- As long as you participate actively in your civic culture and in the wider political community.
- As long as you are tolerant of difference.

These provisos are particularly relevant to both established and migrant ethnic minority groups associated with 'inward migration'. Some of the Government's suggestions for 'managed' migration are captured in these provisos and have been the subject of heated debate on the 'multicultural' paradox with regard to the Labour government's 'race' policies (Bourne 2001; Kundnani 2001a; Back *et al.* 2002; Kushner 2003). These writers suggest that the multicultural paradox at the heart of New Labour is evident in the government being anti-racist on the one hand and seemingly anti-immigration on the other. That is, the government is all for the dismantling of institutional racism from public institutions such as the police (as explored in Chapter 1), yet allegedly racist or more accurately xeno-racist with regard to immigration and asylum policy. I would suggest that both of these strategies, New Labour's anti-racism and its 'tough' policies on asylum, are primarily concerned with the avoidance of social disorder and with improving (or increasing) social or more accurately community cohesion. It is time to face the facts: the Labour government is no longer working towards a multicultural society; it is now working towards a cosmopolitanized society. Within this strategy, the heat of counter-modern emotions associated with immigration and asylum are being systematically cooled to allow the nation, in all its current diversity, to become more comfortable with its irrevocable diversity, through the tougher management of inward migration. This process is thus a prophylactic actuarial strategy dedicated to avoiding further disorder (dis-ease) in the social body through attempting to pacify 'Middle England' at the same time as attempting to draw established minority groups into the wider political community through offering them greater protection from racism (in the form of racist incidents/crimes and dealing with institutional racism) in exchange for their increased commitment to, and participation in, the wider political community. When viewed in this way, the contradictions disappear and the Labour government's wider strategy is exposed. What is different about this strategy is that it is not concerned with protecting 'the British way of life' from an invasion of 'alien' races and cultures; rather, this is a strategy dedicated to attempting to re-imagine a new British way of life. Managed migration is part of this strategy, as is the management of established migrant communities and other minority groups through encouraging them into centripetal strategies associated with dialogue, participation and inclusive protectionism. At the same time, the bad habit of minority group segregation and social detachment is supposedly being disrupted through the strategy of protective inclusionism, in which various hate crime and other laws are being introduced to send a clear message to society that discrimination, violence, hatred and the incitement to hatred are no longer appropriate in the new Britain.

Activating the institutional complex in civil society

Whereas the cosmopolitan elite, the affluent competent consumer and other 'winners' in the context of late-modern globalization are trusted to live an ethical existence in which they increasingly 'seek to manage themselves and their conduct in an ethical fashion according to principles that they have chosen themselves' (Rose 1999: 190),[15] the communities that will be subjected to cosmopolitan strategies in the process of creating the new Britain, as suggested above, will be treated rather differently through a politics that 'attempts to technically manage the way in which each individual should conduct him or herself and his or her relations to others in order to produce politically desired ends' (Rose 1999: 191). Rose describes this as a new game of power, which he refers to as the 'community-civility game'.

It is significant that 'community', that centre-left and centre-right staple, is to remain so central to the dream of dialogic, participatory democracy beyond the multicultural ethos of respecting culture, tradition and identity. Above and in earlier chapters 'community' has been evoked to describe a diverse range of associations, including minority communities (ethnic, religious, sexual), marginalized and excluded communities ('host' and minority), active and passive communities, as well as vulnerable and targeted communities. The recourse to community in Third Way political discourse, according to Rose (2000), is a means of creating novel links between *the personal* and *the political*; here 'communities' are first and foremost associated with citizens (that is, 'communities of citizens') rather than other community formations (especially communities of identity, culture and tradition). It is these communities of citizens that are the location for the emergence of 'active citizenship'. Thus in this process of ushering in the new Britain, communities will also be subjected to a process of reorientation through sanitizing the potential 'difficulty' communities pose to the goal of active citizenship. Giddens makes the following observation, obviously with implications beyond the social problems explored in this book in mind, but with relevance to the government's conception of the process of encouraging 'active communities' which coincide with themes explored above and in earlier chapters:

> community doesn't imply trying to recapture lost forms of local solidarity: it refers to practical means of furthering the social and material refurbishment of neighbourhoods, towns and larger cities.[16]
>
> (Giddens 1998: 79)

Thus, in the context of Third Way politics, 'the community', when purged of strong emotion, emerges as a significant territory for the administration of individual and collective existence. The community becomes a plane or surface upon which micro-moral relations among persons are conceptualized and administered, in which community becomes a *means* of government (Rose 1996b). Communities in this context are expected to work with local government, the police and other organizations to take responsibility for their own capacity-building, conflict-resolution and management in community-based practices (Marinetto 2003).

What is evident here is that individuals are to be made responsible through their individual choices for themselves and those to whom they owe allegiance in their community and in adjacent communities, through the shaping of a lifestyle according to 'grammars of living' which are widely disseminated, yet do not depend upon political calculations and strategies (Rose 1996a). Back *et al.* warn against the emphasis on communities and local empowerment in Third Way politics. The main problem that Back *et al.* identify in relation to this strategy is that in complex multi-faith, multi-ethnic settings:

> 'the community' is not a simplistic or homogeneous formation. Rather than the arbiter of moral worth it becomes a battleground of competing ethics. The local can be the arena for the expression of 'rights for White' tenant groups, foundational Christianity and a complex variety of articulations of Islam . . . Put simply a desire to empower the local, set within a plethora of initiatives to promote participatory democracy, highlights the contradictory nature of apparent localized autonomy.
>
> (Back *et al.* 2002: 5)

However, Solomos (one of Back's co-authors) points out in an earlier article that to some degree, antagonism, disagreement and conflict are essential to the democratic process. That is: 'solidarity itself is not impermeably solid but depends to a certain degree on antagonism and uncertainty' (Solomos 2001: 207). Solomos qualifies this statement by insisting (as does David Blunkett above) that there is a need to develop a shared vision of democratic community, through retaining 'some kind of moral, ethical and political ground – albeit a provisional one – from which to negotiate among multiple interests' (Solomos 2001: 207). At this point, a certain circularity of argument is discernable in both academic and New Labour discourses with regard to how commonality in the form of the shared commitment to the wider political community is to be achieved through communities sharing core values, which in turn facilitates dialogue in the form of participatory democracy between and among communities whereby shared values are forged and reinforced.

What becomes clear from the above is that communities, as well as the cultures, traditions and identities associated with them, are to be subject to a process of realignment in the ethos of cosmopolitan citizenship and participatory democracy. Social groups in the future, in scenarios depicted by Back *et al.*, will increasingly lose their positions of political contest and thus will no longer remain so focused on increasing or protecting *their* rights and entitlements in competition with other social groups. This is to be achieved through attempting to encourage 'community-mindedness' in local areas, yet at the same time ensuring that people do not become *too* community minded. In this context, the emphasis will be less on demands for the special rights and entitlements associated with specific communities and more on the obligations and responsibilities associated with communities within the emergent 'community of communities' (Parekh 2000a). To achieve this transformation, communities, like attachments to identity, culture and tradition, will also be subjected to processes of modification and sanitization so that they can fulfil their role as the location of future-orientated active citizens.

Many of these changes in the British social landscape will be achieved through the 'new levels of attentiveness' (Stevenson 2002) evident in many public institutions and organizations, mostly associated with the police and local government. Working under statutory obligations, these institutions and organizations are already encouraged to liaise, consult and encourage the participation of marginal (and often historically marginalized) ethnic, religious, migrant and sexual and many more minority community groups. The 'institutional complex' (Connolly 2002) of community groups, families, neighbourhood attachments and associations, together with voluntary associations in wider civil society[17] and reflexive public institutions attempting to become attached to these groups (and other agencies in multi-agency networks) in meaningful consultative ways, have all become 'activated' in the Third Way socio-political context, which has as its ultimate agenda the shaping of 'the objective dimensions of institutional life' (Connolly 2002) to facilitate the emergence of the new Britain. The objective dimensions of community life according to Connolly include:

> specific ways in which one materialized institution meshes with, grates on, or collides with others, engendering complex mesh works of dependence and interdependence that recoil back upon individual desires, constituency pursuits, ethical injunctions, and state agendas.
> (Connolly 2002: 19)

This is a potent micro-political dimension which plays a critical role below the threshold of political visibility inside every domain of life (Connolly 2002). 'Unity' is to be established here through attempting to encourage loyalty to the wider political community. This, in turn, encourages dialogue between separated cultural social groups (Stevenson 2002), and this is all to be achieved in the context of an active institutional complex composed of attachments and networks in civil society and attachments and networks to and between public institutions and third-sector organizations. Thus, the reflexivity of public institutions is a component of wider future-orientated reflexive modernization (Beck 1997). The focus of attention of this particular multi-institutional reflexivity is the reduction of the social risks associated with disorder, intolerance, hatred and associated social problems such as democratic and social detachment (segregation), marginalization and the hardening of identities. The generic response to such risks is one of institutional and community reorientation to the other. That is, of both public institutions (central government, local government, police, etc.) and the institutions of civil society (including social institutions such as 'the community' alongside other groups, such as voluntary associations) opening out to the others in their midst primarily through opening up channels of communication and laying the foundations for dialogue. This commitment to dialogue is founded on the belief that toleration of diversity (for example, associated with liberal toleration and multicultural strategies) fosters indifference. Therefore, it is through dialogue that indifference to difference is to be overcome and a new Britain populated by cosmopolitan citizens is to emerge. This is a progressive strategy in terms of inclusive protectionism, and the encouragement of greater participation in marginal communities; yet, at the same time, this strategy has the potential for introducing radical social transformations which might initiate unintended as well as intended consequences in the new Britain which rather than being progressive could be seen as draconian.

Notes

Introduction

1 According to Young-Breuhl, 'the homosexual' is an all-purpose victim of hate, in that homosexuals: are (or have been thought to be) clannish and dangerous 'like' Jews; sexually obsessed and predatory 'like' people of colour; are perceived as gender-deviants who are deemed 'abnormal' (Young-Breuhl 1996: 34); are depicted as men wanting to be women (in the case of male homosexuals), or women who compete with men for women (in the case of lesbian women) (Fone 2000).

2 That is, theory that takes its cues from anthropology and psychoanalysis (Sibley 1995).

3 Lash and Wynne (1992) suggest that although Beck's theory of reflexive modernization has its origins in the sociology and critique of scientific knowledge, it is applicable throughout society.

4 The latter is in turn related to the Home Office's institutional reflexivity, in which they reflect on their failure to adequately integrate migrant communities in the past and to devise policies that prepare migrant and 'host' communities better to reduce tension and potential future disorder, especially in relation to integrating asylum seekers into British society (see Chapter 3).

Chapter 1

1 Bowling (1999) reports that many international news agencies and newspapers around the world included reports on the murder of Stephen Lawrence and the Stephen Lawrence Inquiry on 24, 25 and 26 February 1999, including *Frankfurther Allegemeine Zeitung*, *Le Monde*, Reuters, The Associated Press, Asian Intelligence Wire, *Vancouver Sun*, *Los Angeles Times*, *The Columbian*, *Pittsburg Post-Gazette*, *The Arizona Republic*, *Washington Post*, *Sydney Morning Herald*, *The Toronto Star* and *China Daily*.

2 According to Bourne (2001), the Stephen Lawrence Inquiry made headlines in British newspapers across the political spectrum, including: 'Watershed for a fairer Britain' (*Evening Standard*), 'An historic race relations revolution' (*Daily Mail*), 'Dossier of shame that will change the face of Britain's race relations' (*Daily Mirror*), 'Racists won't win' (*Sun*), 'Never ever again' (*Daily Express*),

'Findings should open all of our eyes' (*Daily Telegraph*), 'Damning verdict on Met' (*Yorkshire Post*).

3   Police stop and search provisions with 'reasonable suspicion' were introduced in England and Wales under the Police and Criminal Justice Act 1984 (Kennison 2000). Stop and search provisions, without 'reasonable suspicion', were introduced in the rest of England and Wales under Section 60 of the Crime, Justice and Public Order Act 1994 by the then Home Secretary Michael Howard in an attempt to more effectively police mostly White 'ravers' and football 'hooligans' (Dodd 2003).

4   The public hearings held in London were conducted between 24 September and 7 October 1998 at Hannibal House. These hearings were followed by public hearings held between 8 October and 13 November in Ealing/Southall, Manchester, Tower Hamlets, Bradford, Bristol and Birmingham (MacPherson 1999: 45.3–45.4).

5   'Unwitting racism' was defined by the inquiry in the following terms:

> Unwitting racism can arise because of lack of understanding, ignorance or mistaken beliefs. It can arise from well intentioned but patronising words or actions. It can arise from unfamiliarity with the behaviour or cultural traditions of people or families from minority ethnic communities. It can arise from racist stereotyping of black people as potential troublemakers. Often this arises out of uncritical self-understanding born out of inflexible police ethos of the 'traditional' way of doing things. Furthermore such attitudes can thrive in tightly knit communities, so that there can be a collective failure to detect and to outlaw this breed of racism. The police canteen can too easily be its breeding ground.
>
> MacPherson 1999: 6.17)

6   The five suspects were all 16 or 17 years old at the time of the murder. They were: Neil and Jamie Acourt, David Norris, Gary Dobson and Luke Knight.

7   According to the Home Office's Crime Reduction Toolkits, racist incidents and harassment cover wide-ranging behaviour, including assault (grievous bodily harm, aggravated bodily harm, common assault), criminal damage (slogans/graffiti), offensive behaviour (threatening/abusive/insulting), harassment (designed to cause the victim alarm or distress), stalking, sending a letter/article conveying indecent or grossly offensive messages or threats, nuisance telephone calls, and arson (http://www.crimereduction.gov.uk/toolkits/rh0204.htm).

8   In their Crime Reduction Toolkit on racist incidents and harassment, the Home Office define a 'racial group' as 'a group of persons defined by reference to race, colour (including citizenship) or ethnic or national origin' (http://www.crimereduction.gov.uk/toolkits/rh0202.htm). This is the same definition

used in the Race Relations Act 1976 (section 3) and the Public Order Act 1986 (Part III, section 17).

9 The ACPO's guide published in 2000 also included a definition of a 'homophobic incident' (see Chapter 5).

10 Racially aggravated sentence enhancement legislation is a reversal in the logic of sentencing associated with heated-emotional offences and cool-calculated offences. Hatred, usually associated with passion, emotion and strong feelings, is being subjected to sentence enhancement here, whereas offences associated with passion and high emotion are usually associated with sentence reduction as 'crimes of passion' (relative to offences motivated by 'cold-blooded' calculation) due to extenuating circumstances (Jacobs and Potter 1998).

11 Jacobs and Potter (1998) follow Durkheim in suggesting that in denouncing crime and the criminal, the population reaffirms its commitment to the society's core values and norms. Their concern, however, is that by incorporating identity politics into the criminal law through provisions offering special protection to 'vulnerable groups', this function of the criminal law of bolstering social solidarity will be undermined through generating inter-group conflicts through the exaggeration of these conflicts in hate crime statistics and through the establishment of victim hierarchies and resentment between groups who are not protected by such provisions.

12 According to the Home Office's Crime Reduction Toolkit information sheets, the reasons why racist incidents are often unreported include suspicion that racist incidents will not be taken seriously, effective action will not be taken, fear of reprisal if the perpetrator discovers that the incident has been reported, and victims are unaware of how to approach the organization concerned (http:www.crimereduction.gov.uk/toolkits/rh0213.htm). The under-recording of racist incidents is in turn the result of victims failing to mention evidence or perceptions of racism, the failure of police to record racist allegations, and some incidents may be recorded by the police but not as racist (http:www.crimereduction.gov.uk/toolkits/rh0214.htm).

13 In relation to police race relations, the requirement for and failure of policing by consent of all communities was brought home to Sir William MacPherson, especially in the public meetings that were held as part of the Stephen Lawrence Inquiry:

> Wherever we went we were met with inescapable evidence which highlighted the lack of trust which exists between the police and the minority ethnic communities. At every location there was a striking difference between the positive descriptions of policy initiatives by senior officers, and the negative expressions of the minority communities, who clearly felt themselves to be discriminated against by the police and others.
>
> MacPherson 1999: 1.2)

14 Some of the Metropolitan Police Services, draft Race and Diversity Review findings were reported on national TV news (BBC1 and Channel 4 News) on 10 March 2004. This review suggested that the retention of ethnic minority police officers in the Service was poor relative to that of White officers and that there was an element of segregation or 'ethnic clustering' in relation to specific areas of the Service. At the same time, the findings from the review suggested that ethnic minority officers were subjected to more formal disciplinary procedures than their White counterparts – it was suggested that the disproportionate recourse to these formal procedures was the means whereby White officers in the Service were attempting to protect themselves from the accusation of racism when dealing with even minor grievances and problems with an ethnic minority officer. Many of the findings from the review echo the findings of the Report on Career Progression of Ethnic Minority Police Officers (Bland *et al.* 1999), which suggested that: ethnic minority officers in the eight forces that participated in the study across England and Wales were twice as likely to resign than Whites; the rate of dismissal for ethnic minority officers was two to three times higher for ethnic minority officers as for White officers; and there were differences in the percentages of White and ethnic minority officers with experience of working in some key posts.

15 In other police forces across the country, similar units have been set up, sometimes called Community Support Teams (see Chapter 5).

16 Stanko (2001) suggests an uneasy fit between the three forms of violence (racist, homophobic and domestic) that are referred to Community Safety Units (CSU). Domestic violence became part of CSU remit because these units were formed using the staff from previously established domestic violence units and so-called vulnerable persons units. However, incidents of domestic violence are not deemed to be hate crime incidents (see Chapter 5) like homophobic and racist crimes, which target a vulnerable minority group. Domestic violence cannot be defined as a hate crime against women, because occasionally men can also be the victims of domestic violence, even though women are victims in four of five recorded cases.

17 According to the Home Office, the Race Relations Amendment Act 2000 strengthens the Race Relations Act 1976. The 2000 Act outlawed discrimination (direct and indirect) and victimization in all public authority functions not covered by the Race Relations Act 1976, with only limited exceptions. It also placed a general duty on specified public authorities to work towards the elimination of unlawful discrimination and to promote equality of opportunity and good relations between persons of different racial groups in carrying out their functions. The general duty is supported by specific duties, which are enforceable by the Commission for Racial Equality (Home Office, http://www.homeoffice.gov.uk/comrac/race/raceact/amendact.html).

18 See endnote 3, above, for a discussion of non-PACE stop and search provisions.

19 It was proposed that from 2003 police officers in the Metropolitan Police

Service would be given pocket computers to record every suspect stopped on the streets to ensure, following the Stephen Lawrence Inquiry recommendations, that stop and search procedures are monitored, and those stopped will receive an 'on the spot' electronic receipt with a reference number for the purposes of complaining if they feel they have been treated unfairly (Ahmed 2002).

20   These figures refer to Bowling's research published in 2003 on PACE stop and search with reasonable suspicion. However, Bowling's figures for stop and search under the Crime, Justice and Public Order Act 1994 (without reasonable suspicion) has a much higher African-Caribbean to White ratio of 27.5:1, with the Asian to White ratio also high at 18:1 (Bowling, in Dodd 2003: 1). See Chapter 4 for the dramatic rise of 'Asian', particularly Muslim, stop and search figures since 9/11.

Chapter 2

1   Alexander (2000) suggests that concerns about Asian young men were largely invisible (relative to concerns about African-Caribbean young men) until the late 1990s. However, she takes issue with the notion that Asian communities, before recent events, should be viewed as being 'unproblematic' and unthreatening. This erases the history of especially the Muslim community as being perceived as being outside of and opposed to British values.

2   In both the CCRT and GCC definitions, disparities in wealth and unequal life-opportunities between people and groups can be described as being relatively de-emphasized in favour of community and group relationships. This de-emphasis of material deprivation and socio-economic factors in these documents will be the focus of later sections of the chapter.

3   The Oldham Independent Review and the Burnley Task Force Review do include more references to deprivation indexes, unemployment and the structural problems associated with these areas than these more high-profile 'national' reports. The Denham Report also includes references to deprivation in these areas, including Bradford. However, the Denham Report does emphasize or at least prioritize cultural factors over material factors.

4   Taken from Mr Blunkett's speech to a regional conference of the Federation of Small Businesses in Sheffield on 5 September 2002. The 'maniacs' he is referring to are young British-Asian men sentenced by Judge Gullick under the charge of 'rioting'.

5   For the charge of riot to be brought, the West Yorkshire Police Force was granted the prior consent of the Director of Public Prosecutions.

6   For example, the first notable outbreak of public disorder to merit official attention in the Manningham area of Bradford occurred between 9 and 11 June 1995. Police heavy-handedness while dealing with a group of young Asian

men playing football on the street resulted in an escalation of disorder in which large numbers of police officers were drafted in. According to Bowling and Phillips (2002), Foundation 2000, an community organization based in Manningham, concluded that these disturbances were directly related to the communities, 'severe loss of confidence in the police' because police action was 'highly questionable, extremely provocative and unreasonable' (in Bowling and Phillips 2002: 11).

Chapter 3

1 For example, in February 2004 the government attempted to follow the lead of many other EU countries by tightening the restrictions on 'White' economic migrants from new EU member states, after the restrictions on their movement was lifted on 1 May 2004. Tony Blair and Jack Straw's safeguards include proposals for: (1) tightening the 'habitual residence' rule that prevents EU migrant workers from seeking unemployment and housing benefit; and (2) all employers will be required to seek work permits for those they hire from the new entrant states. Either or both of these restrictions, or others permitted under EU laws, could be implemented only if immigration numbers prove higher than the 12,000–13,000 a year predicted (White 2004).

2 There are many examples of local communities being divided by proposals to house asylum seekers in their midst. The most high profile case close to Southampton, for example, is the seaside town of Lee-on-Solent in Hampshire. Lee-on-Solent is a small town of roughly 6000 residents close to Gosport and a short ferry journey away from Portsmouth (Kushner 2003). The Home Office announced in February 2003 that plans to build accommodation centres in rural areas (South Glamorgan and Lincolnshire) were being abandoned in favour of new areas. Lee-on-Solent was top of the list of proposed sites (Kushner 2003). Plans were announced by the Home Office to convert the former naval airbase HMS Daedalus into temporary housing for asylum seekers. This resulted in 7000 local protesters attending an anti-asylum rally in the town and eventually handing a 32,000 strong petition to Downing Street. According to Kushner, the Lee-on-Solent campaigners stressed that the town did not have a 'race problem'; however, they were trying to protect their community from being 'swamped' by asylum seekers and were attempting to make sure that a race problem did not arise in the area due to competition between locals and asylum seekers for the already inadequate resources and service provision in the area (Kushner 2003). In April 2003, in Nottinghamshire, a similar protest was provoked in response to plans to convert the former RAF base near Bingham into accommodation for asylum seekers.

3 The Home Office's use of 'host' communities here refers to all non-recent immigrant 'White' communities (so-called indigenous communities).

4 Ontology is the science of being, therefore ontological security is the security of being, the maintenance of identity and the self.

5 The first citizenship ceremonies for immigrants were held on Thursday 26 February 2004 with Prince Charles in attendance.

6 This particular threat, in the form of 'the Muslim menace', will be explored in Chapter 4 in relation to the impact the Anti-Terrorism, Crime and Security Act 2001 on the British Muslim community and on Muslim asylum seekers.

7 Ignatieff's reading of Freud's theory was first introduced to me through a brief reference to it in Jock Young's article 'To these wet and windy shores: recent immigration policy in the UK' published in 2003.

8 Robina Qureshi, head of the Glasgow Campaign to Welcome Refugees, was concerned that after Mr Dag's murder 'every ingredient necessary for race riots is alive and kicking in Sighthill . . . Combat 18 and the BNP are back in the area and people are in such a heightened state of fear that many younger asylum seekers are arming themselves' (in Hill 2001: 4–5).

9 However, there have been some developments in the Sighthill area of Glasgow to ease some of the inter-community tensions in the form of events designed to promote understanding and contact between groups. For example, in June 2002, the second 'cultural fiesta' organized by Strathclyde Police Force and community leaders was held to calm tensions in the area (Khan 2002). It seems that Sighthill's recent 'multicultural' events will be rolled out in other areas of the UK, including Greater Manchester and West Yorkshire (Khan 2002) for the same purpose.

10 In relation to the disturbances, 19 people including a 13-year-old boy were charged with violent disorder. A total of 47 arrests were made and 30 people were charged (Smith 2003).

11 Trevor Phillips is the Chairman of the Commission for Racial Equality. He was addressing the Housing Corporation's 'Design and Diversity Conference' held in London on 1 July 2003.

12 Les Back (1996) refers to similar phenomena, which he calls 'neighbourhood nationalisms' (p. 49).

13 Renton suggests that although the BNP's recent election successes is a matter of concern, they should be put into perspective. The BNP is a vote-gathering party; it is not yet an organization that people join in any number. At 3500, the BNP's claimed membership is only one-sixth of the figure claimed by the National Front in the 1970s and the numbers attending the BNP's national rallies, the 'Red, White and Blue' festival, have not risen, despite considerable press coverage of the events, remaining at around 300–400 in both 2001 and 2002. This is simply too low to sustain the street-level presence that the organization will need if it is to achieve wider electoral success (Renton 2003).

Chapter 4

1 An attempt to include religious discrimination in the 1976 Act failed (Hepple and Choudhury 2001).

2 According to the House of Lords Select Committee, 'incitement' is in origin a common law offence. In common law, for there to be incitement there has to be both some form of communication with a person whom it is intended to incite and, in that communication, some attempt to persuade or encourage that person to commit a criminal offence. However, for there to be incitement at common law it is not necessary to prove that the person who it was attempted to incite was in fact affected by the attempt. The incitement also does not have to be directed towards a specified person or group of persons but, rather, may be general (HL Select Committee on Religious Offences 2003: para. 70). According to Iganski (1999a), the main limitation of the inclusion of 'incitement' in these provisions is that incitement is defined to occur through the use of words or material which are 'threatening, abusive and insulting' and the strength of feeling conveyed by these words arguably excludes many relatively more moderate and subtle expressions, which could be just as likely to stir up hatred.

3 The concept of 'hatred' is a novel one in the criminal law, and under the 'aggravated offences' provisions of the Crime and Disorder Act 1998, the episodes of hatred have to be 'something very extreme' (HL Select Committee on Religious Offences 2003: para. 89). The reason for this is that hatred itself is not a crime, unlike, for example, violence. The Home Office in their oral evidence to the House of Lords Select Committee suggested that it is important to:

> make the distinction . . . between incitement to violence, which is a crime in itself, and the specific area of incitement to hatred, hatred not being a crime, so it is a very specific, narrow range of behaviour that we are talking about which falls between on the one side incitement and on the other aggravated offences.
>
> (Home Office, HL Select Committee on Religious Offences 2003: para. 130)

Iganski (1999a), suggests (see also endnote 2) that hatred in these provisions defines a very severe sentiment which might, like incitement, exclude many other less severe reactions and expressions which could in turn lead to unlawful behaviour. Thus the limitations of both incitement and hatred in the Public Order Act 1986 and in the proposed Bill is that Far Right groups will attempt to keep their propaganda within the law (or in the grey areas of the law) by avoiding severe sentiments and active instigations.

4 The definitions of religion and belief are too complex to be dealt with here; for a detailed examination, see Hepple and Choudhury (2001). This legislation introduced nine new religiously aggravated offences, which expanded the

existing racially aggravated offences introduced in the Crime and Disorder Act; like the latter these new offences are sentence enhancement provisions (see Chapter 1). Clause 39 was eventually dropped from the Anti-Terrorism, Crime and Security Act 2001. This clause became Section II of the Religious Offences Bill 2002. There were a number of problems associated with the inclusion of Clause 39 in the 2001 Act. Many felt that the issues were too large and complex and thus needed to be included under separate legislation; at the same time, many Muslim groups supported the removal of the clause as a matter of timing in that its inclusion would have connected Islam too closely to high-profile terrorist activities, for example 9/11. This concern of the Muslim community will be explored further below.

5 The leading case on what constitutes a 'racial group' is *Mandla v. Dowell Lee* 1983 1 All ER 1062, where the House of Lords held that Sikhs did constitute an 'ethnic group' within the subcategories of 'racial group'. Lord Fraser went on to outline the characteristics of an ethnic group. Two characteristics were essential: a long shared history and a cultural tradition of its own, including social customs and manners but not necessarily associated with religious observance. Other factors would assist the case, including a common geographical origin, a common language and literature, or common religion different from neighbouring groups. The Jewish community has since been treated as having the same protection because the House of Lords, in seeking the meaning for 'ethnic origin', relied on a New Zealand (*King-Ansell v. Police* [1979] 2NZLR 531) decision on the same point under similar legislation, concerning a pamphlet published with the intent to incite ill-will against the Jews (HL Select Committee on Religious Offences 2003: para. 13).

6 For example, the 2001 census figures indicate that Muslims constitute over 3 per cent of the population. Other estimates suggest that about 700,000 Muslims are of Pakistani origin; 300,000 are of Bangladeshi origin; 240,000 are from India; 375,000 are from the Middle East and Africa; 200,000 are from diverse countries such as Malaysia, Turkey, Iran and the Balkans; and about 10,000 are African-Caribbean or White converts (HL Select Committee on Religious Offences 2003: para. 15).

7 For more details on the articles of the European Convention on Human Rights, see http://conventions.coe.int/treaty/en/Treaties/Html/005.htm.

8 Young British men who become suicide bombers or volunteered to fight in the Taliban are increasingly connected to the media-coined Muslim 'hate clerics' in the UK, such as Sheik Abu Hamza Al-Masri, Sheik Abdullah El-Faisal, Sheik Omar Bin Muhammad Bakri and Sheikh Omar Abu Omar (Abu Qatada). For example, Omar Khan Sharif from Derby and his accomplice Asif Muhammed Hanif from Hounslow, West London (who died in the incident), killed three people in Tel Aviv on 1 May 2003. The *Daily Mail* describes Mr Sharif as 'hooked by the Sheik of hate' in their headline on 2 May 2003. The article went on to describe how the assimilated 'westernised' university-educated father of

two from Derby from a middle-class family was transformed by Sheik Abu Hamza Al-Mazir into a fanatic terrorist (Seamark and Taylor 2003) when he attended the Finsbury Park mosque in North London, also frequented by the alleged 'shoe-bomber' Richard Reid, who attempted to blow up a transatlantic flight, and Zacharias Moussaoui, the man accused in the USA of being the twentieth hijacker in the 9/11 attacks (Sears 2003).

9   For example, in October 2003, the day after the bombing in Istanbul in which 27 people died, Denis MacShane (MP Rotherham) caused a stir when he suggested that British Muslims should choose between 'the British way' of democratic dialogue and the way of Islamist terrorism (Press Association 2003a,b). MacShane later apologized to the British Muslim community when he admitted in an article in the *Sheffield Star* that 'he should have chosen some of his words more carefully' (MacShane, in Press Association 2003b: 1). Muslim anger, according to Taylor, was directed not at the apparent suggestion that UK Muslims did not share British values, but at the need for them to condemn terrorism. Inayat Bunglawala, a spokesman for the Muslim Council of Britain, said: 'the Muslim community has consistently condemned terrorism and we condemn this attack on the consulate and HSBC in Turkey' (Taylor 2003: 2). In a similar vein, the BBC morning talk-show host Robert Kilroy-Silk caused outrage in an article he wrote for the *Sunday Express* in April 2003 where he described all Arabs as 'despotic, barbarous, corrupt suicide bombers' (in Arlidge 2004: 1). As a result, Kilroy-Silk's talk show has been suspended and he was investigated by police for inciting racial hatred (Arlidge 2004).

10   As with the Public Order Act 1986, the proposed Bill's provisions stipulate under Section 18(2) that an offence may be committed, in a public or a private place. No offence is committed, however, where the words or behaviour are used, or the written material is displayed, by a person inside a dwelling and are not heard or seen except by other persons in that or another dwelling. The inadvertent use of words that are threatening, abusive or insulting is not an offence. A police officer may arrest without a warrant anyone he or she reasonably suspects is committing the offence.

11   At Select Committee, evidence of incitement in the form of the written and especially published word was prioritized over the spoken word:

> it is probably best to concentrate on published material: the spoken insult seems to be conveyed in a context where the point at issue is probably a public order or harassment offence, and so susceptible to prosecution. Although many of the examples given to us by witnesses consist of offensive conduct or remarks made to individual persons, it is the slogans and inflammatory publications which are at the core of the perceived problem.
>
> (HL Select Committee on Religious Offences 2003: para. 84)

12   The following safeguards were suggested by the Forum Against Islamophobia and Racism:

1. Legislation should include a Note of Guidance setting out the criteria for the exercise of the Attorney General's discretion.
2. The exercise of the discretion by the Attorney General should be subject to scrutiny via parliament via the presentation of an annual report to the Home Affairs Select Committee and the Joint Committee on Human Rights.
3. The Joint Committee on Human Rights be asked to give an opinion and publish an annual report on the practical enforcement of incitement legislation and its compliance with the ECHR, especially article 10.
4. Law enforcement agencies are trained, supervised, monitored and held accountable for the way in which they enforce incitement legislation.
5. An independent 'Ombudsman' be appointed to monitor the implementation of this legislation. He or she should be asked to publish an annual report that is submitted to the Home Affairs Select Committee on Human Rights.

   (Forum Against Islamophobia and Racism 2002: 25–6).

13   Another even more high-profile case is that of Abu Hamza (also know in the tabloids as the one-eyed, hook-handed, Muslim 'hate cleric' at the Finsbury Park mosque in London), who was arrested in May 2004 in London and is likely to be the first test of the new 'fast track' extradition agreement reached between the USA and Britain after the September 2001 attacks, with regard to terrorist charges.

14   The intention of the proposal for a Framework Decision is twofold. First, the intention is to ensure that racism and xenophobia are punishable in all member states by effective, proportionate and dissuasive criminal penalties, which can give rise to extradition or surrender. And, second, to improve and encourage judicial cooperation by removing potential obstacles. This proposed instrument provides that the same racist and xenophobic conducts would be punishable in all member states, which would define a common EU criminal law approach to this phenomenon (Commission of the European Communities 2001: 6).

15   Of course, this comprehensive legislation on the incitement to hatred would have other effects, such as prohibiting or punishing activities across and between some of the groups officially designated as being vulnerable to hate and the incitement of hatred. For example, the more extreme forms of Islamic intolerance targeting lesbians and gays might come under consideration.

Chapter 5

1   However, issues surrounding sexual minorities and immigration and asylum policy and procedures sometimes also coincide. For example, in my first book *Homosexuality, Law and Resistance* (McGhee 2001), I examine the plight of gay male asylum seekers and their application for refugee status in the UK and New Zealand based on their fear of being persecuted in their country of origin as a result of their sexual orientation.

2   This is not to suggest that racism and homophobia do not intersect. For information about the intersection of racist and homophobic violence, see GALOP's (2001) black services needs assessment report, *The Low Down*, in which the racist and homophobic violence experienced by African, Asian and Caribbean lgb people in London was reported.

3   The word homophobia (first coined in North America in the 1960s) was first used in an academic setting in K.T. Smith's (1971) article 'Homophobia: a tentative personality profile'. In 1972, Weinberg defined homophobia in his book *Society and the Healthy Homosexual* as 'the dread of being in close quarters with homosexuals' (p. 4). In an article in 1975, Freedman described homophobia as 'an extreme rage and fear reaction to homosexuals' (p. 19). For an overview, see Fone (2000).

4   According to Whittle (2000), 'transgender' is an umbrella term used to define a political and social community which is inclusive of transsexual people, transgender people, cross-dressers (transvestite) and other groups, such as 'gender-variant' people.

5   This auditing process has been (and will be) conducted in every city and, increasingly, in many towns across the UK. For example, see Stonewall and the LGBT Advisory Group Community *News Digest* for recent homophobic crime surveys, and news on various homophobic crime initiatives, at: http://www.stonewall.org.uk and http://www.lgbtag.org/info/localnews.htm, respectively. See also Blackbourn and Loveday (2004) for a review of several local homophobic crime audits, including Portsmouth's 'Speaking Out' audit, Southampton's Hidden Targets Report and Birmingham's Pink Shield Project.

6   Willmott (1987) offers a similar, yet slightly different typology of how individuals and groups are attached to and experience and define community in the form of: the 'territorial community' (those who live in a particular area), the 'interest community' (those people who have something in common over and above the geographical area in which they live) and the 'attachment community' (people who have a sense of belonging to a place).

7   Sanderson (1999) defines stakholders as professionals, managers and public service workers, user-recipients and representatives of all citizens with an interest in services. This definition is closer to the idea of stakeholders used in the context under discussion, which is in contrast to stakeholding

defined in terms of economic and labour market terms (Clarke and Newman 1997).

8 For an introductory discussion of 'public deliberation' or 'deliberative democracy' in the context of 'social policy making', see Ellison (1999), especially pages 72–7.

9 That is, the Crime and Disorder Act is best known for its authoritarian provisions that cater for the Prime Minister's much quoted ambition of getting 'tough on crime, tough on the causes of crime', especially in relation to youth crime. According to Fairclough, 'tough' is a New Labour buzzword (already encountered in Chapter 3 in relation to asylum seekers) which moves the government to the centre in an attempt to court 'middle-class' 'Middle England' (Fairclough 2000). The consensus-building element of the youth crime provisions in the Crime and Disorder Act was that such measures were presented as being for young people's own good. They were in the order of early preventive interventions, tackling anti-social rather than necessarily 'criminal' activities. Muncie (1999) suggests that the authoritarian toughness of the provisions was, as a result, legitimized in the name of welfare.

10 In Chapter 6, the Home Office's depiction of ethnic, religious and sexual minority groups, as well as others, as 'hard to reach groups', will be explored. In particular, the 'historical reasons' why some of these groups, including the lgbt community, do not trust the police will be examined.

11 See Canadian research conducted by Bagley and Tremblay (1997).

12 See American and British research conducted by Hershberger and D'Augelli (1997) and Rivers (2000), respectively.

13 See Chapter 1.

14 Other members of this multi-agency group are the Portsmouth Gay Men's Health Promotion Service, Portsmouth Domestic Violence Project, and North and Mid-Hampshire Gay Men's Health Project.

15 The reduction in suicide rates to zero since 1994 is the result of a policy of cautioning first-time gross indecency offenders along with an automatic referral to the GCHS.

16 This report was a victim survey and an agency audit. Agencies surveyed in this report were: Breakout Youth Project, Victim Support Service, Solent Lesbian and Gay Switchboard, Southampton City Council Housing Department, Winchester Rape and Sexual Abuse Counselling, The Rainbow Project, No Limits Youth Information and Advise Centre, Options Drug and Alcohol Counselling Service, Southampton Women's Aid, Southampton Rape Crisis and Sexual Counselling Service, and Society of Dismas.

17 Community policing and community consultation in Southampton has been carried out within the context of significant changes, especially in relation to the creation of a centralized police division in the city. For example, in 1998 Portswood and Southampton Central stations joined forces; in April 2001, Shirley and Bitterne were added to form a new city-wide police division. This

larger police division now matches the local authority area covered by South-ampton City Council. This reorganization will have an impact on the future local authority and police statutory partnerships and community policing programmes, especially in the light of the appointment, in February 2002, of a new Community Policing Chief Inspector.

18 According to Rose (1999), an 'analytics of government' should 'start by asking what authorities of various sorts want to happen, in relation to problems defined how, in pursuit of what objectives, through what strategies and techniques' (p. 22).

19 In summary, 279 people took part in the study. The average age of the sample was 29 years, with a range of 16–63 years. The sample consisted of more men than women: 69 per cent male, 28 per cent women and 3 per cent identified as transgender. The sample was predominantly White (93.6 per cent) (Mallett 2001: 19–20).

20 There is a need to be more specific about the members of the lgbt community most 'at risk' of homophobic incidents in Southampton; these are the resi-dents of SO14 (the city centre including the Newtown-Nicholson area and the Northam Estate). SO14 is also the location of most of the city's lgbt venues and the site of the vast majority of homophobic incidents reported.

21 Cruikshank's analysis 'focuses on such technologies of citizenship' as the 'war on poverty' in Community Action Programs in the USA in the 1960s (Cruikshank 1994), and the California Task Force set up in the early 1990s to promote self-esteem and social and personal responsibility in the long-term jobless (Cruikshank 1996). Even though these programmes are very different from the attempts to promote confidence and boost self-esteem in the lgbt community, there are exploitable parallels between these 'social' projects.

Chapter 6

1 In the two moments of 'sexual minority citizenship re-negotiation' under examination here, the focus of policing and legislative reform shifts, as will be demonstrated in the chapter, from 'homosexuals' in the 1950s and 1960s to the lesbian and gay community in the 1980s to lesbian, gay, bisexual and transgender communities from the late 1990s to the present.

2 Certain notorious and high-profile trials in 1953 and 1954, especially one involving a member of the aristocracy, Lord Montagu, also provoked strong comment in the national press, much of it critical of the authorities (West 1977). As a result, the Home Secretary, bowing to popular demand, agreed to set up a departmental committee to look into the law and practice relating to both homosexual offences and prostitution. In this chapter, the analysis shall be limited to homosexual offences.

3 According to Smith (1990), the 'badness' of a bad gay lies in his unfixity and excessiveness, his insatiable drive towards expansion and self-reproduction, and his contamination of the 'space of normalcy'. This non-private homosexuality is seen as a potential social threat, as homosexuality unrestricted is homosexuality that has the potential to spread (see McGhee 2000, 2001).

4 According to Plummer, the concept of intimate citizenship

> starts to organize a series of somewhat disparate concerns around the personal life. For the time being I will see intimate citizenship as a sensitizing concept which sets about analyzing a plurality of public discourses and stories about how to live the personal life in a late modern world where we are confronted by an escalating series of choices and difficulties around intimacies.
>
> (Plummer 2001: 238)

5 According to Plummer, there are examples of subaltern queer cultures

> that will not be mainstreamed or co-opted into the citizenship culture. Seeing the roots of gay and lesbian life in transgression, there remain strands – queer strands – that seek to keep (at least some) gay cultures on the borders, challenging dominant cultural forms and assumptions, and seeking to highlight 'the trouble with normal'.
>
> (Plummer 2001: 245)

For example, the queer activist and academic Michael Warner (1999) is particularly opposed to the culture of privatization and the culture of shame that is unfolding in North America to police the boundaries of public space, especially public sex cultures. Warner declares that his

> aim has been to bring to articulacy the public-ness of sex publics, in all their furtive ephemerality, as a substantive good. I want to inspire queers to be more articulate about the world they have already made, with all the variations from the norm . . . with its refusal of the tactful silences that preserves hetero privilege, and with the full range of play and waste and public activity that goes into making a world.
>
> (Warner 1999: 192–3)

6 Richardson (2000) reminds us that there is an interesting tension in the use of the term 'private' to demarcate the boundaries of (homo)sexual citizenship, because while lesbians and gay men are banished from the public to the private realm, they are, in many senses, simultaneously excluded from the private where this is conflated with 'the family'. As a result, Richardson suggests that:

> notions of privacy, as well as of public space, are exclusionary, the right to privacy being primarily a right of legally married

heterosexuals. In this sense, both the public and the private need to be understood as sexualized concepts.

(Richardson 2000: 78)

This spatialization of homosexuality and heterosexuality will inevitably intensify in the USA as President Bush attempts to garner support for his amendment to the US Constitution to ensure the continued exclusion of same-sex couples from the institution of marriage. However, at the same time, there is evidence in Britain, especially in the reform of sex offences, of a familialization of 'the normal gay' (see below).

7 Plummer does suggest that 'intimacy' can move away from the focus on love and sexuality to focus on other areas, including domestic violence. He cites Elizabeth Stanko's work on women's experiences of male violence, especially her 1985 book *Intimate Intrusions*, but only to make the point that 'rape' is a 'sexual' or 'intimate' form of violence, and it is his suggestion that Stanko's use of the term intimate 'does connect back to its original meaning: rape is, after all, an inmost violation of the being and the body' (Plummer 2003: 13). Thus, Plummer curtails his discussion of violence as another example of an 'intimate' experience connecting the public and the intimate.

8 For Ellison (1997), contemporary citizenship is a defensive strategy (more accurately, following de Certeau (1984), a defensive tactic) 'involving attempts to retain a sense of integration – in a complex and potentially hostile social and political environment' (p. 712).

9 For example, Jones and Newburn (2001) suggest that even in areas where police have developed extensive consultative links with the 'out' lesbian and gay community, this will not necessarily help in fostering positive links with those gay men and women who are not 'out'.

10 The CPS (2002a) describes this as an 'entirely understandable reluctance' on the part of members of lgbt communities due to 'the way in which members of the lgbt communities have historically been treated by individuals within the Criminal Justice agencies' (p. 7).

11 The Crime and Disorder Act 1998 included racially aggravated incidents as a crime, but did not include a similar provision that defined incidents motivated by homophobia as crime. As a result, according to Baxendale (2001), homophobia is confirmed as the prejudice that dare not speak its name. Baxendale notes, however, that despite not being written into law, homophobic – and indeed transphobic – incidents are being taken seriously by many police forces in England and Wales, and the police, unlike the Home Office, 'have no problem in understanding the thematic link between racism and homophobia, and improving their practices with both' (Baxendale 2001: 60). The CPS has gone as far as to regard homophobia as an aggravating factor (like racism), and that homophobia might be the motivating factor in the commissioning of other crimes that police must bring to the attention of the courts (CPS 2002a).

12   Associated with the inclusion of the European Convention on Human Rights (ECHR) in UK law in the Human Rights Act 1998.
13   The discriminatory nature of Section 13 of the Sexual Offences Act 1956 was noted by the European Court of Human Rights in the case of A.D.T. *v.* the UK in 2000. Section 13 states that:

> It is a crime for a man to commit an act of gross indecency with another man, whether in public or private, or to be party to the commission by an act of gross indecency with another man, or to procure the commission of an act of gross indecency with another man.

It was noted by the European Court that there are no provisions under domestic law for the regulation of private homosexual acts between consenting adult women; nor is there domestic legislation affecting heterosexual behaviour which corresponds to Section 13. 'Thus acts of oral sex and mutual masturbation between more than two consenting adult heterosexuals (as long as there are no homosexual acts between two males) do not constitute an offence' (A.D.T. *v.* the UK 2000: paras. 18–19).

In relation to prosecutions under Section 13 of the Sexual Offences Act 1956, the European Court found that there had been a violation of Article 8 of the ECHR as 'the reasons submitted for the maintenance in force of legislation criminalizing homosexual acts between men in public . . . are not sufficient to justify the legislation and the prosecution' (A.D.T. *v.* the UK 2000: 38–9).

14   According to the European Court of Human Rights, 'gross indecency' is not defined by statute. It appears to cover any act involving 'sexual indecency' between two male persons (A.D.T *v.* UK 2000: para. 15).
15   The common law offence of outraging public decency includes 'all open lewdness, grossly scandalous behaviour and whatever openly outrages public decency or is offensive and disgusting, or injurious to public morals by tending to corrupt the mind and destroy the law of decency, morality and good order'.
16   The ACPO attempted to ameliorate the historical area of conflict relating to the policing of 'gross indecency' by suggesting that police forces take into account how they police similar types of offences among the heterosexual community. They suggest that 'alternative solutions should be sought, including liaison with the gay community' (ACPO, in Morrison and MacKay 2000: Appendix D). An example of an alternative solution to policing gross indecency can be found in Southampton (see also Chapter 5), where a cautioning policy is in operation in public sex areas in the city. When a first-time public sex offender is apprehended by police officers in Southampton, they are not arrested, but rather are cautioned and then referred to the Southampton Gay Community Health Service (GCHS) for counselling. Initiatives such as these will become more commonplace in England and Wales, under the recommendations for a generic public sex offence that suggest that offenders

should be given a warning 'in order to end the nuisance before any offence is committed' (Home Office 2000: 126).

Chapter 7

1 For example, in Chapter 1, the Stephen Lawrence Inquiry's recommendation that police stop and search methods remain outside of race relations legislation, thus perpetuating tensions between police and ethnic minority communities; in Chapter 2, the emergence of a 'cohesive' British society, and establishing greater 'cohesion' between White and Pakistani communities in Bradford, was compromised by the scorched earth sentencing in the authoritarian backlash to the Bradford 'riots'; and the image of the new Britain comfortable with its own diversity was most spectacularly undermined in Chapter 3 in relation to the anxious xeno-racism associated with the Labour government's immigration and asylum policy (more on the latter below).
2 That is the difference between the citizenship status of men and women; men being the public universal citizen and women being the private non-citizen (Lister 1997).
3 The title of this speech was 'Britishness and the Government's agenda on Constitutional Reform', delivered to the Association of Regional Newspaper Executives on 28 March 2000.
4 Parekh is referring to the 'One Nation' discourse found in the Home Office report, *Race Equality in Public Services*, published in March 2000, where the government declared its commitment to creating a country where 'every colour is a good colour . . . every member of every part of society is able to fulfil their potential . . . racism is unacceptable and counteracted . . . everyone is treated according to their needs and rights . . . everyone recognizes their responsibilities . . . and racial diversity is celebrated' (in Parekh 2000a: 40).
5 For example, the BNP has in recent years been involved in a process of embracing multiculturalism in the attempt to present poor White groups as a minority whose culture, tradition and identity are ignored in the multiculturalist agenda.
6 Berlant and Warner define heteronormativity thus.

> By heteronormativity we mean the institutions, structures of understanding and practical orientations that make heterosexuality seem not only coherent – that is, organised as a sexuality – but also privileged. Its coherence is always provisional, and its privilege can take several (sometimes-contradictory) forms: unmarked, as the basic idiom of the personal and the social; or marked as a natural state; or projected as an ideal or moral accomplishment.
>
> (Berlant and Warner 1998: 548)

Heteronormativity is therefore the term used to specify the tendency in the contemporary Western sex-gender system to view heterosexual relations as the norm, and all other forms of sexual behaviour as deviations from this norm (Spargo 1999).

7 According to Knowles (2003), 'Critical White Studies' emerged in the late twentieth century. Richard Dyer (1997), for instance, argues that the effectiveness of Whiteness lies in it occupying a central, yet undeclared and unmarked, position from which the world is known and judged (Knowles 2003: 174–5). There are many similarities between queer theory and Critical White Studies; both attempt to name, mark and locate either Whiteness or heteronormativity as privileged positions.

8 Turner (2002) also suggests that cosmopolitanism has an elitist flavour in the sense that 'the elite, in the comfort of their Beverly Hills mansions, can afford to be generous to other cultures at a safe distance, whereas the slum dwellers of Bradford and Glasgow cannot' (p. 61). Below Beck's theory of cosmopolitanization will be contextualized within a governmental strategy that is attempting to implement a variety of cosmopolitanism in the streets of Bradford and Glasgow among other places.

9 Although some of these communities, for example the Pakistani community in Bradford, are depicted as living 'transnational' lives in relation to their connections with Pakistan in the CCRT Report (see Chapter 2).

10 Feeley and Simon describe the differences between the 'old penology' and the 'new penology' in the following terms:

> the old penology is rooted in a concern for individuals, and preoccupied with such concepts as guilt, responsibility and obligation, as well as diagnosis, intervention and treatment of the individual offender . . . in contrast the new penology . . . is actuarial. It is concerned with techniques for identifying, classifying and managing groups assorted by levels of dangerousness.
>
> (Feeley and Simon 1994: 173)

11 Richard Sennett (1998) also refers to this 'we' as the dangerous pronoun (see also Crow 2002: 4).

12 This project is part of a growing network of projects listed by 'Regeneration Exchange' in information sheet 5 (Conflict Resolution and Procedures) in various locations in the UK. These programmes are mainly 'youth'-based projects dedicated to conflict-resolution and encouraging cross-cultural contact between groups of young people from different ethnic backgrounds. Projects in other areas include the 'Resolving Differences-Building Communities' project based at Leicester College set up to reduce tensions between groups of African-Caribbean and Somalian young women at the college after conflict erupted in the autumn of 2001. At the same time, the 'Aik Saath: Conflict Resolution Peer Group' project has been set up in Slough to ease

conflict between local Asian and Muslim young people in Slough (http://www.regenerationexchange.org).

13 These types of programmes will continue to emerge in the UK. For example, a pioneering 'racism scheme' set up the Social Work Department and Probation Services in Falkirk in 2003 subjects racially aggravated offenders to a structured programme for confronting their offending behaviour through watching videos, filling out questionnaires and participating in discussion groups. According to one of the organizers, the purpose behind these programmes is as follows: 'it's about getting them to challenge their views and getting them to look at Scottish culture and try to get them to realize it is not a mono-culture' (www.monitoring-group.co.uk).

14 According to Mary Douglas (1992), a polluting person 'has developed some wrong condition or simply crossed some line which should not have been crossed and this displacement unleashes danger for someone' (p. 136).

15 Rose (1999) suggests that the practices and styles of an aestheticized life-choice that were previously the monopoly of cultural elites have been generalized in 'new habitats of subjectification' within consumer markets and advertising images which have added to a culture in which individuals believe that they can shape an autonomous identity for themselves through choices in taste, music, goods, styles and habitus. This culture embodies a shift, according to Rose, away from obedience to externally imposed codes of conduct and values in the name of the collective good and towards ethics, 'the active and practical shaping by individuals of the daily practices of their own lives in the name of their own pleasures, contentments or fulfilments' (pp. 178–9).

16 In later work, Giddens (2001) favours 'civil society' over 'community', as communities can turn 'bad' – from the point of view of Third Way politics – in that they often become 'too strong' and can 'breed' identity politics and exclusivity and thus are difficult to reconcile with the principles of tolerance and diversity upon which an effective civil society depends. Giddens attempts to distinguish between the unproblematic (communitarian) celebration of 'community' by locating communities within civil society and thus referring to them as 'the communities of civil society' (p. 51). I concur with this position by suggesting below that communities are one component in the 'institutional complex' of wider 'civil society', which also includes voluntary associations and social institutions that are all being 'activated' as a means of government in the Third Way socio-political context.

17 Within this institutional complex, all attachments and associations, in a much wider definition of 'civil society' usually tolerated by communitarians or social capital theorists, are to be included in the strategy of 'activation'.

Bibliography

Aaronovitch, D. (2004) Stop and search: a defining moment, *The Guardian*, 6 July, p. 5.

Ahmed, K. (2002) Met launches new 'sus' patrols, *The Observer*, 6 October (retrieved from: http://society.guardian.co.uk/crimeandpunishment/story/0,8150,806091,00.html).

Alexander, C. (2000) *The Asian Gang: Ethnicity, Identity & Masculinity*. Oxford: Berg.

Alexander, C. (2003) Violence, gender and identity: re-imagining 'the Asian gang'. Paper presented to the *Youth and Gender: Transnational Identity and Islamophobia Seminar*, European Commission, Brussels, 22–24 May 2003.

Alexander, C. (in press) Embodying violence: 'riots', dis/order and the private lives of 'the Asian gang', in C. Alexander and C. Knowles (eds.) *Making Race Matters: Bodies, Space & Identity*. Basingstoke: Palgrave.

Alibhai-Brown, Y. (2000) *After Multiculturalism*. London: Foreign Policy Centre.

Allen, C. (2003) *Fair Justice: The Bradford Disturbances, the Sentencing and the Impact*. London: Forum Against Islamophobia and Racism.

Allport, G. (1954) *The Nature of Prejudice*. New York: Addison-Wesley.

Al Yafai, F. (2003) The brick that turned fear and rumour into riot, *The Guardian*, 25 June (retrieved from: http://society.guardian.co.uk/asylumseekers/story/0,7991,984600,00.html).

Amin, A. (2002) *Ethnicity and the Multicultural City: Living with Diversity*. Draft report for the ESRC Cities Programme and the Department of Transport, Local Government and the regions (DTLR) (retrieved from: http://www.livjim.ac.uk/cities/papers/ash_amin.pdf).

Anthias, F. (1999) Institutional racism, power and accountability, *Sociological Research Online*, 4 (1), 1–12 (retrieved from: http://www.socresonline.org.uk/4/lawrence/anthias.html).

Appiah, K.A. (1998) Cosmopolitan patriots, in P. Cheah and R. Robbins (eds.) *Cosmopolitics: Thinking and Feeling Beyond the Nation*, pp. 34–48. Minneapolis, MN: University of Minnesota Press.

Archbishop's Council of the Church of England (2003) Memorandum: House of Lords – Religious Offences in England and Wales – Minutes of Evidence (retrieved from: http://www.parliamentthestationery-office.co.uk/pa/ld200203/ldselect/ldrelof/95/207.htm).

Arendt, H. (1968) *Between Past and Future*. New York: Viking Press.

Arlidge, J. (2004) Mr Silk, *The Observer*, 11 January (retrieved from: http://www.guardian.co.uk/race/story/0,11374,1120618,00.html).

Association of Chief Police Officers (2000) *Guide to Identifying and Combating Hate Crime* (retrieved from: www.acpo.police.uk).

Audit Commission (2000) *Another Country: Implementing Dispersal Under the Immigration and Asylum Act 1999* (retrieved from: www.audit-commission.gov.uk).

Back, L. (1996) *New Ethnicities and Urban Culture: Racism and Multiculture in Young Lives*. London: UCL Press.

Back, L., Keith, M., Khan, A., Shukra, K. and Solomos, J. (2002) The return of assimilationism: race, multiculturalism and New Labour, *Sociological Research Online*, 7 (2), 1–13 (retrieved from: http://www.socresonline.org.uk/7/2/back.html).

Bagley, P. and Tremblay, A. (1997) Suicidal behaviours in homosexual and bisexual males, *Crisis*, 18 (1), 24–34.

Ballintyne, S. and Fraser, P. (2000) It's good to talk, but it's not good enough, in S. Ballintyne, K. Pease and V. McLaren (eds.) *Secure Foundations: Key Issues in Crime Prevention, Crime Reduction and Community Safety*, pp. 164–88. London: Institute of Public Policy Research.

Bauman, Z. (1995) *Life in Fragments*. Oxford: Blackwell.

Bauman, Z. (1998) *Globalization: The Human Consequences*. Cambridge: Polity Press.

Bauman, Z. (2000) *Liquid Modernity*. London: Polity Press.

Baxendale, G. (2001) Soft on hate crime, soft on the causes of hate crime, *Gay Times*, October, p. 60.

BBC News (2001) Oldham hit by fresh violence, 28 May (retrieved from: http://news.bbc.co.uk/1/hi/uk/1355379.stm).

BBC, Bradford and West Yorkshire, News (2001) 'Serious disorder' flares in city, 8 July (retrieved from: http://www.bbc.co.uk/bradford/news/indepth/bradford_riot080701_seriousdisorder.shtml).

BBC2 (2002) *Trouble Up North*, 16 December 2002.

Beck, U. (1992) *Risk Society: Towards a New Modernity*. London: Sage.

Beck, U. (1997) *The Reinvention of Politics: Rethinking Modernity in the Global Social Order*. Cambridge: Polity Press.

Beck, U. (2002) The cosmopolitan society and its enemies, *Theory, Culture and Society*, 19 (1–2), 17–44.

Bell, D. and Binnie, J. (2000) *The Sexual Citizen: Queer Politics and Beyond*. Cambridge: Polity Press.

Benhabib, S. (1992) *Situating the Self: Gender, Community and Postmodernism in Contemporary Ethics*. Cambridge: Polity Press.

Benyon, J. (1984a) The riots, Lord Scarman and the political agenda, in J. Benyon (ed.) *Scarman and After: Essays Reflecting Lord Scarman's Report, the Riots and their Aftermath*, pp. 3–19. Oxford: Pergamon Press.

Benyon, J. (1984b) The policing issues, in J. Benyon (ed.) *Scarman and After: Essays Reflecting Lord Scarman's Report, the Riots and their Aftermath*, pp. 101–13. Oxford: Pergamon Press.

Benyon, J. (1984c) Scarman and after, in J. Benyon (ed.) *Scarman and After: Essays*

Reflecting Lord Scarman's Report, the Riots and their Aftermath, pp. 233–43. Oxford: Pergamon Press.

Berlant, L. (1997) *The Queen of America Goes to Washington City*. Durham, NC: Duke University Press.

Berlant, L. and Warner, M. (1998) Sex in public, *Critical Inquiry*, 24 (Winter), 547–66.

Bersani, L. (1995) *Homos*. Cambridge, MA: Harvard University Press.

Bhabha, H. (1990) The third space: an interview with Homi Bhabha, in J. Rutherford (ed.) *Identity: Community, Culture, Difference*, pp. 206–12. London: Lawrence & Wishart.

Bhabha, H.K. (1995) *The Location of Culture*. London: Routledge.

Bhattacharyya, G. (2002) *Sexuality and Society: An Introduction*. London: Routledge.

Blackbourn, D. and Loveday, B. (2004) Community safety and homophobic crime, *Community Safety Journal*, 3 (2), 15–22.

Black Information Link (2003) New asylum bill will boost racist BNP, 28 November (retrieved from: http://www.blink.org.uk).

Blair, T. (1995) Speech to the 1995 Labour Party Conference, 3 October. London: Labour Party.

Blair, T. (1999) Facing the modern challenge: the Third Way in Britain and South Africa. Speech to the South African Parliament, Pretoria, 6 January.

Blair, T. (2000) Britishness and the government's agenda of constitutional reform. Speech to the Association of Regional Newspaper Executives, 28 March (retrieved from: http://www.britembassy.at/speeches/003pm_britishness.rtf).

Blair, T. (2001) The power of community can change the world. Speech to the Labour Party Conference, Brighton 2001 (retrieved from: http://www.labout.org.uk/lp/news/labour/docs/LONGSPEE . . ./TBCONFSPEECH2001.TX).

Bland, N., Mundy, G., Russell, J. and Tuffin, R. (1999) *Career Progression of Ethnic Minority Police Officers*. London: PRC Unit Publication, Home Office.

Blunkett, D. (2001a) Securing order, basic safety, and underpinning our freedoms. Speech to the Labour Party Conference, Brighton 2001 (retrieved from: http://www.number-10.gov.uk).

Blunkett, D. (2001b) Blunkett calls for honest and open debate on citizenship and community, 10 Downing Street Newsroom (retrieved from: http://www.number-10.gov.uk/news.asp?newsID=3255).

Bocock, R. (1980) *Freud and Modern Society: An Outline and Analysis of Freud's Sociology*. Walton-in-Thames: Thomas Nelson.

Bohman, J. (2000) *Public Deliberation: Pluralism, Complexity and Democracy*. Cambridge, MA: MIT Press.

Bonnett, A. (2000) *Anti-Racism*. London and New York: Routledge.

Bourdieu, P. (1977) *Outline of a Theory of Practice*. Cambridge: Cambridge University Press.

Bourne, J. (2001) The life and times of institutional racism, *Race and Class*, 43 (2), 7–22.

Bourne, J. (2002) Does legislating against racial violence work?, *Race and Class*, 44 (2), 81–5.

Bowles, S. and Gintis, H. (2002) Social capital and community governance, *The Economic Journal*, 112 (November), 419–36.

Bowling, B. (1999) *Violent Racism: Victimization, Policing and Social Context*. Oxford: University Press.

Bowling, B. and Phillips, C. (2002) *Racism, Crime and Justice*. Harlow, UK: Longman-Pearson Education.

Bradford Vision (2001) *Community Pride Not Prejudice: Making Diversity Work in Bradford*. Bradford District Race Review. Bradford: Bradford Vision.

Branigan, T. (2003) Salvation Army boy who converted to campaign of hate, *The Guardian*, 25 February (retrieved from: http://www.guardian.co.uk/race/story/o_11374_90256_00.html).

Bridges, L. (1999) The Lawrence Inquiry – incompetence, corruption, and institutional racism, *Journal of Law and Society*, 26 (3), 298–322.

Bridges, L. (2001) Race, law and the state, *Race and Class*, 43 (2), 61–76.

Bristow, J. (1997) *Sexuality*. London: Routledge.

Brooks, J. (1999) (Can) modern local government (be) in touch with the people?, *Public Policy and Administration*, 14 (1), 42–59.

Bucek, J. and Smith, B. (2000) New approaches to local democracy: direct democracy, participation and the 'Third Sector', *Environment and Planning C: Government and Policy*, 18, 3–16.

Burney, E. (2002) The uses and limits of prosecuting racially aggravated offences, in P. Iganski (ed.) *The Hate Debate: Should Hate be Punished as a Crime?*, pp. 103–13. London: Profile Books.

Burnley Task Force (2001) *Burnley Speaks, Who Listens?* Burnley: Burnley Task Force.

Campbell, B. (1993) *Goliath: Britain's Dangerous Places*. London: Methuen.

Carlen, P. (1992) Criminal women and criminal justice: the limits to, and potential of, feminist and left realist perspectives, in R. Mathews and J. Young (eds.) *Issues in Realist Criminology*, pp. 51–69. London: Sage.

Casciani, D. (2003) Analysis: battle over Asylum Bill, *BBC News*, 26 November (retrieved from: http://news.bbc.co.uk/1/hi/uk_politics/324095.stm).

Chahal, K. (1999) The Stephen Lawrence Inquiry Report, racist harassment and racist incidents: changing definitions, clarifying Meaning?, *Sociological Research Online*, 4 (1), 1–5 (http://www.socresonline.org.uk/4/lawrence/Chahal.html).

Chandler, D. (2001) Active citizenship and the therapeutic state: the role of democratic participation in local government reform, *Policy and Politics*, 29 (1), 3–14.

Clarke, J. and Newman, J. (1997) *The Managerial State: Power, Politics and Ideology in the Remaking of Social Welfare*. London: Sage.

Cohen, P. (1996) All white on the night? Narratives of natavism on the Isle of Dogs, in T. Butler and M. Rustin (eds.) *Rising in the East*, pp. 170–214. London: Lawrence & Wishart.

Cohen, R. (1994) *Frontiers of Identity: The British and the Others*. London: Longman.

Coleman, C. and Moynihan, J. (1996) *Understanding Crime Data: Haunted by the Dark Figure*. Buckingham: Open University Press.

Collier, R. (1998) *Masculinities, Crime and Criminology*. London: Sage.

Commission of the European Communities (2001) *Council Framework Decision on Combating Racism and Xenophobia*, Brussels (retrieved from: http://europa.eu. int/comm/employment_social/news/2002/feb/proposal_jai_664_en.pdf).

Connolly, W.E. (2002) *Neuropoltics: Thinking, Culture, Speed*. Minneapolis, MN: University of Minnesota Press.

Court, D. (2003) Direct work with racially motivated offenders, *Probation*, 50 (1), 52–8.

Crawford, A. (1998) *Crime Prevention and Community Safety*. London: Longman.

Crawford, A. (2001) Joined-up but fragmented: contradiction, ambiguity and ambivalence at the heart of New Labour's 'Third Way', in R. Mathews and J. Pitts (eds.) *Crime, Disorder and Community Safety*, pp. 54–80. London: Routledge.

Crawley, H. (2003) Tackling the causes of asylum, *The Observer*, 11 May (retrieved from: http: //observer.guardian.co.uk/asylum/story/0,1084,953265,00.html).

Creppell, I. (2003) *Toleration and Identity: Foundations in Early Modern Thought*. London: Routledge.

Crow, G. (2002) *Social Solidarities: Theories, Identities and Social Change*. Buckingham: Open University Press.

Crown Prosecution Service (2002a) *Guidance on Prosecuting Cases of Homophobic Crime*. London: Equality and Diversity Unit/Policy Directorate.

Crown Prosecution Service (2002b) *Zero Tolerance for Homophobic Crime* (retrieved from: http://www.cps.gov.uk/Home/PressArchive/150–02.htm).

Cruikshank, B. (1994) The will to empower: technologies of citizenship and the war on poverty, *Socialist Review*, 23 (4), 29–55.

Cruikshank, B. (1996) Revolutions within: self-government and self-esteem, in A. Barry, T. Osborne and N. Rose (eds.) *Foucault and Political Reason*, pp. 231–52. London: UCL Press.

Davies, W. (2003) Complex truth behind Wrexham riots, *BBC News*, 24 June (retrieved from: http://news.bbc.co.uk/1/hi/wales/north_east/3016678.stm).

Davis, M. (1990) *City of Quartz: Excavating the Future of Los Angeles*. London: Verso.

Dean, M. (1999) *Governmentality: Power and Rule in Modern Society*. London: Sage.

Dean, M. (2002) Racists can learn not to hate, *The Guardian*, 4 December (retrieved from: http://society.guardian.co.uk/comment/column/0,7882,852892,00. html).

de Certeau, M. (1984) *The Practices of Everyday Life*. Berkeley, CA: University of California Press.

Denham, J. (2002) *Building Cohesive Communities: A Report of the Ministerial Group on Public Order*. London: HMSO.

Department for Education and Employment (2000) *Sex and Relationship Education Guidance*. Nottingham: DfEE.

Department of the Environment, Transport and the Regions (1998a) *Modernising Local Government: Local Democracy and Community Leadership*. London: DETR.

Department of the Environment, Transport and the Regions (1998b) *Modern Local Government in Touch With the People*. London: DETR.

Department of the Environment, Transport and the Regions (1998c) *Guidance on Enhancing Public Participation in Local Government*. London: DETR.

Dilley, R. (2000) Any port in a storm, *BBC News*, 25 January (retrieved from: http://news.bbc.co.uk/1/hi/uk/612347.stm).

Dobash, R. and Dobash, R. (1979) *Violence Against Wives: A Case Against Patriarchy*. New York: Open Books.

Dobe, K. (2000) Muslims, ethnicity and the law, *International Journal of Discrimination and Law*, 4 (1), 369–86.

Dodd, V. and Seenan, G. (2001) Fleeing asylum seekers ordered back to London, *The Guardian*, 10 August (retrieved from: http://society.guardian.co.uk/asylumseekers/story/0,7991,534855,00.html).

Dodd, V. (2003) Black people 27 times more likely to be stopped, *The Guardian*, 21 April (retrieved from: http://society.guardian.co.uk/raceequality/story/0,8150,940330,00.html).

Dollimore, J. (1992) The cultural politics of perversion: Augustine, Shakespeare, Freud, Foucault, in J. Bristow (ed.) *Sexual Sameness: Textual Differences in Lesbian and Gay Writing*, pp. 9–25. London: Routledge.

Douglas, M. (1966) *Purity and Danger: An analysis of the Concepts of Pollution and Taboo*. London: Routledge.

Douglas, M. (1992) *Purity and Danger: An analysis of the Concepts of Pollution and Taboo*, 2nd edn. London: Routledge.

Doward, J. and Hinsliff, G. (2004) British hostility to Muslims 'could trigger riots', *The Observer*, 30 May (retrieved from: http://observer.guardian.co.uk/uk_news/story/0,6903,1227962,00.html).

Driver, S. and Martell, L. (1997) New Labour's communitarianisms, *Critical Social Policy*, 17 (3), 27–46.

Driver, S. and Martell, L. (2002) *Blair's Britain*. Cambridge: Polity Press.

Durkheim, E. (1956) *Education and Sociology* (translated by S.D. Fox). Glencoe, IL: Free Press.

Dyer, R. (1997) *White*. London: Routledge.

Eisenstein, Z. (1996) *Hatreds: Racialized and Sexualized Conflicts in the Twenty-First Century*. London: Routledge.

Ellison, N. (1997) Towards a new social politics: citizenship and reflexivity in late modernity, *Sociology*, 31 (4), 697–717.

Ellison, N. (1999) Beyond universalism and particularism: rethinking contemporary welfare theory, *Critical Social Policy*, 19 (1), 57–86.

Erjavec, K. (2003) Media construction of identity through moral panics: discourses of immigration in Slovenia, *Journal of Ethnic and Migration Studies*, 29 (1), 83–101.

Escoffier, J. (1998) *American Homo: Community & Perversity*. Berkeley, CA: University of California Press.

Etzioni, A. (1993) *The Spirit of Community: Rights, Responsibilities and the Communitarian Agenda*. New York: Simon & Schuster.

Etzioni, A. (1997) *The New Golden Rule: Community and Morality in a Democratic Society*. London: Profile Books.

Etzioni, A. (2001) *The Monochrome Society*. Princeton, NJ: Princeton University Press.

European Commission Against Racism and Intolerance (2001) *Second Report on the United Kingdom*, Strasbourg, 30 April (retrieved from: www.ecri.coe.int).

European Convention on Human Rights (1950) *Convention for the Protection of Human Rights and Fundamental Freedoms*, Rome (retrieved from: http: conventions.coe.int/treaty/en/Treaties/Html/005.htm).

European Monitoring Centre on Racism and Xenophobia (2002) *Anti-Islamic Reactions in the EU after the Terrorist Acts Against the USA (United Kingdom)* (retrieved from: http://www.eumc.eu.int/eumc/material/pub/112001/uk-en.pdf).

Evans, D. (1993) *Sexual Citizenship: The Material Construction of Sexualities*. London: Routledge.

Evans, D.T. (1995) (Homo)sexual citizenship: a queer kind of justice, in A.R. Wilson (ed.) *A Simple Matter of Justice? Theorizing Lesbian and Gay Politics*, pp. 116–32. London: Cassell.

Fairclough, N. (2000) *New Labour, New Language?* London: Routledge.

Fair Justice for All (2003) http://www.nationrecs.demon.co.uk/fjfa/history.htm (retrieved 17 January 2003).

Feeley, M. and Simon, J. (1992) The new penology: notes on the emergent strategy of corrections and its implications, *Criminology*, 30 (4), 449–79.

Feeley, M. and Simon, J. (1994) Actuarial justice: the emerging new criminal law, in D. Nelken (ed.) *The Futures of Criminology*, pp. 173–201. London: Sage.

Fekete, L. (2001a) The emergence of xeno-racism, *Race and Class*, 43 (2), 23–40.

Fekete, L. (2001b) The death of Firsat Dag and the failure of Scottish dispersal, *Independent Race and Refugee News Network* (retrieved from: http://www.irr.org.uk/euroebulletin/united_kingdom/asylum_seekers_refugees/2001/akO.html).

Fekete, L. (2002) All in the name of security, in P. Scraton (ed.) *Beyond September 11: An Anthology of Dissent*, pp. 102–7. London: Pluto Press.

Fish, S. (1994) *There is No Such Thing as Free Speech: And It's a Good Thing, Too*. Oxford: Oxford University Press.

Flyvberg, B. (1998) Habermas and Foucault: thinkers for civil society?, *British Journal of Sociology*, 49 (2), 210–33.

Fone, B. (2000) *Homophobia: A History*. New York: Metropolitan Books.

Forrest, R. and Kearns, A. (2000) Social cohesion, social capital and the neighbourhood. Paper presented to *ESRC Cities Programme Neighbourhoods Colloquium*, Liverpool, 5–6 June.

Forum Against Islamphobia and Racism (2002) *The Religious Offences Bill: A Response* (retrieved from: http://www.fairuk.org/policy05.htm).

Fraser, N. (1997) *Justice Interruptus: Critical Reflections on the 'Postsocialist' Condition.* London: Routledge.

Freedman, M. (1975) Homophobia: the psychology of a social disease, *Body Politic*, 24, 19–29.

Furedi, F. (2004) *Therapy Culture: Cultivating Vulnerability in an Uncertain Age.* London: Routledge.

Fuss, D. (1995) *Identification Papers*. London: Routledge.

GALOP (2001) *The Low Down: Black Lesbians, Gay Men and Bisexual People Talk about Their Experiences and Needs.* London: GALOP.

Garland, D. (2001) *The Culture of Control*. Oxford: Oxford University Press.

Gelsthorpe, L. (1997) Feminism and criminology, in M. Maguire, R. Morgan and R. Reiner (eds.) *The Oxford Handbook of Criminology*, 2nd edn, pp. 511–25. Oxford: Clarendon Press.

Giddens, A. (1990) *The Consequences of Modernity*. Cambridge: Polity Press.

Giddens, A. (1994a) Living in a post-traditional society, in U. Beck, A. Giddens and S. Lash (eds.) *Reflexive Modernization: Politics, Tradition and Aesthetics in the Modern Social Order*, pp. 56–109. Cambridge: Polity Press.

Giddens, A. (1994b) Risk, trust, reflexivity, in U. Beck, A. Giddens and S. Lash (eds.) *Reflexive Modernization: Politics, Tradition and Aesthetics in the Modern Social Order*, pp. 184–97. Cambridge: Polity Press.

Giddens, A. (1998) *The Third Way: The Renewal of Social Democracy*. Cambridge: Polity Press.

Giddens, A. (2000) *The Third Way and its Critics*. Cambridge: Polity Press.

Giddens, A. (2001) Introduction, in A. Giddens (ed.) *The Global Third Way Debate*, pp. 1–22. Oxford: Polity Press.

Gillan, A. (2003) Detained Muslim cleric is spiritual leader to militants, hearing told, *The Guardian*, 20 November (http:politics.guardian.co.uk/homeaffairs/story/0,1088874,00.html).

Gilling, D. and Barton, A. (1997) Crime prevention and community safety: a new home for social policy?, *Critical Social Policy*, 17 (3), 63–84.

Gilroy, P. (1992) *There Ain't No Black in the Union Jack*. London: Routledge.

Gilroy, P. (2004) *After Empire: Melancholia or Convivial Culture*. London: Routledge.

Giroux, H. (1994) Living dangerously: identity politics and the new cultural racism, in H. Giroux and P. McLaren (eds.) *Between Borders: Pedagogy and the Cultural Politics of Cultural Studies*, pp. 29–55. London: Routledge.

Glavanis, P. (1998) Political Islam within Europe: a contribution to the analytic framework, *Innovations*, 11 (4), 391–410.

Gordon, C. (1991) Governmental rationality: an introduction, in G. Burchell, C. Gordon and P. Miller (eds.) *The Foucault Effect*, pp. 1–52. London: Harvester Wheatsheaf.

Hall, R. (1985) *Ask Any Woman*. Bristol: Falling Wall Press.

Hall, S. (1996) Introduction: who needs 'identity'?, in S. Hall and P. Du Gay (eds.) *Questions of Cultural Identity*, pp. 1–17. London: Sage.

Hall, S. (1998a) The great moving nowhere show, *Marxism Today*, November/December, pp. 9–14.

Hall, S. (1998b) New ethnicities, in *ICA Document 7: Black British Cinema*, pp. 27–31. London: ICA.

Hall, S. and Held, D. (1990) Citizens and citizenship, in S. Hall and M. Jacques (eds.) *New Times: The Changing Face of Politics in the 1990s*, pp. 173–90. London: Lawrence & Wishart.

Hampshire Constabulary (2000) *Policing Our Communities: A Practical Guide*. Basingstoke: Hampshire Constabulary.

Hampshire Police Authority (2001) *Hampshire Police Authority Annual Policing Plan 2001/02*. Basingstoke: Hampshire Police Authority.

Hanmner, J. and Saunders, S. (1984) *Well Founded Fear*. London: Hutchinson.

Harris, P. (2001) Race riots ignite Bradford, *The Observer*, 8 July (retrieved from: http://observer.guardian.co.uk/uk_news/story/0,6903,518610,00.html).

Hepple, B. and Choudhury, T. (2001) *Tackling Religious Discrimination: Practical Implications for Policy-Makers and Legislators*, Home Office Research Study 221. London: Home Office.

Herek, G.M. and Berrill, K.T. (1992) Introduction, in G.M. Herek and K.T. Berrill (eds.) *Hate Crimes: Confronting Violence Against Lesbians and Gay Men*, pp. 1–10. Newbury Park, CA: Sage.

Her Majesty's Inspectorate of Constabularies (1997) *Winning the Race: Policing Plural Communities*. HMIC Thematic Inspection Report on Police Community and Race Relations 1996/1997.

Her Majesty's Inspectorate of Constabularies (2000) *Winning the Race: Embracing Diversity* (retrieved from: http://www.homeoffice.gov.uk/hmic/wtr3-int. pdf).

Her Majesty's Inspectorate of Constabularies (2001) *Winning the Race: Policing Plural Communities Revisited* (retrieved from: http://www.homeoffice.gov.uk/hmic/wtrrev.htm).

Her Majesty's Inspectorate of Constabularies (2003) *Diversity Matters*, Home Office Communication Directorate, February 2003 (retrieved from: http://www.homeoffice.gov.uk).

Herrnstein, R.J. and Murray, C. (1994) *The Bell Curve: Intelligence and Class in American Life*. New York: Free Press.

Hershberger, D. and D'Augelli, R. (1997) Predictors of suicide attempts among gay, lesbian and bisexual youth, *Journal of Adolescent Research*, 12 (4), 477–97.

Heyd, D. (1996) *Toleration: An Elusive Virtue*. Princeton, NJ: Princeton University Press.

Hier, S. (2003) Risk and panic in late modernity: implications of the converging sites of social anxiety, *British Journal of Sociology*, 54 (1), 3–20.

Hill, A. (2001) Racism has turned the good people here bad, *The Observer*, 12 August (retrieved from: http://observer.guardian.co.uk/asylum/story/0,1084,537978, 00.html).

Hillyard, P. (2002) In defence of civil liberties, in P. Scraton (ed.) *Beyond September 11: An Anthology of Dissent*, pp. 107–12. London: Pluto Press.

Holdaway, S. (1996) *The Racialisation of British Policing*. London: Macmillan.

Home Office (1991) *Safer Communities: The Local Delivery of Crime Prevention through the Partnership Approach* (the Morgan Report). London: Home Office.

Home Office (1998a) Crime and Disorder Act Guidelines: Racially Aggravated Offences (retrieved from: http://www.homeoffice.gov.uk/docs/racagoff.html).

Home Office (1998b) *Guidance on Statutory Crime and Disorder Partnerships: Crime and Disorder Act 1998*. London: HMSO.

Home Office (1998c) *Fairer, Faster and Firmer*. London: Home Office.

Home Office (2000) *Setting the Boundaries: Reforming the Law on Sexual Offences*. London: HMSO.

Home Office (2001a) *Community Cohesion: A Report of the Independent Review Team*. London: Home Office.

Home Office (2001b) *Policing a New Century: A Blueprint for Reform*. Cm 5326. London: Home Office.

Home Office (2002a) *Protecting the Public: Strengthening Protection Against Sex Offenders and Reforming the Law on Sexual Offences*, Cm 5668. London: HMSO.

Home Office (2002b) *Secure Borders, Safe Haven: Integration with Diversity in Modern Britain*, February 2002, Cm 5387. London: Home Office.

House of Commons Select Committee on Home Affairs (2001) *The Anti-Terrorism, Crime and Security Bill, First Report* (retrieved from: http://www.publications. parliament.uk/pa/cm200102/cmselect/cmhaff/351/35108.htm).

House of Lords Select Committee (2003) *Religious Offences in England and Wales, First Report* (retrieved from: http://www.parliament.the-stationery-office.co.uk/ pa/ld200203/ldselect/ldrelof/95/950.htm).

Hughes, G. (1996) Communitarianism and law and order, *Critical Social Policy*, 16 (4), 17–41.

Hughes, G. (1998) *Understanding Crime Prevention: Social Control, Risk and Late Modernity*. Buckingham: Open University Press.

Huntington, S.P. (1993) The clash of civilizations?, *Foreign Affairs*, 72 (4), 22–49.

Hussain, Y. and Bagguley, P. (2003) *Citizenship, Ethnicity and Identity: British Pakistanis after the 2001 'Riots'*. Working Paper, Department of Sociology and Social Policy. Leeds: University of Leeds.

Hyland, J. (2001) British Muslims threatened with treason charges, *World Socialist Web Site*, 10 November (retrieved from: http://www.wsws.org/articles/2001/ nov2001/trea-n10.shtml).

Iganski, P. (1999a) Legislating against hate: outlawing racism and anti-semitism in Britain, *Critical Social Policy*, 19 (1), 129–41.

Iganski, P. (1999b) Why make 'hate' a crime?, *Critical Social Policy*, 19 (3), 386–95.

Ignatieff, M. (1996) Nationalism and toleration, in R. Caplan and J. Feffer (eds.)

Europe's New Nationalism: States and Minorities in Conflict, pp. 213–32. Oxford: Oxford University Press.

Ignatieff, M. (1998) *The Warrior's Honour: Ethnic War and Modern Conscience*. New York: Metropolitan Books.

Institute of Race Relations (1999) Institute of Race Relations Evidence submitted to Part 2 of the Inquiry into Matters Arising from the Death of Stephen Lawrence, 19 February (retrieved from: http://www.irr.org.uk/cgi-bin/news/printable.pl).

Isin, E.F. and Wood, P.K. (1999) *Citizenship and Identity*. London: Sage.

Jacobs, J.B. and Potter, K. (1998) *Hate Crimes: Criminal Law and Identity Politics*. Oxford: Oxford University Press.

James, A. (2003) Peace of mind, *The Guardian*, 9 July (retrieved from: http://society.guardian.co.uk/societyguardian/story/0,7843,993957,00.html).

Jefferson, T. (1991) Discrimination, disadvantage and police-work, in E. Cashmore and E. McLaughlin (eds.) *Out of Order? Policing Black People*, pp. 166–88. London: Routledge.

Jenks, C. (2003) *Transgression*. London: Routledge.

Jenness, V. and Broad, K. (1997) *Hate Crimes: New Social Movements and the Politics of Violence*. New York: Aldine de Gutter.

Johnson, P. (2003) Cleric from London unmasked as inspiration for Muslim terrorists, *The Telegraph*, 21 May, pp. 1–2.

Johnson, P. and Womack, S. (2003) Asylum seekers facing deportation may be tagged, *The Telegraph*, 28 November (retrieved from: http://www.telegraph.co.uk/news/main.jhtml?xml=/news/2003/11/28/nasy28.xml&sS.htm).

Jones, T. and Newburn, T. (2001) *Widening Access: Improving Police Relations with Hard to Reach Communities*, Police Research Series Paper No. 138, Research, Development and Statistics Directorate. London: Home Office.

Karla, V.S. (2002) Riots, race and reports: Denham, Cantle, Oldham and Burnley inquiries, *Sage Race Relations Abstracts*, 27 (4), 20–30.

Keane, J. (1998) *Civil Society: Old Images, New Visions*. Cambridge: Polity Press.

Keith, M. (1991) Policing a perplexed society? No-go areas and the mystification of police-black conflict, in E. Cashmore and E. McLaughlin (eds.) *Out of Order? Policing Black People*, pp. 189–214. London: Routledge.

Keith, M. (1993) *Race, Riots and Policing: Lore and Disorder in a Multi-Racist Society*. London: UCL Press.

Kennison, P. (2000) Being realist about stop and search, in A. Marlow and B. Loveday (eds.) *After Macpherson: Policing After the Stephen Lawrence Inquiry*, pp. 61–72. London: Russell House.

Khan, S. (2002) Sighthill shows way to harmony, *The Observer*, 26 May (retrieved from: http://observer.guardian.co.uk/asylum/story/0,1084,722558,00.html).

Knowles, C. (2003) *Race and Social Analysis*. London: Sage.

Kristeva, J. (1982) *Powers of Horror: An Essay in Abjection*. New York: Columbia University Press.

Kundani, H. (1999) Loss of nerve, *The Guardian*, 8 December (retrieved from: http://society.guardian.co.uk/societyguardian/story/0,7843,391361,00.html).

Kundnani, A. (2001a) From Oldham to Bradford: the violence of the violated, *Race and Class*, 43 (2), 105–31.

Kundnani, A. (2001b) In a foreign land: the new popular racism, *Race and Class*, 43 (2), 41–60.

Kushner, T. (2003) Meaning nothing but good: ethics, history and asylum seeker phobia in Britain, *Patterns of Prejudice*, 37 (3), 257–76.

Kushnick, L. (1999) Over policed and under protected: Stephen Lawrence, institutional and police practices, *Sociological Research Online*, 4 (1), pp. 1–14 (retrieved from: http://www.socresonline.org.uk/4/lawrence/Kushnick.html).

Lash, S. (1994a) Reflexivity and its doubles: structure, aesthetics, community, in U. Beck, A. Giddens and S. Lash (eds.) *Reflexive Modernization: Politics, Tradition and Aesthetics in the Modern Social Order*, pp. 110–73. Cambridge: Polity Press.

Lash, S. (1994b) Expert-systems or situated interpretations? Culture and institutions in disorganized capitalism, in U. Beck, A. Giddens and S. Lash (eds.) *Reflexive Modernization: Politics, Tradition and Aesthetics in the Modern Social Order*, pp. 198–215. Cambridge: Polity Press.

Lash, S. (1999) *Another Modernity: A Different Rationality*. Oxford: Blackwell.

Lash, S. and Wynne, B. (1992) Introduction, in U. Beck, *Risk Society: Towards a New Modernity*, pp. 1–8. London: Sage.

Lawrence, P.A. (1976) *Georg Simmel: Sociologist and European*. Walton-on-Thames: Thomas Nelson.

Laville, S. and Cowan, R. (2004) Gay murder victim survived Soho bomb, *The Guardian*, 2 November, http://www.guardian.co.uk/print/0,3858,5052995-103690,00.html, 1–2.

Laxer, G. (2003) Radical transformative nationalisms confront the US Empire, *Current Sociology*, 51 (2), 133–52.

Lea, J. (2000) The Macpherson Report and the question of institutional racism, *The Howard Journal*, 39 (3), 219–33.

Lea, J. and Young, J. (1984) *What Is to Be Done About Law and Order? Crisis in the Eighties*. Harmondsworth: Penguin Books.

Lemert, C. (1997) *Postmodernism Is Not What You Think*. Oxford: Blackwell.

Levitas, R. (1998) *The Inclusive Society? Social Exclusion and New Labour*. Basingstoke: Palgrave.

Lister, R. (1997) *Citizenship: Feminist Perspectives*. London: Macmillan.

Lister, R. (2001) New Labour: a study in ambiguity from a position of ambivalence, *Critical Social Policy*, 21 (4), 425–47.

Local Government Association (2002) *Guidance on Community Cohesion*. London: Home Office.

Lombardi, E.L., Wilchins, R.E., Priesing, D. and Malouf, D. (2001) Gender violence: transgender experiences with violence and discrimination, *Journal of Homosexuality*, 42 (1), 89–101.

Lupton, D. (1999) *Risk*. London: Routledge.

MacPherson, W. (1999) *The Stephen Lawrence Inquiry: Report of an Inquiry by Sir William MacPherson*, Cm 4262–1. London: Home Office.

Maffesoli, M. (1991) The ethic of aesthetics, *Theory, Culture and Society*, 8 (1), 7–20.

Malik, K. (1996) *The Meaning of Race: Race, History and Culture in Western Society*. London: Macmillan.

Mallett, L. (2001) *Hidden Targets: Lesbian Women and Gay Men's Experiences of Homophobic Crime and Harassment in Southampton*. Southampton: Southampton City Council.

Marinetto, M. (2003) Who wants to be an active citizen: the politics and practice of community involvement, *Sociology*, 37 (1), 103–20.

Marks, D. (2001) Disability and cultural citizenship: exclusion, 'integration' and resistance, in N. Stevenson (ed.) *Culture and Citizenship*, pp. 153–66. London: Sage.

Marshall, T.H. (1977) *Class, Citizenship and Social Development*. Chicago, IL: University of Chicago Press.

Martin, S.E. (1999) Police and the production of hate crimes: continuity and change in one jurisdiction, *Policing Quarterly*, 2 (4), 417–37.

Mason, G. (2002) *The Spectacle of Violence: Homophobia, Gender and Knowledge*. London: Routledge.

Mathews, R. and Pitts, J. (2001) Introduction: beyond criminology?, in R. Mathews and J. Pitts (eds.) *Crime, Disorder and Community Safety*, pp. 1–26. London: Routledge.

Mawby, R.I. and Walklate, S. (1994) *Critical Criminology: International Perspectives*. London: Sage.

McDowell, L. (2003) *Redundant Masculinities? Employment Change and White Working Class Youth*. Oxford: Blackwell.

McGhee, D. (2000) Wolfenden and the fear of 'homosexual spread': permeable boundaries and legal defences, *Studies in Law, Politics and Society*, 21, 65–97.

McGhee, D. (2001) *Homosexuality, Law and Resistance*, Routledge Research in Gender and Society. London: Routledge.

McLaughlin, E. (2002) Rocks and hard places: the politics of hate crime, *Theoretical Criminology*, 6 (4), 493–8.

McLaughlin, E. and Murji, K. (1999) After the Stephen Lawrence Report, *Critical Social Policy*, 19 (3), 371–85.

McManus, J. and Rivers, D. (2001) *Without Prejudice: A Guide for Community Safety Parterships on Responding to the Needs of Lesbians, Gays and Bisexuals* (retrieved from: www.nacro.org.uk).

McRobbie, A. (1997) Pecs and penises: the meaning of girlie culture, *Soundings*, 4, 205–44.

Miller, J., Quinton, P. and Bland, N. (2000) *Police Stops and Searches: Lessons from a Programme of Research Briefing Note*, Police Research Series Papers Nos. 127–32, Research, Development and Statistics Directorate. London: Home Office.

Minson, J. (1981) The assertion of homosexuality, *m/f*, 5 & 6, 19–36.

Misztal, B.A. (1996) *Trust in Modern Societies: The Search for the Bases of Social Order.* Cambridge: Polity Press.

Mooney, J. and Young, J. (2000) Policing ethnic minorities: stop and search in North London, in A. Marlow and B. Loveday (eds.) *After Macpherson: Policing After the Stephen Lawrence Inquiry*, pp. 73–88. London: Russell House.

Moran, L.J. (1996a) *The Homosexual(ity) of Law.* London: Routledge.

Moran, L.J. (1996b) The homosexualization of human rights, in C. Gearty and A. Tomkins (eds.) *Understanding Human Rights*, pp. 313–35. London: Mansell.

Moran, L.J. (2000) Victim surveys and beyond: researching violence against lesbians, gay men, bisexuals and transgender people, *SCOLAG Journal*, September, pp. 10–12.

Moran, L.J. (2001) Affairs of the heart: critical reflections on hate crime, *Law and Critique*, 12 (3), 1–15.

Moran, L.J. and McGhee, D. (1998) Perverting London: the cartographic practices of law, *Law and Critique*, IX (2), 207–24.

Moran, L.J and Skeggs, B. (2004) *Sexuality and the Politics of Violence and Safety.* London: Routledge.

Morris, S. (2003) Press whips up asylum hysteria, *The Guardian*, 24 January (retrieved from: http://society.guardian.co.uk/asylumseekers/story/o, 7991,881252,00.html).

Morrison, C. and MacKay, A. (2000) *The Experience of Violence and Harassment of Gay Men in the City of Edinburgh.* Edinburgh: Scottish Executive Central Research Unit.

Mouffe, C. (1992) Democratic politics today, in C. Mouffe (ed.) *Dimensions of Radical Democracy: Pluralism and Citizenship*, pp. 7–17. London: Verso.

Muncie, J. (1999) Institutionalized intolerance: youth justice and the 1998 Crime and Disorder Act, *Critical Social Policy*, 19 (2), 147–76.

Murray, C. (1990) *The Emerging British Underclass.* London: IEA Health and Welfare Unit.

Muslim Council of Britain (2003) Memorandum: House of Lords – Religious Offences in England and Wales – Minutes of Evidence (retrieved from: http://www.parliament_thestationery-office.co.uk/pa/ld200203/ldselect/ldrelof/95/210.htm).

Myslik, W.D. (1996) Renegotiating the social/sexual identities of places: gay communities as safe havens or sites of resistance, in N. Duncan (ed.) *Bodyspace: Destabilizing Geographies of Gender and Sexuality*, pp. 156–69. London: Routledge.

Newburn, T. and Jones, T. (2002) *Consultation By Crime and Disorder Partnerships*, Police Research Series Paper No. 148, Research, Development and Statistics Directorate. London: HMSO.

Oldham Independent Review (2001) *One Oldham One Future.* Oldham: Oldham Independent Review.

O'Malley, P. (1996) Indigenous governance, *Economy and Society*, 26, 301–26.

Osborne, T. (1998) *Aspects of Enlightenment: Social Theory and the Ethics of Truth.* London: UCL Press.

Parekh, B. (2000a) *The Future of Multi-Ethnic Britain.* London: Profile Books.

Parekh, B. (2000b) *Rethinking Multiculturalism: Cultural Diversity and Political Theory.* London: Macmillan.

Parker, S. (2003) BNP trebles seats, *The Guardian*, 2 May (retrieved from: http://society.guardian.co.uk/localgovelections/story/0,8150,948245,00.html).

Passerin d'Entrèves, M. (1994) *The Political Philosophy of Hannah Arendt.* London: Routledge.

Patton, C. (1993) Embodying subaltern memory: kinesthesia and the problematics of gender and race, in C. Schwichtenberg (ed.) *The Madonna Connection: Representational Politics, Subcultural Identities, and Cultural Theory*, pp. 81–105. Oxford: Westview Press.

Peacemaker (2001a) Youth justice boards small bids for voluntary organizations, 13 August 2001 (retrieved from: http://www.peace-maker.co.uk/projects/projects.asp?ID=3).

Peacemaker (2001b) Getting to know you – 'strangers' find they have a lot in common, 1 December (retrieved from: http://www.peace-maker.co.uk/projects/projects.asp?ID=5).

Phelan, S. (2001) *Sexual Strangers: Gays, Lesbians, and Dilemmas of Citizenship.* Philadelphia, PA: Temple University Press.

Plummer, K. (ed.) (1981) *The Making of the Modern Homosexual.* London: Hutchinson.

Plummer, K. (1995) *Telling Sexual Stories: Power, Change and Social Worlds.* London: Routledge.

Plummer, K. (2001) The square of intimate citizenship: some preliminary proposals, *Citizenship Studies*, 5 (3), 237–53.

Plummer, K. (2003) *Intimate Citizenship: Private Decisions and Public Dialogues.* Seattle, WA: University of Washington Press.

Powell, M. (2000) New Labour and the Third Way in British Welfare State: a new distinctive approach? *Critical Social Policy*, 20 (1), 39–60.

Press Association (2003a) Police officers injured in Wrexham violence, *The Guardian*, 24 June (retrieved from: http://society.guardian.co.uk/asylumseekers/story/0,7991,984058,00.html).

Press Association (2003b) New MacShane apology to UK Muslims, 3 December (retrieved from: http://politics.guardian.co.uk/labour/story/0,9061,1099154,00.html).

Probyn, E. (1998) *Mc*-identities: food and the familial citizen, *Theory, Culture and Society*, 15, 155–73.

Putnam, R.D. (2000) *Bowling Alone: The Collapse and Revival of American Community.* New York: Simon & Schuster.

Rattansi, A. (1992) Changing the subject? Racism, culture and education, in

J. Donald and A. Rattansi (eds.) *Race, Culture and Difference*, pp. 11–48. Sage Publications and Open University Press.

Rt. Hon. The Lord Goldsmith QC, Attorney General (2003) Memorandum: House of Lords – Religious Offences in England and Wales – Minutes of Evidence (retrieved from: http://www.parliamentthestationeryoffice.co.uk/pa/ld200203/ldselect/ldrelof/95/30116o.htm).

Ray, L. and Smith, D. (2002) Hate crime, violence and cultures of racism, in P. Iganski (ed.) *The Hate Debate: Should Hate be Punished as a Crime?*, pp. 88–102. London: Profile Books.

Raz, J. (1986) *The Morality of Freedom*. Oxford: Clarendon Press.

Renton, D. (2003) Examining the success of the British National Party, 1999–2003, *Race and Class*, 45 (2), 75–85.

Rhodes, R.A.W. (1997) *Understanding Governance: Polity Networks, Governance, Reflexivity and Accountability*. Buckingham: Open University Press.

Richardson, D. (1996) Heterosexuality and social theory, in D. Richardson (ed.) *Theorizing Heterosexuality: Telling it Straight*, pp. 1–20. Buckingham: Open University Press.

Richardson, D. (1998) Extending citizenship: cultural citizenship and sexuality, in N. Stevenson (ed.) *Cultural Citizenship*, pp. 42–59. London: Sage.

Richardson, D. (2000) *Rethinking Sexuality*. London: Sage.

Rivers, I. (2000) Going against the grain: supporting lesbian, gay and bisexual clients as they 'come out', *British Journal of Guidance and Counselling*, 28 (4), 503–13.

Rose, N. (1987) Beyond the public/private division: law, power and the family, *Journal of Law and Society*, 14 (1), 61–76.

Rose, N. (1990) *Governing the Soul*. London: Routledge.

Rose, N. (1994) Expertise and the government of conduct, *Studies in Law, Politics and Society*, 24, 359–67.

Rose, N. (1996a) Governing 'advanced' liberal democracies, in A. Barry, T. Osborne and N. Rose (eds.) *Foucault and Political Reason: Liberalism, Neo-liberalism and Rationalities of Government*, pp. 27–64. London: UCL Press.

Rose, N. (1996b) The death of the social? Re-figuring the territory of government, *Economy and Society*, 25 (3), 327–56.

Rose, N. (1999) *The Powers of Freedom: Reframing Political Thought*. Cambridge: Cambridge University Press.

Rose, N. (2000) Community, citizenship, and the Third Way, *American Behavioral Scientist*, 43 (9), 1395–1411.

Rubin, G. (1992) Thinking sex, in C.S. Vance (ed.) *Pleasure and Danger*, pp. 267–319. London: HarperCollins.

Runnymede Trust (2001) *Addressing the Challenge of Islamophobia*. London: Commission on British Muslims and Islamophobia.

Runnymede Trust (2002) *The Nature of Islamophobia* (retrieved from: http://www.runnymedetrust.org/meb/islamophobia/nature.html).

Sanderson, I. (1999) Participation and democratic renewal: from 'instrumental' to 'communicative rationality'?, *Policy and Politics*, 27 (3), 325–41.

Scarman, Lord (1981) *The Brixton Disorders 10–12 April 1981: Report of an Inquiry by the Rt. Hon. Lord Scarman*, Cmnd. 8427. London: HMSO.

Schedler, P. and Glastra, F. (2001) Communicating policy in late modern society: on the boundaries of interactive policymaking, *Policy and Politics*, 29 (3), 337–49.

Scheerer, S. (1998) The delinquent as a fading category of knowledge, in V. Ruggerio, N. South and I. Taylor (eds.) *The New European Criminology: Social Order in Europe*, pp. 425–42. London: Routledge.

Schuster, L. and Solomos, J. (2001) Asylum, refuge and public policy: current trends and future dilemmas, *Sociological Research Online*, 6 (1) (retrieved from: http://www.socresonline.org.uk/6/1/Schuster.html).

Schuster, L. and Solomos, J. (2002) Rights and wrongs across European borders: migrants, minorities and citizenship, *Citizenship Studies*, 6 (1), 37–54.

Seamark, M. and Taylor, B. (2003) Hooked by the Sheik of hate, *Daily Mail*, 2 May, p. 1.

Sears, N. (2003) Prep school charmer who joked that he shared a film star's name, *Daily Mail*, 2 May, p. 6.

Seidman, S. (2002) *Beyond the Closet: The Transformation of Gay and Lesbian Life*. London: Routledge.

Sennett, R. (1974) *The Fall of Public Man*. Cambridge: Cambridge University Press.

Sennett, R. (1998) *The Corrosion of Character: The personal Consequences of Work in the New Capitalism*. New York: Norton.

Shearing, C.D. and Stenning, P.C. (1996) From the Panopticon to Disney World: the development of discipline, in J. Muncie, E. McLaughlin and M. Langan (eds.) *Criminological Perspectives: A Reader*, pp. 413–22. London: Sage in association with the Open University.

Sibley, D. (1995) *Geographies of Exclusion*. London: Routledge.

Simmel, G. (1950) *The Sociology of Georg Simmel* (translated and edited by K.H. Wolff). London: Collier Macmillan.

Sivanandan, A. (2000) *Macpherson and After*, Institute of Race Relations (retrieved from: http://www.irr.org.uk/cgi-bin/news/printable.pl).

Sivanandan, A. (2001) Poverty is the new black, *Race and Class*, 43 (2), 1–6.

Sivanandan, A. (2002) Poverty is the new black: beyond 9/11, in P. Scraton (ed.) *Beyond September 11: An Anthology of Dissent*, pp. 113–17. London: Pluto Press.

Smart, C. (1990) Feminist approaches to criminology or postmodern woman meets atavistic man, in A. Morris and L. Gelsthorpe (eds.) *Feminist Perspectives in Criminology*, pp. 71–84. Milton Keynes: Open University Press.

Smith, A.N. (1990) A symptomology of an authoritarian discourse, *New Formations*, 10 (Spring), pp. 41–65.

Smith, A.N. (1994) *New Right Discourse on Race and Sexuality: Britain 1968–1990*. Cambridge: Cambridge University Press.

Smith, K.T. (1971) Homophobia: a tentative personality profile, *Psychological Reports*, 29 (1), 1091–4.

Smith, L. (2001) Britain: Bradford is fourth city hit by riots, *World Socialist Web Site*, 10 July (retrieved from: http://www.wsws.org/articles/2001/jul2001/brad-j10.shtml).

Smith, L. (2003) Asylum-seekers targeted by rioters in Wales, *World Socialist Web Site*, 9 July (retrieved from: http://www.wsws.org/articles/2003/jul2003/asyl-j09.shtml).

Solomos, J. (1993a) Constructions of black criminality: racialization and criminalization in perspective, in D. Cook and B. Hudson (eds.) *Race and Criminology*, pp. 118–35. London: Sage.

Solomos, J. (1993b) *Race and Racism in Britain*, 2nd edn. London: Macmillan.

Solomos, J. (1999) Social research and the Stephen Lawrence Inquiry, *Sociological Research Online*, 4 (1), pp. 1–7 (retrieved from: http://www.socresonline.org.uk/4/lawrence/Solomos.html).

Solomos, J. (2001) Race, multi-culturalism and difference, in N. Stevenson (ed.) *Culture and Citizenship*, pp. 198–211. London: Sage.

Solomos, J. and Rackett, T. (1991) Policing and urban unrest: problem constitution and policy response, in E. Cashmore and E. McLaughlin (eds.) *Out of Order? Policing Black People*, pp. 42–64. London: Routledge.

Southampton City Council (2001) *The Renaissance of the City – Southampton City Strategy, Southampton: The Inclusive City* (retrieved from: http://www.southampton.gov.uk/citylife/city_strategy/inclusive.htm).

Spargo, T. (1999) *Foucault and Queer Theory*. Cambridge: Totem Books.

Stanko, E. (1985) *Intimate Intrusions: Women's Experience of Male Violence*. London: Routledge & Kegan Paul.

Stanko, E. (2001) Re-conceptualising the policing of hatred: confessions and worrying dilemmas of a consultant, *Law and Critique*, 12, 309–29.

Stenson, K. (1998) Beyond histories of the present, *Economy and Society*, 27 (4), 333–52.

Stevenson, N. (2002) Cosmopolitanism, multiculturalism and citizenship, *Sociological Research Online*, 7 (1), pp. 1–17 (retrieved from: http://www.socresonline.org.uk/7/1/stevenson.html).

Stevenson, N. (2003) *Cultural Citizenship: Cosmopolitan Questions*. Basingstoke: Open University Press/McGraw-Hill Education.

Sullivan, A. (1995) *Virtually Normal: An Argument about Homosexuality*. New York: Picador.

Taylor, C. (1992) *Multiculturalism and 'The Politics of Recognition': An Essay by Charles Taylor*. Princeton, NJ: Princeton University Press.

Taylor, M. (2003) Minister's call to choose outrages British muslims, *The Guardian*, 22 November (retrieved from: http://politics.guardian.co.uk/foreignaffairs/story/0,1090902,00.html).

Taylor, M. (2004) BNP faces internal revolt and financial turmoil, *The Guardian*, 2 August, p. 5.

Taylor, S. (1984) The Scarman Report and explanations of riots, in J. Benyon (ed.) *Scarman and After: Essays Reflecting Lord Scarman's Report, the Riots and Their Aftermath*, pp. 20–36. Oxford: Pergamon Press.

Tempest, M. (2004a) It boils down to intolerance, *The Guardian*, 2 July (retrieved from: http://politics.guardian.co.uk/homeaffairs/story/0,1252905,00.html).

Tempest, M. (2004b) Doubts grow over religious hate law, *The Guardian*, 7 July (retrieved from: http://society.guardian.c.uk/crimeandpunishment/story/0,8150,1256002,00.html).

Thompson, S. and Hoggett, P. (2001) The emotional dynamics of deliberative democracy, *Policy and Politics*, 29 (1), 351–64.

Tomsen, S. and Mason, G. (2001) Engendering homophobia: violence, sexuality and gender conformity, *Journal of Sociology*, 37 (3), 257–73.

Travis, A. (2002) Anger at Blunkett 'Whining maniacs' attacks, *The Guardian*, 6 September, p. 6.

Travis, A. (2003) Law Lords to reappraise anti-terror rules, *The Guardian*, 5 August (retrieved from: http://politics.guardian.co.uk/homeaffairs/story/0,1012351,00.html).

Turner, B.S. (2001) The erosion of citizenship, *British Journal of Sociology*, 52 (2), 189–209.

Turner, B.S. (2002) Cosmopolitan virtue, globalization and patriotism, *Theory, Culture and Society*, 19 (1–2), 45–63.

Valier, C. (2002) Punishment, border crossings and the powers of horror, *Theoretical Criminology*, 6 (3), 319–37.

Valier, C. and Lippens, R. (2004) Moving images, ethics and justice, *Punishment and Society*, 6 (3), 319–33.

Valverde, M. (1996) 'Despotism' and ethical liberal governance, *Economy and Society*, 25 (3), 357–72.

Van Krieken, R.V. (1999) The barbarism of civilization: cultural genocide and the 'stolen generations', *British Journal of Sociology*, 50 (2), 297–315.

Van Loon, J. (2002) *Risk and Technological Culture: Towards a Sociology of Virulence*. London: Routledge.

Viscount Colville of Culross (2003) Lords report predicts that amending legislation on religious offences is likely to be controversial (retrieved from: http://www.parliament.uk/parliamentary_committees/lords_press_notices/pn100603ro.cfm).

Waddington, P.A. (1999) Discretion, respectability and institutional police racism, *Sociological Research Online*, 4 (1), 1–12 (retrieved from: http://www.socresonline.org.uk/4/lawrence/waddington.html).

Walklate, S. (1996) Community and crime prevention, in E. McLaughlin and J. Muncie (eds.) *Controlling Crime*, pp. 293–331. London: Sage.

Walklate, S. (1998) Excavating the fear of crime: fear, anxiety or trust, *Theoretical Criminology*, 2 (4), 403–18.

Warner, M. (1993) Introduction, in M. Warner (ed.) *Fear of a Queer Planet*, pp. vii–xxxi. Minneapolis, MN: University of Minnesota Press.

Warner, M. (1999) *The Trouble With Normal: Sex, Politics, and the Ethics of Queer Life*. Cambridge, MA: Harvard University Press.

Weaver, M. (2003) CRE head blames asylum dispersal for riots, *The Guardian*, 1 July (retrieved from: http://society.guardian.co.uk/asylumseekers/story/0,7991,988966,00.html).

Weber, L. and Bowling, B. (2002) The policing of immigration in the new world disorder, in P. Scraton (ed.) *Beyond September 11: An Anthology of Dissent*, pp. 123–9. London: Pluto Press.

Weekly Worker (2002) Blair's Bradford witch-hunt: injury to one is injury to all, *Weekly Worker*, 1 August (retrieved from: http://www.cpgb.org.uk/wprker/443/bradford.html).

Weeks, J. (1977) *Coming Out*. London: Quartet.

Weeks, J. (1986) *Sexuality*. London: Routledge.

Weeks, J. (1989) *Sex, Politics and Society*. London: Longman.

Weeks, J. (1995) *Invented Moralities: Sexual Values in the Age of Uncertainty*. Cambridge: Polity Press.

Weeks, J. (1996) The idea of a sexual community, *Soundings*, 2 (Spring), 71–84.

Weeks, J. (1999) 'Sexual citizenship', *Theory, Culture and Society*, 15 (3–4), 35–52.

Weeks, J., Heaphy, B. and Donovan, C. (2001) *Same Sex Intimacies: Families of Choice and Other Life Experiments*. London: Routledge.

Weinberg, G. (1972) *Society and the Healthy Homosexual*. New York: St. Martin's Press.

Weissberg, R. (1998) *Political Tolerance: Balancing Community and Diversity*. London: Sage.

Weller, P., Feldman, A. and Purdam, K. (2001) *Religious Discrimination in England and Wales*, Home Office Research Study No. 220. London: Home Office.

Werbner, P. (1997) Essentialising essentialism, essentialising silence: ambivalence and multiplicity in the constructions of racism and ethnicity, in P. Werbner and T. Modood (eds.) *Debating Cultural Hybridity: Multi-cultural Identities and the Politics of Anti-racism*, pp. 226–56. London: Zed Press.

West, D.J. (1977) *Homosexuality Re-Examined*. London: Duckworth.

White, M. (2004) Migrants: Blair acts on benefits, *The Guardian*, 18 February, p. 1.

Whittle, S. (2000) *The Transgender Debate: The Crisis Surrounding Gender Identities*. Reading, UK: South Street Press.

Willmott, P. (1987) Introduction: policing and the community, in P. Willmott (ed.) *Policing and the Community*, pp. 1–16. London: Policy Studies Institute.

Wilson, A.R. (1993) Which equality? Toleration, difference or respect, in J. Bristow and A.R. Wilson (eds.) *Activating Theory: Lesbian, Gay, Bisexual Politics*, pp. 171–89. London: Lawrence & Wishart.

Wintour, P. (2001) Blunkett told to drop hate clause, *The Guardian*, 12 December (retrieved from: http://www.guardian.co.uk/Archive/Article/0,4273.4318092,00.html).

Wolfenden, Lord (1957) *Report of the Departmental Committee on Homosexual Offences and Prostitution*, Cmnd 247. London: HMSO.

Yanay, N. (2002) Hatred as ambivalence, *Theory, Culture and Society*, 19 (3), 71–88.

Yeatman, A. (2001) Feminism and citizenship, in N. Stevenson (ed.) *Culture and Citizenship*, pp. 138–52. London: Sage.

Young, I.M. (1990) *Justice and the Politics of Difference*. Princeton, NJ: Princeton University Press.

Young, I.M. (1997) Difference as a resource for democratic communication, in J. Bohman and W. Rehg (eds.) *Deliberative Democracy: Essays on Reason and Politics*, pp. 383–406. Cambridge, MA: MIT Press.

Young, J. (1999a) *The Exclusive Society: Social Exclusion, Crime and Difference in Late Modernity*. London: Sage.

Young, J. (1999b) Cannibalism and bulimia: patterns of social control in late modernity, *Theoretical Criminology*, 3 (4), 387–407.

Young, J. (2003) To these wet and windy shores: recent immigration policy in the UK, *Punishment and Society*, 5 (4), 449–62.

Young-Breuhl, E. (1996) *The Anatomy of Prejudices*. Cambridge, MA: Harvard University Press.

Yuval-Davis, N. (1994) Women, ethnicity and empowerment, *Feminism and Psychology*, 4 (1), 179–97.

Zizek, S. (1990) Eastern European republics of Gilead, *New Left Review*, 183, 50–62.

Zizek, S. (1994) *The Metastases of Enjoyment: Six Essays on Woman and Causality*. London: Verso.

Index

n/ns refers to note/s, *passim* indicates numerous scattered mentions within page range.

abjection theory, 80
ACPO *see* Association of Chief Police
    Officers
active citizenship, 75, 122, 136–7, 159, 182
active communities, 182
adiaphorization, 111–12
African-Caribbean community/youth,
    18–35 *passim*
    and Asian community, 41–2, 190*n*
    stop and search, 36–7, 38, 189–90*n*
Ahmed, Lord, 102, 103
Al Yafai, F., 85, 86
Alexander, C., 41–2, 60, 61, 99, 100, 102
Alibhai-Brown, Y., 166, 167
anti-hate crime and emergent subjectivities,
    137–40, 199*n*
Anti-Nazi League, 44
Anti-Terrorism, Crime and Security Act
    (2001), 95–6, 97–102, 193–4*n*
    Clause, 39 101–2, 105–6, 110–11
Arendt, H., 51–2, 55, 170–1
Asian community/youth, 36–7, 41–2, 190*n*
    see also Bradford; Burnley; community
    cohesion; Muslim community; Oldham
Association of Chief Police Officers (ACPO),
    27–8, 32
    homophobia issue, 125–7, 128, 129, 134–5,
    148–9, 153, 154–5, 158
Asylum Bill (2003), 90–1
asylum issue, 65–7
    case studies, 82–7, 192*ns*
    deterrence, 67–71
    dispersal policy, 69–70, 71, 78–82, 87,
    191*n*
    Far Right organisations, 83, 87–9
    managed integration, 71–5
    post, 9/11 responses, 75–8
Attorney-General, role of, 107–9
Audit Commission, 68, 69, 70, 81–2
authoritarian populism, Bradford, 58–63
Azam, M., 90

Back, L. *et al.*, 58, 77, 181, 183
'bad apples thesis', 21, 24
'balkanization' of criminal law, 31, 32
Bauman, Z., 112, 166, 176
BDRR *see* Bradford District Race Review
    Report
Beck, U., 4, 5, 42, 62, 68, 165, 168, 170, 171,
    174, 176, 185
Bell, D. and Binnie, J., 147, 159
Benhabib, S., 51, 52, 173–4
Benyon, J., 19
Bishop, Lord, 105, 110
Blair, Tony, 101, 163, 164, 177, 203*n*
blasphemy, 95, 96
Blunkett, David, 58–61 *passim*, 70–1, 72, 74–
    5, 79–80, 100–1, 116, 123, 165–6, 171,
    190*n*
BNP *see* British National Party
Bourdieu, P., 54–5
Bourne, J., 22, 24, 25, 30, 31, 181
Bowling, B., 16–17, 18, 21, 37
    and Phillips, C., 21, 25, 32
Bradford, 44–5, 48, 57–8, 71
    'community' defence and authoritarian
    populism in, 58–63
    sentences, 58–61, 62–3, 190*ns*
Bradford District Race Review (BDRR) Report,
    48–50, 51, 53
Bradfordian People Programme, 49–50, 53
Bridges, L., 36, 37
Bristow, J., 145
British citizenship, 45, 149, 159
    asylum/immigration policy, 72–3, 74–5
    crisis in, 6–8
    emergent, 11–12
    second generation immigrants, 58, 62
    see also citizenship
British National Party (BNP), 43, 44, 62, 83,
    88
    anti-Islamic publications, 104, 112
    policy, 88–9

Brixton (Scarman Inquiry), 18–23, 24,
33–4
Brooks, Duwayne, 16, 20, 27
Burnley, 44, 45, 48, 57–8, 59, 61, 62, 71

Caia Park Estate, Wrexham (asylum case
study), 85–7
Campbell, B., 86, 89
CBMI *see* Commission on British Muslims
and Islamophobia
CCRT *see* Community Cohesion Review
Team Report
Chandler, D., 121, 124, 132
citizenship
active, 75, 122, 136–7, 159, 182
cosmopolitan, 169–73
cultural, 170–2
identity and, 172
'intimate citizenship', 146–7, 200n
reflexive, 149
sexual, 146–9, 151–2, 160, 200–1ns
'technologies of citizenship', 139, 199n
see also British citizenship
Cohen, P., 67, 89
Colville, Viscount, 115
Combat, 18 61, 83
Commission on British Muslims and
Islamophobia (CBMI), 99, 100
'commonality in difference', 167
community cohesion
facilitation of, 51–5
lack of, 45–51
and managed integration, 71–5
Community Cohesion Review Team (CCRT)
Report, 46–8, 55–6, 190n
'community' defence, Bradford, 58–63
community safety and homophobia,
122–3
community safety units, 35, 189n
'community/ies' and Third Way politics,
182–4, 205n
Connolly, W.E., 184
consultation, politics of, 32–5
cosmopolitan citizenship, 169–73
cosmopolitanization, 173–82
CPS *see* Crown Prosecution Service
Crawford, A., 123
Crawley, H., 68, 70–1
Creppell, I., 8–9, 10, 32, 92, 163–4
Crime and Disorder Act (1998)
community safety, 122, 123, 198n

racial minorities, 28, 30, 33, 34, 95, 96–7
sexual minorities (lgbt), 120, 127, 142,
150–6
Crime Reduction Toolkit, 187–8ns
Criminal Libel Act (1819), 95, 96
Crown Prosecution Service (CPS), 133,
154–5, 158, 160
Cruikshank, B., 54, 137, 138–79
cultural citizenship, 170–2

Dag, Firsat, 82, 83, 84, 85
de-homosexualization of sex offences,
156–60
decriminalization of homosexuality, 143–50,
200–1n
Denham, J., 73
Denham Report, 43, 44, 57, 60
Department of the Environment, Transport
and the Regions (DETR), 120, 121, 123,
124
deprivation
family circumstances, 22–3
host community, 82–3, 86
vs. cultural factors, 55–7
Dilley, R., 81
dispersal policy, 69–70, 71, 78–82, 87, 191n
disturbances, 99–100
see also Bradford; Brixton; Burnley; Caia
Park Estate, Wrexham; Oldham;
Sighthill, Glasgow
Dodd, V. and Seenan, G., 84, 85
Dohlakia, Lord, 113
Doward, J. and Hinsliff, G., 99

el-Faisal, Sheikh Abdullah, 112
elites, 182, 205n
Ellison, N., 149
emergent British citizenship, 11–12
emergent subjectivities, 137–40, 199n
emotion in contemporary culture, 5–6
Erjavec, K., 77, 80
European Commission Against Racism and
Intolerance (ECRI), 69, 70, 95
European Convention on Human Rights
(ECHR), 98, 105, 157, 194n, 202ns
European Monitoring Centre on Racism and
Xenophobia, 101, 103
Evans, D., 145–6, 170

Fair Justice For All, 59–60, 61, 62
Fairclough, N., 57, 121, 177

'familial citizen', 159
family circumstances, African-Caribbeans, 22–3
Far Right perspectives
    asylum issue, 83, 87–9
    post-9/11 100, 103–5, 110, 111
    see also specific organizations
Fekete, L., 68, 69, 79, 82, 83–4, 97, 98
Fish, S., 113
Forum Against Islamophobia and Racism, 97, 103–4, 107–8, 196*n*
Fraser, N., 56, 57
freedom of expression and incitement to religious hatred, 105–7, 112–13
Freud, S., 78, 79, 192*n*
Furedi, F., 5, 172, 177, 179
Fuss, D., 53, 55

Garland, D., 63
gay, lesbian, bisexual and transgendered (lgbt) communities, 118, 119, 197*ns*
    see also homophobia; sexual minorities
gendered issue of disturbances, 85–6, 99
Giddens, A., 4, 5, 11–12, 33, 72–3, 78, 121, 146, 149, 173, 182, 205*n*
Gilroy, P., 22, 35, 37
'gross indecency', 159–60
Guidance on Community Cohesion (GCC) Report, 47, 51, 52, 53–4
Gullick, Judge Stephen, 59–61

habitus, 54–5
Hall, S., 12, 53, 169
Hampshire Constabulary, 130
Hampshire Police Authority, 130
'hard to reach' groups, 151–2
hate
    and institutional reflexivity, 4–8
    social problem of, 1–4, 124–9
'hate crimes'
    ACPO definition, 27–8
    homophobia (lgbt), 125–8, 151–5
    initiatives, 34–5
    legislation, 7–8, 28–32, 34–5
    probation services programmes, 178–9, 205*n*
    sentence enhancement, 29–30
Her Majesty's Inspectorate of Constabularies (HMIC), 34, 38, 149, 153, 154–5, 158
Herek, G.M. and Berrill, K.T., 126
heteronormativity, 169, 203–4*n*

Heyd, D., 10
Hill, A., 82–3, 84
Hillyard, P., 100–1
HL *see* House of Lords Select Committee on Religious Offences
Holdaway, S., 33–4
Home Affairs Select Committee, 87–8
Home Office, 28, 37–8
    CCRT Report, 46–8, 55–6, 190*n*
    Crime Reduction Toolkit, 187–8*ns*
    Fair Justice For All campaign, 59–60
    immigration/asylum, 67, 69–75 *passim*, 77, 79–80, 85
    Morgan Report/community safety, 122–3
    sexual minorities (lgbt), 150, 151, 152, 156–8, 159–60, 162, 202–3*n*
homophobia, 118–20
    anti-hate crime and emergent subjectivities, 137–40, 199*n*
    community safety, 122–3
    New Labour modernisation agenda, 120–2, 139–40
    social harm of hate, 124–9
    Southampton (case study), 129–37, 198–9*ns*
homosexuality *see* sexual minorities
House of Lords (HL) Select Committee on Religious Offences, 94, 95, 102, 104, 105–7, 108–9, 109–11, 113–15, 195*ns*, 196*ns*
housing stocks and dispersal policy, 81–2
Hughes, G., 111
Human Rights Act (1998), 105
Hussain, Y. and Bagguley, P., 43, 57–8, 62, 170

ICPS *see* Inter-Community Peer Support Project
identity and citizenship, 172
Iganski, P., 28–9, 112
Ignatieff, M., 41, 42, 78, 79, 178
Immigration and Asylum Act (1999), 67–8, 69–70, 80, 88
incitement to racial hatred, 95, 96–7, 107, 109, 193*ns*
incitement to religious hatred, 96, 97, 101–2, 104–5, 107–9
    and freedom of expression, 105–7, 112–13
    in international law, 94–5
    message of legislation, 109–15
    UK religious offences and, 95–102

Institute of Race Relations, 23–4
'institutional complex', 184–5, 205*n*
institutional racism, 21–2, 23, 24–6
institutional reflexivity, 4–8, 9
institutionalized homophobia, 128–9, 154
integration
  managed, 71–5
  multicultural strategies, 6–7, 186*n*
Inter-Community Peer Support (ICPS)
    Project, 177–8, 204–5*n*
International Covenant on Civil and
    Political Rights, 94–5
'intimate citizenship', 146–7, 200*n*
Islamophobia, 80, 98, 99, 101–2
  see also Muslim community

Jacobs, J.B. and Potter, K., 1, 7, 29–31, 32,
    93, 110, 177
James, A., 178
Jefferson, T., 41
Jenness, V. and Broad, K., 17–18, 93
'joined up government', 120–2

Karla, V.S., 50, 55
Khan, Imran (Lawrence family solicitor),
    20, 27
Khan, Sadiq, 99
Knowles, C., 67, 89
Kristeva, J., 80
Kundnani, H., 50, 77, 79, 80–1, 82, 181
Kushner, T., 77, 181
Kushnick, L., 37

'language clusters', asylum seeker policy,
    81, 82, 84
Lash, S., 4, 6, 34, 165
Laville, S. and Cowan, R., 118
Lawrence family, 17, 18, 20, 26, 27
Lawrence, Stephen (MacPherson Inquiry/
    Report)
  criticisms of Inquiry, 20–1, 25–6, 32
  Institute of Race Relations, 23–4
  institutional racism, 24–5
  Report recommendations, 27, 28, 33, 34,
    35–6, 37–9, 187–8*ns*
  and Scarman Inquiry (Brixton), 18–21,
    38
  significance of, 16–18
legislation
  asylum/immigration, 65–6
  'hate crimes', 7–8, 28–32, 34–5

incitement to racial hatred, 95, 96–7, 107,
    109, 193*ns*
  Race Relations, 36, 94, 189*n*
  sexual offences, reform, 143–50, 156–60,
    200–1*n*
  see also incitement to religious hatred;
    specific Acts
Levitas, R., 57
Local Government Act (1999), 120, 122, 123
Local Government Association/GCC Report,
    5, 47, 51, 52, 53–4
local government, stakeholder-oriented, 121,
    197–8*n*
loyalty, 101, 166, 195*n*
Lucas, Lord, 106, 107
Lupton, D., 80

McLaughlin, E., 7–8
  and Murji, K., 17, 20, 26, 36
McManus, J. and Rivers, D., 126, 127, 128–9
MacPherson Inquiry/Report *see* Lawrence,
    Stephen
Malik, K., 65, 66, 101
Mallet, L., 130, 131, 134, 135–6
managed integration, 71–5
managed migration, 181
Mandla v. Dowell Lee, 96–7
'marginalization boxes', 175
Mathews, R. and Pitts, J., 132
Metropolitan Police Service, 18, 19, 20, 33–4
  criticisms of, 20–1
  'minority ethnic staff', 34–5, 189*n*
  stop and search, 36–7, 189–90*n*
Miller, J. *et al.*, 37–8
Misztal, B.A., 6, 9–10, 133–4
mixophilia/mixophobia, 176–7
modernisation agenda, New Labour, 120–2,
    139–40
modernisation, reflexive, 4–5, 12, 185
modernity
  reflexive, 165
  to late modernity, 175
Mooney, J. and Young, J., 38–9
moral neutrality (adiaphorization), 111–12
moral panics, 60–1, 75, 76–7
Moran, L.J., 126, 128, 138
  and Skeggs, B., 8, 127–8
Morgan Report/community safety, 122–3
Mouffe, C., 171, 172
multi-agency groups (lgbt), 130–3, 134,
    135–6, 198*n*

multiculturalism, 56, 57, 165–9
  integration strategies, 6–7, 186n
  paradox, 181
  vs. cosmopolitanization, 173
Muslim community
  asylum seekers, 80
  ethnic and cultural diversity, 97, 194n
  impact of anti-terrorism laws, 98–102,
    194–5ns
  Islamophobia, 80, 98, 99, 101–2
  lack of legal protection, 94, 96, 97, 102–5,
    112
  see also asylum issue
Muslim Council of Britain, 94, 102, 108

narcissism of minor differences, 78, 79
Naseri, Davoud Rasui, 83
National Front, 44–5, 61, 62
negative aspects of tolerance, 8–10
neighbourhood nationalism, 89, 192n
'new' Britain, 165–9
New Labour, 66–7, 124, 180, 181, 183
  modernisation agenda, 120–2, 139–40
  politics of deterrence, 67–71
Newburn, T. and Jones, T., 151–2
9/11 attacks, 75–8, 92, 97, 102–4

Oldham, 43, 45, 48, 57–8, 59, 61, 62, 71
  ICPS Project, 177–8, 204–5n
Operation Swamp (Swamp '81), 19–20
Osborne, T., 179–80
'other', 1, 9
  self and, 53
Ousely, Lord, 87

Pakistani community see Asian community/
  youth; Bradford; Burnley; community
  cohesion; Muslim community; Oldham
Parekh, B., 167, 170, 184
participation and cosmopolitanization,
  173–5
Phillips, Trevor, 86, 87, 192n
Plummer, K., 52, 146–7, 170
Police and Criminal Evidence Act (1984), 34
policing
  and racial minorities, 18–21
  and sexual minorities, 124–9, 150–6
  stop and search powers, 19, 20, 35–9, 187n,
    189–90ns
  see also specific communities and police
    sevices/organizations

political theory of judgement, 51–2
politics
  of consultation, 32–5
  of deterrence, 67–71
  of managed integration, 71–5
'polluting persons', 179
Powell, Enoch, 66
prejudice, forms of, 1–2, 3
print media perspectives, 26, 70, 72, 77,
  79–80, 81, 84
privacy and homosexuality, 143–50, 161–2,
  200–1n
probation services programmes, 178–9,
  205n
problem-oriented approach to crime,
  124–5
prostitution see Wolfenden Committee/
  Report
'protective inclusionism', 3
psychoanalytical perspectives, 2–3, 78–9,
  192n
Public Order Act (1986), 95, 96–7, 107, 108,
  109, 112, 193ns
Putnam, R.D., 48, 50, 53, 176

race and policing, 18–21
Race Relations Act (1976), 95, 96, 193n
Race Relations legislation, 36, 94, 189n
'racial group', legal definition, 96–7, 194n
racial hatred, incitement to, 95, 96–7, 107,
  109, 193ns
'racial incident', 29
  ACPO definition, 27–8, 188n
  under-reporting, 31, 33, 188n
'racially aggravated offences', 28–9, 95, 96–7,
  188n
racism
  institutional, 21–2, 23, 24–6
  print media perspectives, 26, 70
  social problem of race vs., 23–4
  xeno-racism, 68, 78, 191n
Raz, J., 9
reflexive citizenship, 149
reflexive modernisation, 4–5, 12, 185
reflexive modernity, 165
Religious Offences Bill (2002), 96, 105
  see also House of Lords (HL) Select
    Committee on Religious Offences
religiously aggravated offences, 95–6, 97,
  193–4n
Renton, D., 80, 90

Richardson, D., 141, 148, 150, 161, 170
risk sensibility, 77–8
risk society, 4–5, 186*n*
Rose, N., 54, 55, 110–11, 121, 122, 131–2,
    138–9, 144, 166–7, 175, 182, 183
Rubin, G., 144–5
Runnymede Trust, 103
Rushdie (Salman) affair, 96

Scarman Inquiry (Brixton disturbances),
    18–23, 24, 33–4
Schedler, P. and Glastra, F., 121–2, 136
second generation immigrants, 58, 62
security issue, 72–3, 76
    see also Anti-Terrorism, Crime and Security
    Act (2001)
Seidman, S., 155, 160, 161
self and 'other', 53
Sennett, R., 5
sentence(s)
    Bradford disturbances, 58–61, 62–3, 190*ns*
    enhancement, 29–30, 97
sexual citizenship, 146–9, 151–2, 160,
    200–1*ns*
sexual minorities, 141–2
    lgbt communities, 118, 119, 197*ns*
    and policing, 124–9, 150–6
    and privacy, 143–50, 161–2, 200–1*n*
    see also homophobia
Sexual Offences Acts, 142, 144–5, 157,
    202*ns*
sexual offences, reform of legislation,
    143–50, 156–60, 200–1*n*
Sighthill, Glasgow (asylum case study),
    82–5, 192*ns*
Sivanandan, A., 17, 25, 26, 67–8, 78
Smith, A.M., 65, 145
Smith, Glen, 99
social capital
    bonding/bridging, 48, 50, 51, 53, 57,
    172–3
    and habitus, 54–5
social problems
    of hate, 1–4, 124–9
    of race vs. racism, 23–4
Solomos, J., 17, 25, 66, 168–9, 170, 183
    and Rackett, T., 22, 23
Southampton Gay Community Health
    Service (GCHS), 130
Southampton (homophobia case study),
    129–37, 198–9*ns*

space *see* privacy and homosexuality
stakeholder-oriented local government,
    121, 197–8*n*
Stevenson, N., 169, 170, 171, 172, 173,
    180, 184–5
Stone, Richard, 99
stop and search powers, 19, 20, 35–9,
    187*n*, 189–90*ns*
Straw, Jack, 20, 69, 150
subjectivities, emergent, 137–40, 199*n*

Tebbitt, Norman, 101
'technologies of citizenship', 139, 199*n*
Terrorism Act (2000), 97–8, 99
Thatcher, Margaret, 65–6, 101
Third Way politics, 11–12, 32, 45
    community, 182–4, 205*n*
toleration
    definitions/models, 9–11
    negative aspects of, 8–10
    and Third Way politics, 11–12
Travis, A., 58–9, 60, 87–8, 98
'trust building', 7, 34, 133–5, 152–3

under-reporting of crime, 31, 33, 128–9,
    188*n*
United Nations (UN) Human Rights
    Committee, 94–5
United States (USA), 30–1, 155, 160,
    177
    9/11 attacks, 75, 75–8, 92, 97, 102–4

Valier, C., 60, 61, 76–7
    and Lippens, R., 18
Van Loon, J., 73, 74, 76, 77–8
violence, homophobic, 148–9, 201*n*
voucher system, 68–9

Weaver, M., 86, 87
Weber, L. and Bowling, B., 75, 76
Weeks, J., 144, 146, 162, 170
Weissberg, R., 177
Werbner, P., 96
West, D.J., 143
West Yorkshire Police Force, 61
Widdecombe, A., 100
Wilkinson, S., 85
Wolfenden Committee/Report, 138–46
    passim, 154–61 *passim*

xeno-racism, 67–8, 78, 191*n*

Young, I.M., 56, 122, 144
Young, J., 3, 57–8, 71, 111, 166, 167–8, 175
   Mooney, J. and, 38–9

Young-Breuhl, E., 1–2

Zizek, S., 2

Related books from Open University Press

Purchase from www.openup.co.uk or order through your local bookseller

WORK, CONSUMERISM AND THE NEW POOR
SECOND EDITION

Zygmunt Bauman

Reviewers' comments on the first edition:

> It will be of great interest and value to students, teachers and researchers in sociology and social policy . . . [Bauman] provides a very forceful and sophisticated statement of the case; and a very well written one too. As a wide ranging analysis of our present discontents it is an admirable example of the sort of challenge which sociology at its best can offer to us and our fellow citizens to reassess and re-think our current social arrangements.
>
> *Work, Employment and Society*

> This is a stylish and persuasive analysis of the transition between the age of the 'society of producers' to that of the 'society of consumers'.
>
> *Political Studies*

It is one thing to be poor in a society of producers and universal employment; it is quite a different thing to be poor in a society of consumers, in which life projects are built around consumer choices rather than on work, professional skills or jobs. Where 'being poor' was once linked to being unemployed, today it draws its meaning primarily from the plight of a flawed consumer. This has a significant effect on the way living in poverty is experienced and on the prospects for redeeming its misery.

Work, Consumerism and the New Poor traces this change over the duration of modern history. It makes an inventory of its social consequences, and considers how effective different ways of fighting poverty and relieving its hardships are. The new edition of this seminal work features:

- Updated coverage of key thinkers in the field
- Discussion of recent work on redundancy, disposability and exclusion
- Current thinking on the effects of capital flows on different countries and the changes on the shop floor through, for example, business process re-engineering
- New material on security and vulnerability

Key reading for students and lecturers in sociology, politics and social policy, and those with an interest in contemporary social issues.

Contents:
Series editor's foreword – Acknowledgements – Introduction – The meaning of work: producing the work ethic – From work ethic to the aesthetic of consumption – The rise and fall of the welfare state – The work ethic and the new poor – Prospects for the new poor – References – Index.

144pp   0 335 21598 X (Paperback)   0 335 21599 8 (Hardback)